GANGS

A Reference Handbook

Other Titles in ABC-CLIO's
Contemporary
World Issues
Series

Books in the Contemporary World Issues series address vital issues in today's society such as terrorism, sexual harassment, homelessness, AIDS, gambling, animal rights, and air pollution. Written by professional writers, scholars, and nonacademic experts, these books are authoritative, clearly written, up-to-date, and objective. They provide a good starting point for research by high school and college students, scholars, and general readers, as well as by legislators, businesspeople, activists, and others.

Each book, carefully organized and easy to use, contains an overview of the subject; a detailed chronology; biographical sketches; facts and data and/or documents and other primary-source material; a directory of organizations and agencies; annotated lists of print and nonprint resources; and an index.

Readers of books in the Contemporary World Issues series will find the information they need in order to better understand the social, political, environmental, and economic issues facing the world today.

GANGS

A Reference Handbook

Karen L. Kinnear

**CONTEMPORARY
WORLD ISSUES**

ABC-CLIO

Santa Barbara, California
Denver, Colorado
Oxford, England

Library of Congress Cataloging-in-Publication Data

Kinnear, Karen L.
    Gangs : a reference handbook / Karen L. Kinnear.
       p.   cm. — (Contemporary world issues)
    Includes bibliographical references and index.
    ISBN 0-87436-821-9 (alk. paper)
    1. Gangs—United States—Handbooks, manuals, etc. I. Title.
II. Series.
    HV6439.U7K55   1996
    364.1'06'60973—dc20

01 00 99 98 97   10 9 8 7 6 5 4 3

ABC-CLIO, Inc.
130 Cremona Drive, P.O. Box 1911
Santa Barbara, California 93116-1911

This book is printed on acid-free paper ∞.

Manufactured in the United States of America

*To all those who are out in the streets
working with gang members and children at risk—
they deserve our praise and support*

Contents

Preface

Juvenile gangs and the growing violence that is frequently associated with gangs are becoming a major concern to many states and cities. More and more cities are enacting tough new laws to control the violence, while police departments and other agencies are trying to find an effective way to control violent youth groups. In the meantime, people living in areas most affected by gang violence are trying to cope with the fear that they may become innocent victims of that violence.

Like other books in the Contemporary World Issues series, this book provides a survey of the available literature and other resources on the topic of juvenile gangs and directs readers to sources for further research. Research into and knowledge about gangs have grown in recent years. The literature and resources discussed here provide insight into the causes, treatment, and prevention of juvenile gangs and gang behavior. This book is a useful reference for students, writers, and researchers as well as professionals who deal with gangs.

Chapter 1 introduces the topic and reviews the literature concerning gangs. Chapter 2 provides a chronology of the significant events relevant to gang issues. Chapter 3 offers biographical sketches of individuals who have played or are currently playing key roles in many areas of gang research, intervention, and prevention activities. Chapter 4 provides statistical information on gangs and gang activities and offers excerpts from a variety of state laws in this area. Chapter 5 provides a directory of organizations, associations, and government agencies that deal with gang members or attempt to keep children from joining gangs. In Chapter 6, books, handbooks, manuals, and periodicals are described; the literature varies from popular accounts to primary research and provides a wide perspective on this problem. Chapter 7 includes an annotated list of nonprint resources, including films, videocassettes, and Internet resources.

Introduction 1

Most young people join some type of social group. These groups can help youths develop social skills, fulfill many of their emotional needs, offer an environment in which they are valued, provide them with goals, and give direction and structure to their lives. Some youths will join groups that society considers prosocial, such as Boy or Girl Scouts, Little League, or fraternities and sororities. Others will join groups that are considered antisocial, such as gangs. What makes a youth decide to join a group? How can society steer children into prosocial groups? How can the influence of gangs be diminished? Researchers and other professionals are trying to answer these questions.

What Is a Gang?

One of the first problems encountered by those who study gangs and gang behavior is how to define a gang. Is it just a group of people who hang around with each other? Can adults in a group be defined as a gang? Do the people in the group have to engage in some type of criminal behavior? Defining gangs is often a highly political issue that reflects the interests and agendas of the various individuals and agencies involved with gangs, including law-enforcement personnel, politicians, advocates, social workers, the media, and researchers.

Researcher Frederic Thrasher offered this early definition in 1927: "A gang is an interstitial group, originally formed spontaneously, and then integrated through conflict. It is characterized by the following types of behavior: meeting face to face, milling, movement through space as a unit, conflict, and planning. The result of this collective behavior is the development of tradition, unreflective internal structure, esprit de corps, solidarity, morale, group awareness, and attachment to a local territory" (page 57). Thrasher believed that gangs were interstitial in that they were created in the cracks or along the boundaries of society. Gang members are not in the mainstream and do not have the advantages that others do; they are often lower class, left out, and ignored by the rest of society.

Thrasher's definition of gangs influenced other definitions made by researchers who followed him. Malcolm Klein (1971) added the element of delinquency: "any denotable adolescent group of youngsters who (a) are generally perceived as a distinct aggregation by others in their neighborhood; (b) recognize themselves as a denotable group (almost invariably with a group name); and (c) have been involved in a sufficient number of delinquent incidents to call forth a consistent negative response from neighborhood residents and/or enforcement agencies" (page 13).

Desmond Cartwright also built on Thrasher's definition. He believed that a gang was "an interstitial and integrated group of persons who meet face to face more or less regularly and whose existence and activities as a group are considered an actual or potential threat to the prevailing social order" (Cartwright, Thomson, and Schwartz 1975, 4).

Walter Miller (1980), after talking with criminal-justice system professionals and others working with youth, defined a gang as "a self-formed association of peers, bound together by mutual interests, with identifiable leadership, well defined lines of authority, and other organizational features, who act in concert to achieve a specific purpose or purposes which generally include conduct of illegal activity and control over a particular territory, facility, or type of enterprise" (page 121).

S. Gardner (1983) included territory and delinquency in his definition: "An organization of young people usually between their early teens and early twenties, which has a group name, claims a territory or neighborhood as its own, meets with its members on a regular basis, and has recognizable leadership. The key element that distinguishes a gang from other organizations of young people is delinquency: its members regularly participate in activities that violate the law" (page 5).

In 1987 the California Office of Criminal Justice Planning defined a gang as "a group of associating individuals which (a) has an identifiable leadership and organizational structure; (b) either claims control over particular territory in the community, or exercises control over an illegal enterprise; and (c) engages collectively or as individuals in acts of violence or serious criminal behavior" (pages 3–4).

George Knox (1993) believes a group can be considered a gang when "it exists for or benefits substantially from the continuing criminal activity of its members. Some element of crime must exist as a definitive feature of the organization for it to be classified as a gang. That need not be income-producing crime, because it could also be crimes of violence" (page 5).

Dan Korem (1994), who studied suburban gangs, defined a gang as "a group of youths who are banded together in a specific context and whose activities include, but are not limited to, criminal acts. Adults may or may not be a part of this group, but when there is adult involvement, they will only represent a small minority of the gang membership" (page 35).

As these definitions show, several major elements can be found in most current definitions of gangs: some type of organization, identifiable leadership, identifiable territory, a specific purpose, continual association, and participation in some type of illegal activity.

Most gangs today have other behaviors in common: they use graffiti to mark their territory and to communicate with other gangs; they dress alike, often adopting a particular color as a gang color (for example, red for the Bloods, blue for the Crips); they often tattoo themselves with gang names or symbols; they abide by a specific code of conduct; they have their own specific language; and they have their own set of hand signs that help them recognize other gang members. For example, the Discipline Nation and its affiliates have a distinctive style and refer

> to themselves as the Folks, their major insignia is the Six Pointed Star, and their dress is "tight." Their basic color is black and if they wear an earring it will be in the right ear. They wear their hat tilted to the right . . . , they will wear one glove on the right hand, they may have one pocket on the right side turned inside out and it will be dyed in the gang's color or colors, they

will roll up the right pants leg, they may have two of the fingernails on the right hand colored with the gang's colors, the hood of their sweatshirt will be dyed with the gang's colors, their shoes will either be colored or the laces of the right shoe will be in the gang's color, their belt buckle will be loose on the right side, and they may wear a bandanna in the gang's colors anywhere on the right side of their body (Illinois State Police 1989, 9–10).

Gang Organization

Gangs form for many reasons. They also are organized in a variety of ways, depending on their primary purpose, their level of structure, and the degree of control that the gang leaders have. Carl Taylor (1990) categorizes gangs, based on the reasons for their existence, as scavenger gangs, territorial or turf gangs, and instrumental or corporate gangs. Scavenger gangs are loosely organized with a leadership that may change often, and this type of gang provides its members with a purpose for their lives. Many members are low achievers or school dropouts and are likely to exhibit violent behavior. Their crimes are usually not serious and are spontaneous. Territorial gangs may claim blocks, neighborhoods, specific buildings, or even schools as their home turf. These gangs are highly organized and have elaborate initiation rites as well as rules and regulations for controlling members' behavior. Members usually wear gang colors. Instrumental or corporate gangs usually have a clearly defined leader and a finely defined hierarchy of leadership, often a military-type structure. Youth generally become members if the gang views their contribution as necessary to the success and survival of the gang itself. Crimes are committed for a specific purpose, usually profit of some sort, and not just for fun. Gangs may start off as scavenger gangs and, over time, become instrumental or corporate gangs.

Lewis Yablonsky (1970) also distinguished three types of gangs, with a somewhat different definition; he referred to them as social, delinquent, and violent gangs. Social gangs are fairly permanent and cohesive, have a permanent location, and usually do not engage in delinquent or criminal activity. Delinquent gangs are organized for some type of illegal activity, usually for profit. They tend to be small, cohesive, exclusive, and well organized, and they participate in violent as well as social activity in the process of gaining illegal profits. Violent gangs are formed for the purpose of engaging in violent activity; these gangs are loosely organized and highly unstable, membership is uncertain, and core members often are emotionally unstable.

Other researchers also have organized gangs into a variety of categories. Most gang typologies contain four general types: social gangs, retreatist gangs, conflict gangs, and criminal gangs. Social gangs, which are the most common type, are also known as territorial or street-corner gangs. They are primarily involved in social activities, which may or may not include illegal activities, have some structure, and are identified with a specific territory. Alcohol and drug use are common among retreatist gang members and often are a major focus for this type of gang—one whose members pull back or retreat from society. Conflict gangs often are involved in serious criminal and violent activities. Criminal gangs, somewhat rare among juvenile gangs according to some experts, have strong leadership and a strong profit motive, are highly disciplined, and do not like to draw attention to themselves (Covey, Menard, and Franzese 1992).

Gangs are also made up of a variety of member types. "Wannabes" are usually younger people who want to become gang members or are seen as potential recruits by current members. Core members and leaders are the most consistently identified group of members; core members are more likely to be involved in the major activities of the gang. Veterans or "O.G." (for "old gangsters") are usually older youths or adults who are not actively involved in gang activity; many have the respect and admiration of younger gang members and work with gang leaders to help them achieve their goals.

Why Join a Gang?

Young people join gangs for many reasons. Some join for the same reasons that they might join Scouts or Little League or later join fraternities or sororities: they want to hang out with their friends who are part of a certain group or they are looking for ways to distinguish themselves from their parents, to develop their own identities. Other young people join for economic reasons; if the gang is selling drugs or stolen goods, many youngsters see gang membership as an easy way to make some money.

Many people believe that kids join gangs and then get in trouble by going along with the dictates of the group. Fellow gang members display values that are conducive to crime, provide opportunities for violent and sociopathic behavior, show how to gain material wealth that would otherwise be unavailable to most inner-city youth, and provide an environment in which young men are supposed to prove their manhood by following these examples. Other people believe that kids who join gangs are already troublemakers and are seeking an outlet for their criminal tendencies. Travis Hirschi (1969) found that gangs harbored members who had little respect for others' opinions; therefore, it is likely that those juveniles who joined gangs already knew what they wanted to do—they did not need the encouragement of others in the gang to help them decide. Earlier researchers also found that some juveniles were already delinquent before they joined juvenile gangs (Glueck and Glueck 1950).

Many theories attempt to explain why juveniles join gangs. Several of these theories are sociological in nature, focusing on structural and dynamic variables as causes of gang formation and behavior. Some of these variables include social environment, family, and economic conditions and opportunity. Most of the theories fall into five categories: bonding and control theory, opportunity and strain theory, labeling theory, subcultural or cultural-conflict theory, and radical or sociopolitical theory.

Bonding and Control Theory

The basic social institutions in American society, including home, school, church, and workplace, can teach children socially acceptable behavior. These institutions reward children who follow the rules and punish those who don't. Family processes and interaction play a particularly important role in developing social bonds that may prevent young people from committing delinquent or criminal acts. Some researchers have found that families of delinquents tend to spend little time together and provide less support and affection than families of well behaved youths. Parents often are unemployed and have problems with alcohol, and they may provide little or no supervision for their children (Patterson 1982, Snyder and Patterson 1987). Children of such parents may not pay attention in, or even attend, school, and they may not attend church either. These children miss out on multiple opportunities to learn socially appropriate behavior.

Opportunity and Strain Theory

The media often depict the American Dream—to achieve wealth, social position, and personal goals—as attainable for everyone. Many young people have the same dream for themselves, that they will be able to do better than their parents and achieve great things in their lives. However, not all young people have an equal opportunity to achieve this dream. As a result, they grow up frustrated and may develop a sense of hopelessness, believing that they will not receive the same things from society as other people. The resulting depression can lead to delinquent behavior. A number of researchers believe that such social strain explains juvenile and gang delinquency (Cloward and Ohlin 1960, Cohen 1965). Deborah Prothrow-Stith (1991) believes that young people who think they will be able to gain their fair share of what society has to offer are likely to join clubs, scouts, or fraternities, while young people who do not believe that society will provide for them may join gangs. She says that juveniles join gangs, including violent gangs, only when they believe that their future opportunities for success are limited. Other researchers believe that strain theory does not adequately explain why juveniles join gangs. For instance, it does not explain why middle-class youths become delinquent or join gangs. The strain of living with limited opportunities does not lead most inner-city youths to join gangs, only certain youths. While this theory provides one explanation, it also demonstrates the need to examine several factors that may interact to lead youths into delinquent or gang behavior.

Labeling Theory

According to sociologist George Herbert Mead (1934), an individual's self-concept is derived from how others define the individual. This concept provides the basis for labeling theory, which some have called a self-fulfilling prophecy. Several theorists have applied this theory to juvenile delinquency. According to Arnold Goldstein (1991), it "is not the initial act(s) of delinquent behavior (*primary deviance*) that labeling theory seeks to explain, but delinquent acts subsequent to society's official response to the initial act(s) (*secondary deviance*)." An individual's good behavior may not be reinforced if other people believe he is a troublemaker; as opportunities for engaging in delinquent behavior present themselves, the individual may figure that if most people think he is bad, he might as well be bad.

Cultural Conflict or Subcultural Theory

Some researchers believe that delinquent behavior results from an individual conforming to the current norms of the subculture in which he grows up, if these norms vary from those of the larger society (Shaw and McKay 1942, Miller 1958). Several studies have shown that males who admit that some of their friends are delinquent also admit that they have committed delinquent acts (Johnson 1979). Other studies have shown that students who live in neighborhoods with high rates of delinquency are more likely to commit delinquent acts than students living in areas of low delinquency (Rutter and Giller 1983). Youngsters who grow up in areas that have high crime and delinquency rates may come to believe that crime and delinquency are normal aspects of everyday life and therefore do not think that they are doing anything wrong when they misbehave or commit a crime.

Radical Theory

In the late 1970s, several researchers developed a sociopolitical perspective on crime and delinquency, known as radical theory or the "new criminology." Believing that laws in the United States are developed by and for the ruling elite, radical theorists hold that these laws are used to hold down the poor, minorities, and the powerless (Abadinsky 1979, Meier 1976). Radical theory is based on several propositions: (1) American life is structured around an advanced capitalist society; (2) government is organized to serve the needs of the capitalist ruling class; (3) criminal law and crime control protect the interests of the ruling class; (4) society is prepared to oppress the lower economic classes through any means necessary; and (5) only a society based on socialism will solve the crime problem (Quinney 1974).

Other Theories

Some researchers believe that many of today's gangs have evolved into major business enterprises. For example, Felix Padilla (1992) contends that "the gang represents a viable and persistent business enterprise within the U.S. economy, with its own culture, logic, and systematic means of transmitting and re-inforcing its fundamental business virtues" (page 3). Gangs have become big business; many youth may join them as a means of earning money, more money than they would earn at the local fast-food restaurant. The gang may provide the same opportunities that a local business or large corporation might provide to a youth from a middle-class neighborhood.

Looking for ways in which community life affects criminality, researchers have examined such factors as anonymity, mobility, territoriality, population density, and systems of behavior reinforcement and punishment. Peers can alter how an individual views criminal or delinquent behavior. James Wilson and Richard Herrnstein (1985) claim that "the density of human settlement can affect the frequency with which one encounters opportunities for crime (by presenting a chance to steal a purse or a car when one is to the right of his 'crossover point'—that is, when the rewards of crime appear stronger than the delayed rewards of not committing the crime); and the extent of natural surveillance of the streets, provided it is carried out by persons willing to act on the basis of what they see, may affect the probability of being caught and punished" (page 311).

The preceding theories attempt to explain group or gang behavior from a primarily sociological viewpoint. However, the field of psychology also has provided a wealth of theories about why individual youths become delinquent or join gangs. These theories can be grouped into several categories: constitutional, psychoanalytic, personality, and genetic.

Constitutional

These theories focus on body type and physical characteristics and are based on the work of Cesare Lombroso in the early 1900s. Lombroso, an Italian physician, believed that some people were both morally and physically prone to criminal behavior. Some of the major physical characteristics he associated with criminal behavior included large ears, short legs, sloping shoulders, and flat feet as well as a variety of others (Lombroso 1911). Over time, while beliefs about specific physical characteristics fell out of favor, theories about body types and criminality were still being considered. William Sheldon (1949) proposed that specific body builds were related to temperament as well as to overt behavioral tendencies. In his 1949 study of nude photographs of 200 youths incarcerated for delinquent behavior, he found that a significant number were what he termed "mesomorphs," that is, they were muscular, had broad chests and large bones, and had low waists. Although other researchers have supported these findings (Cortes and Gatti 1972, Gibbens 1963, Glueck and Glueck 1950), constitutional factors are no longer believed to determine or influence delinquent behavior to any great extent.

Psychoanalytic

These theories focus on basic psychological needs that may lead to criminal or delinquent behavior when the needs are not met. For example, Freud (1961) believed that criminal behavior resulted from an individual's need for punishment, which grew from unconscious, incestuous wishes. F. Alexander and W. Healy (1935) focused on the criminal's inability to delay gratification, while J. Bowlby (1949) believed that maternal separation from a child and parental rejection played significant roles in turning juveniles into delinquents. Others explain that criminal behavior results from individuals searching for love, nurturing, and attention that they are not receiving at home (Johnson and Szurek 1952).

Personality

Theories focusing on the personality of the juvenile as a factor in delinquency imply that the youth is responsible for becoming delinquent, regardless of all outside influences. Sheldon and Eleanor Glueck (1950) theorize that delinquent youth are more assertive, narcissistic, resentful, suspicious, extroverted, and impulsive and are ambivalent toward authority. Similarly, J. J. Conger and W. C. Miller (1966) found delinquents to be more egocentric and unfriendly than other youths, while J. Arbuthnot and D. A. Gordon (1987) found them less capable of sociomoral reasoning, empathy, and interpersonal problem solving. However, other researchers believe that personality traits of criminals and noncriminals do not differ significantly (Schuessler and Cressey 1950, Feldman 1977).

Genetic/Hormonal

A genetic link to criminality was first proposed in the early 1900s. H. H. Goddard (1916), based on his study of the Kallikak family, believed that feeblemindedness was passed from parent to child and was associated with criminality in 50 percent of all cases he studied. R. L. Dugdale (1942) found a similar relationship in his genealogical study of the Jukes family. The methods of both of these researchers have been questioned by others in the field. Over time, studies of fraternal versus identical twins became the more acceptable and reliable means of measuring the relationship between genetics and criminality. However, even these studies were found to be less reliable than first thought. The possible influence of the social and physical environment could not be ignored. Later studies of siblings who were split up at birth and placed in different social environments indicated that the potential for criminal behavior might indeed be influenced by biological factors (Mednick 1977; Pollock, Mednick, and Gabrielli 1983). L. Ellis (1987) proposes a neurohormonal theory of delinquency in which he suggests that high levels of androgens, especially testosterone, affect brain function. Thus, young males going through puberty are more likely to become delinquent in part because of the increase in testosterone in their systems.

Combination of Theories

Many researchers have found it necessary to combine various theories in order to explain delinquent behavior. For example, social learning theory holds that situational, cognitive, and physiological variables interact to influence behavior (Bandura 1973). Social development theory considers the following variables important: the opportunities available to the child for bonding with the parent, life skills, and the reinforcements that are provided for good behavior (Hawkins and Weis 1985). M. P. Feldman (1977) ties together social learning theory, individual predisposition, and social labeling theory. Differential association-differential reinforcement theory, as proposed by R. L. Burgess and R. L. Akers (1966), is a combination of the differential-association perspective proposed by Edwin Sutherland (1947) and social learning theory from A. Bandura. In *Deviant Behavior* (1985), Akers explains differential association-differential reinforcement theory: one's behavior is shaped by imitating other people's behavior and by observing the consequences (or lack of consequences) of other people's behavior.

Most researchers focus on male juvenile delinquency and gang participation. In *Men, Women, and Aggression*, Anne Campbell observes:

> Women are curiously ignored in all three theories [structural, social control, cultural]. Structural arguments focus almost wholly on classism and racism, but it is women, not men, who bear the brunt of the poverty that results. Any theory arguing that gangs are the result of economic inequality must surely predict

that women would be at least equal partners in the roster of gang members. As for social control theory, women are also exposed to the erosion of family and community control, but they are much less likely to join gangs. . . . The cultural analysis is both detailed and persuasive, but it explains only Chicano gangs. . . . During the course of the last 200 years, the predominant ethnic makeup of gangs has altered time and again. What they all have in common is the gang as a predominantly male response to poverty and lack of opportunity. The culture that has to be examined is that of poverty-level and working-class masculinity (Campbell 1993, 129–130).

In addition to examining masculinity issues when studying gang participation and gang behavior, researchers also must be careful not to generalize about the influence of gangs on the criminality of their members because gangs differ greatly from city to city and from ethnic group to ethnic group.

Social Factors

As can be seen from the many theories concerning the existence and growth of gangs, many factors interact to lead youth to join gangs. Gangs are basically an American product; other countries have seen some gang activity, such as Germany with its skinheads, but gangs have become a major social problem in the United States more than in any other country. As Irving Spergel and his colleagues (1994) say, "Rapid urban population change, community disintegration, increasing poverty (relative and absolute), and social isolation contribute to institutional failures and the consequent development of youth gangs" (page 3).

Growing up in American society today can be a challenge, particularly in an inner-city neighborhood. When young people have little structure in their lives, when they have no purpose or can see no reason to excel in school, they are apparently more likely to join gangs. The gang gives their lives structure, makes them feel important and useful, protects them from a violent environment, and provides some sense of safety in numbers. Gang members are loyal to each other and to the gang, their group gets special attention in the community, and their association may provide financial rewards if the gang is selling drugs or other illegally obtained merchandise. Excitement is a part of gang life; members can get an adrenaline rush from some of their activities, and they may feel empowered by the backing and respect of the other gang members, which gives them the courage to do whatever the gang asks of them.

Racial/Ethnic Gangs

Most gangs are race- or ethnic-specific. That is, whites usually join white gangs, Hispanics usually join Hispanic gangs, and African-Americans usually join African-American gangs. Researchers have found that these racial/ethnic gangs have several characteristics that are specific to their gangs.

Hispanic Gangs

Hispanic gang members often set themselves apart from other gangs by using a slang language that is a combination of English and Spanish. Many gang members are proud to call themselves crazy, hence the common use of the word "loco" in much of their language to denote they are unafraid or macho.

African-American Gangs

According to several researchers, African-American gang members stay in their gangs longer than gang members from other racial/ethnic groups. This can be explained in part by the lack of economic opportunities available to these youths. According to Irving Spergel (1995), legitimate opportunities for African-American youth are more "thoroughly blocked" than in any other community: "More limited systems of illegitimate opportunity have evolved, based pervasively on street-gang structures, than is the case for any other racial or ethnic group. . . . Because of persistent poverty associated with racism, black male youths also become overidentified as gang members" (page 62).

Asian Gangs

Asian youth may join gangs to rebel against the Buddhist principles that many of their parents follow or they may join for reasons similar to those of youth from other cultures. Chinese, Samoan,

Korean, Cambodian, Hmong, Japanese, Tongan, Filipino, and Vietnamese gangs exist in the United States. These gangs are usually organized for economic reasons and members rarely commit crimes against other cultural or racial groups; property crimes are typical. Spergel (1993), in a review of the literature, finds that these gangs, especially Japanese, Taiwanese, and Hong Kong gangs, are the best organized of all gangs, the most secretive, and the best disciplined.

Malcolm Klein (1995) found that Asian gangs were quite selective in choosing members. Non-Asian members were not welcomed, and these gangs threatened their Asian victims with death or great bodily damage if they talked to the police. Because most cities have few police officers, reporters, or researchers who are Asian or understand Asian culture, few outsiders are able to gain the confidence of Asian gang members and victims in order to better understand them.

White Gangs

White gangs have the longest history among all racial/ethnic gangs; they were especially prominent in the late 1800s and early 1900s as many Europeans immigrated to the United States. More recently, they have become less visible. Groups identified as gangs include stoners, heavy metal groups, satanic worshipers, bikers, and skinheads.

White supremacist groups are popular gangs in many areas of the United States. They believe in the doctrines of Adolf Hitler and may be tied in with the Ku Klux Klan and the neo-Nazi movement. Many gang members refer to themselves as 'skin-heads." They tend to wear their hair short, wear black biker boots, and listen to punk-rock music. However, some skinheads may keep their hair longer to keep from being identified as skinheads. They dislike African Americans, Asians, Hispanics, Jews, gays, lesbians, Catholics, and any other group that they do not consider part of the "white Aryan race."

Many people believe that the skinheads are becoming more popular with white youth today because many of these youth believe that the future holds little promise for them. They do not believe that they will be better off than their parents, and they may become disaffected with society, often looking for someone else to blame for their problems. Most research indicates that the skinheads are loosely organized, primarily high school dropouts and working-class youth. Their trademark is violence, which distinguishes them from most street gangs. Skinheads join together to commit violence against anyone they don't like or approve of, while street gangs form for a wider variety of reasons. In fact, some researchers believe that skinheads should not be considered typical street gangs, but rather "constitute what can best be described as a terrorist youth subculture" (Hamm 1993, 65).

Gangs in Affluent Areas

No one appears to be certain about the number of gangs or extent of their influence outside of the inner city. Media reports and gang studies tend to focus on gangs and violence in the inner city rather than those in more affluent neighborhoods. Dan Korem (1994) has studied gangs in affluent neighborhoods and believes that there is a certain "flow of events" that leads to gang formation in these areas. This flow includes the breakdown of families in part of the community; the emergence of styles of dress, music preference, hair styles, and graffiti that are characteristic of youth subculture; increase in drug abuse; and unexpected acts of violence.

Females in Gangs

Early studies of gangs often did not consider females as gang members. They were seen, if at all, as girlfriends of gang members with only a superficial interest in gang activities. As more gang research has been conducted, the role of the female has expanded to include a secondary role in gang activities. Females often help male gang members, usually by carrying weapons, offering alibis, and gathering information on rival gang members. Recent studies indicate that females make up between 10 and 30 percent of all gang members (Campbell 1984, Moore 1991). These same studies suggest that female participation in gangs may be increasing, including participation in all-female gangs, and female roles may be changing. Some researchers believe that females join gangs for many of the same reasons that males do. Others believe that females join for vastly different reasons, often because of psychological factors and problems with society's expectations for young women. Males are more likely to need t̲ support and encouragement of other males as they matur most girls do not need this type of group suppor usually have more freedom in their activities.

A study conducted by Beth Bjerregaard and Carolyn Smith (1993), using data from the Rochester Youth Development Study, found many similarities between female and male participation in gangs. For both males and females, a strong relationship exists between membership in a gang and instances of delinquency, drug use, and sexual activity, and the relationship between gang membership and sexual activity at an early age was stronger for females than for males. Females were also more likely than males to see their opportunities for success limited, especially educationally, and to believe that joining a gang was their best opportunity to become successful.

Anne Campbell (1987) studied female gangs and found that the female gang member is not simply a sexual object, hanging around the male gang members solely to provide sex. She found that the "social talk of delinquent girls generally shows that they not only reject sexual activity outside the context of a steady relationship, but even reject friendships with 'loose' girls whose reputation might contaminate them by association" (pages 451–52). Campbell goes on to say that "[n]ew girls in the group who, unaware of the prevailing norms, slept around with a variety of men were called to account for their behavior at meetings and instructed that serial monogamy was required" (page 461).

Growth of Gangs and Increasing Levels of Violence

Most experts agree that gang activity has increased significantly during the 1980s and 1990s. The news media offer many gang members the recognition that they crave. Stories about gang activities and gang violence are a concrete example to gang members that their gangs and their actions are important. As Prothrow-Stith (1991) explains, in "Boston, it sometimes feels that the only way a kid in the inner city can get any recognition is by joining a gang and doing something criminal" (page 107). Advances in technology have provided the growing news media with the ability to communicate a greater amount of information than ever before and to do it faster. People die every day on the streets of our cities, not always as a result of gang violence, but as a result of drunk driving, exposure, and other non-gang-related violence, but most deaths and shootings that are reported are the more violent, "newsworthy" items. Many researchers believe that while gang violence may have increased over time, it is also likely that news coverage of gangs and gang-related violence has increased, thereby giving the impression that gang-related violence has increased more significantly than is actually the case.

Researchers believe that a variety of factors have led to increasingly violent behavior on the part of gang members. The major factors are guns, territory, and drugs.

Guns

According to Goldstein (1983) there are 200 million privately owned guns in the United States. Guns are involved in two out of every three murders in the country. The number of juveniles arrested for weapon offenses increased by more than 100 percent between 1985 and 1993—from just under 30,000 to more than 61,000 annually (Bureau of Justice Statistics 1995). With their increasing availability, guns have become the weapon of choice for gang members. Many researchers believe that gang members are more likely to carry and to use guns than other juveniles—one gang member shoots a member of another gang, that gang retaliates, then the first gang retaliates, and so on. L. Berkowitz, summarizing a number of studies on the proliferation of guns and the emotions and aggression gun possession leads to, asserts that

> weapons stimulate people to act aggressively because of their aggressive meaning. In other words, many of us associate guns with the idea of killing and hurting. Because of these associations, the mere sight of a weapon can elicit thoughts, feelings and perhaps even muscular reactions in us that we have previously learned to connect with aggressive behavior. If we do not have any strong inhibitions against aggression at that moment, these elicited thoughts, feelings and motor reactions can heighten the chances that we will show open aggression toward others who happen to be available (Berkowitz, no date, 2–3).

Territory

Territory may be more important to gangs today than in the past. With more emphasis on material possessions, territory can be considered a possession. As the distribution and sale of drugs becomes more popular and profitable for gangs, the amount of territory that a gang controls becomes more important. Territory plays a critical part in the life of many gangs. James Vigil (1988), reporting on the importance of territory, quotes one young gang member: "The only thing we can do is build our own little nation. We know that we have complete control in our community. It's like we're making our stand. . . . We take pride in our little nation and if any intruders enter, we get panicked because we feel our community is being threatened. The only way is with violence" (page 131).

Drugs

Many of our images of gangs, based primarily on media reports, include the use of alcohol and drugs. We tend to believe that gangs sell drugs to make extra money or even that many of them are structured as mini-corporations and are heavily involved in the drug trade. However, research suggests that this is generally not the case; while many gang members use alcohol and illegal drugs, most are not heavily involved in selling drugs.

For example, in 1964, I. Chein and his colleagues surveyed New York City Youth Board staff who worked with street-gang members in New York City and found that gangs contacted by these staff members reported little drug use or selling of drugs by gang members. However, also in 1964, Spergel found that gang members who were on the verge of leaving the gang and violent gang activity were more likely than other gang members to be involved in drug use and a limited amount of drug selling. In her studies of Chicano gang members in East Los Angeles, Joan Moore (1991) found that heroin became popular among the older gang members during the late 1940s; many members left the gang to become involved in the heroin trade. Many reports have found that gang members were likely to be using marijuana, even during the 1950s and 1960s, although they report little involvement in heavy sales activities of this substance.

Studying Mexican-American gangs in southern California, James Vigil found that gang members generally started using drugs at the age of 12.7 years and that use of more than one drug was common, but that most gang members were not heavily involved in drug sales. Explaining the popularity of drug use among gang members, Vigil said that "drinking and drugs act as a 'social lubricant' to facilitate the broadening, deepening, and solidifying of group affiliations and cohesiveness. . . . Drug and alcohol usage often facilitates gang youths' release from their felt obligations to social mores and thus increases their willingness to participate in other criminal acts, especially if such behavior seems to help them prove their loyalty and commitment to the group" (Vigil 1988, 126).

During the 1960s and 1970s, changes in the labor market led to a decrease in low-skill jobs, especially in manufacturing, which eliminated the legitimate job market for many lower-class youth. Many of these youth found that the illegal drug trade offered them a chance to make money and gain social status among their peers. According to Spergel, evidence suggests that by the late 1970s several members of black gangs in Chicago, 'particularly those older members with prison experience, were significantly engaged in drug dealing. The Blackstone Rangers, later known as the El Rukns, were a continuing target of the Chicago Police Department for drug dealing, shady property investments, and other organized criminal activities" (Spergel 1995, 45).

Though more gang members than non–gang members use drugs and many also sell drugs, they do not generally appear to be part of larger criminal drug organizations. According to Ira Reiner (1992), former Los Angeles County district attorney, drugs and gangs should be treated as two separate issues, even though some of the same individuals who sell drugs are gang members. Reiner reports that in Los Angeles more than 70 percent of all gang members use drugs, which is four times the percentage of non–gang members, and seven times more gang members sell drugs than non–gang members. Younger gang members tend to focus their time and energy on intergang rivalries and see drugs only as a source of employment, while older gang members lean more toward selling drugs than other activities usually important to gang members.

According to Spergel (1995), 'the youth gang's fluid, unstable, emotionally charged character is not suited to a rational drug organization" (page 47). Leonard Dunston also sees gang structure and drug organization as separate:

> In New York City, drugs are controlled by organized crime groups. Young, weak, undermanned and poorly organized street gangs cannot compete with the older more powerful and violent groups. The fragmented street gangs do not have the network organizations employing youths in various aspects of their drug business. They are employed as steerers, lookouts,

> dealers, enforcers or protectors from robbers and other drug organizations. The primary difference between a drug organization and a youth gang is that in a drug organization all members are employees while youth gang membership only requires affiliation. We do not see our youth gangs become drug organizations (Dunston 1990, 7).

Other researchers also believe that gangs are too unorganized, unfocused, and unable to effectively operate a serious drug organization. Klein, Maxson, and Cunningham (1988) believe the gang-drug connection has been overstated and should not be considered a single social problem.

Gangs have entered into the sale of drugs to some extent, however, especially with the appearance of crack cocaine. According to the General Accounting Office (GAO), the activity of gangs in the use and sale of crack has increased over the years. While the GAO report indicates that black street gang activity began little more than 25 years ago in the South Central Los Angeles area, approximately 15 years ago these gangs became involved in dealing marijuana, LSD, and PCP with a corresponding growth in gang violence associated with the push to establish drug territories. Finally, "in the early 1980s, the gangs began selling crack cocaine. Within a matter of years, the lucrative crack market changed the black gangs from traditional neighborhood street gangs to extremely violent groups operating from coast to coast" (GAO 1989, 47).

Researchers have found inconsistencies in the strength of the relationship between street-gang membership, drug use, drug selling, and violence. Jeffrey Fagan (1988, 1989) found that violent acts committed by gangs did not necessarily occur in relation with drug sales; gangs were involved with violence whether or not they were also involved in drug sales. Klein, Maxson, and Cunningham (1988) found no relation between drug sales and gang homicides in a study of Los Angeles gangs, drugs, and homicides. Lawrence Bobrowski (1988), an analyst for Chicago's Gang Crime Unit, examined the relationship between gang-related drug dealing and violence using statistics from the Chicago Police Department. While he found a relationship between gangs and drug use, he did not find a relationship between arrests for drug dealing or possession by gang members and gang violence. In a 1994 report, the Institute for Law and Justice also reported that it found no strong relationship between drugs and gangs. It claimed that "if gangs were to disappear overnight, drugs would remain a serious problem, and if drugs were to disappear overnight, gangs would still be a serious problem. These two problems intersect and complicate each other, but there are still large areas in which they are independent of each other" (Institute for Law and Justice 1994, 8–9).

Barry Cooper (1987) found that many Detroit youth gangs were organized to distribute crack cocaine. Edward Dolan and Shan Finney (1984) describe the economic temptation that selling drugs has for many gang members, within the framework of the environment in which they grow up and the lack of other legitimate sources of income. They also describe the use of drugs by many gang members.

Some gangs involved in the distribution of drugs may not allow members to become users. For example, Ko-Lin Chin (1990) found that, while many of the early Chinese gangs in New York City distributed heroin, most of these gangs refused to use heroin themselves. While studying gangs in Detroit, Thomas Mieczkowski (1986) found that the street-level juvenile drug runners, primarily running heroin, rejected the use of heroin for themselves. However, many of these youths used other drugs, primarily marijuana and cocaine, for recreational purposes.

In a study comparing the two largest black and two largest Hispanic gangs in Chicago between 1987 and 1990, Block and Block (1993) found that black gangs were more likely than the Hispanics to be involved in drug-related rather than territorial-related violence.

Police Departments and Gangs

Many police departments currently have special units to deal with the problem of gangs. These units range in size from 1 to 500 staff members and are either centrally located or have offices spread throughout the city. The size of the gang unit often depends on the seriousness and extent of the city's gang problems as well as the extent of other problems that may take precedence, the financial strength of the police department, and the importance the public and city officials place on reducing gang problems. For example, in the late 1980s, eight officers were assigned to a variety of tasks within the Preventive Patrol Unit of the Philadelphia Police Department. The unit worked with gang youth, runaways, sexually abused children, and at-risk youth.

During the same time, both the Los Angeles Police Department and Sheriff's Department developed special gang units of approximately 200 officers each. By 1992 the Chicago Police Department's gang unit employed more than 500 specially trained police officers (Spergel 1995).

Federal authorities from such agencies as the Bureau of Alcohol, Tobacco and Firearms, the Federal Bureau of Investigation, the Drug Enforcement Administration, and the Immigration and Naturalization Service sometimes get involved in efforts to intervene in gang activities. At the local, state, and federal levels, the FBI sponsors task forces in 42 cities to fight gang- and drug-related violence (Ostrow 1992).

Within the past 20 years, many law-enforcement agencies have focused on gangs as criminal organizations and have set up or advocated elaborate information and tracking systems, primarily at the local level, though state governments are now beginning to see the value of these types of systems. Robert Philibosian (1989, 55) asserts that the growth of gangs and their involvement with drugs underscores the need for a statewide information system in California: "The expansion of gangs and their importation of drugs throughout the state make it even more critical to design and develop a statewide gang information network and clearing house. The statewide system should provide local law-enforcement officials with gang analysis files. The system would greatly improve communication, cooperation, and coordination among all criminal justice entities through the state."

Police departments use a variety of techniques to gather information about gangs and individual gang members. These techniques include staking out territory where gangs are known to congregate, patrolling and enforcing the law aggressively in gang territories, surveillance of individual gang members and gang hangouts, following up on investigations into gang activities, developing an extensive information system on gang members and their activities, and infiltrating locales in which gangs may be found, such as schools, activity centers, and malls. According to Spergel,

> Gang information systems are expected to improve crime analysis, surveillance, communication, investigation, and other techniques to monitor gang activity, especially gang-related drug trafficking. Law enforcement officials argue that improved data systems and

coordination of information across different justice system agencies will lead to more efficiency, more gang members being removed from the streets, more rapid prosecution, and more imprisonment with "less hassle" for longer periods (Spergel 1995, 195).

Many people believe that law-enforcement officials already spend too much time gathering information and intruding into the lives of suspected gang members and their families and that the police harass blacks in the inner cities. In Los Angeles, police are alleged to pick up gang members and drop them off in a rival gang's territory. Several studies suggest that the police are sometimes out of line. As a result of the Rodney King beating, the Independent Commission on the Los Angeles Police Department, commonly known as the Christopher Commission, found many documented instances of police brutality and harassment of racial minorities. Mexican-Americans, both gang members and non–gang members, experience harassment at the hands of the police in the barrios of Los Angeles, although it is possible that the bad feeling that exists between the police and gangs may lead to some false reports of harassment (Mirande 1981; Vigil 1988).

Legislation and Gangs

Thirty-one states have enacted RICO (Racketeer Influenced Corrupt Organizations) statutes to help their officials combat gang crime. The writers of these statutes portray gangs as a serious, organized threat to society (Spergel 1995). However, according to a recent National Institute of Justice (NIJ) study, only 17 percent of prosecutors in large counties and less than 10 percent in smaller counties have ever used RICO statutes to prosecute gang members (Johnson, Webster, and Connors 1995).

State conspiracy laws have been used to combat gang crime along with state drug-kingpin statutes. The NIJ study found that state conspiracy laws were used against gang members by 37 percent of prosecutors in large jurisdictions and 26 percent of prosecutors in small jurisdictions, while 36 percent of all prosecutors used state drug-kingpin laws against gang members (Johnson, Webster, and Connors 1995). Many cities have tried arranging gang treaties and truces to lessen gang crime. In some cases, these truces have worked for a while, but in most cases something eventually triggers an end to the truce.

Street Terrorism Enforcement and Prevention (STEP) acts have been passed in five states (California, Florida, Georgia, Illinois, and Louisiana) to combat gang activities. STEP acts are based on RICO statutes and deal with gangs in a comprehensive way, with one law, and they address constitutional issues related to the prosecution of street-gang activities (see chapter 4 for excerpts from California's STEP Act).

Other states and local jurisdictions have passed legislation to deal with their specific gang-related problems. These statutes focus on such gang activities as drive-by shootings, member recruitment, weapon possession, loitering, and pointing weapons from a vehicle. The statutes also address law-enforcement issues like vehicle forfeiture, witness protection programs, accessibility of juvenile records, the age limit for juvenile offenses, and automatic adult/juvenile certification for any gang-related crime.

Other Legal Responses to Gangs

Prosecutors often take what they call a vertical approach to dealing with gang youth. Once assigned to a case, they stay with the case from the beginning to end. As a result of this strategy, the conviction rate has gone up. Prosecutors have become more experienced, more specialized, and often more community-oriented in dealing with gang crime. A 1992 NIJ study found that 30 percent of prosecutors in large jurisdictions have formed gang units in their offices, use vertical prosecution, and have a staff of two to four people (Johnson, Webster, and Connors 1995).

Prosecutors are responsible for protecting witnesses in all criminal cases; they often must resort to extraordinary measures to protect witnesses in gang-related cases. The 1992 NIJ survey found that 89 percent of prosecutors in large jurisdictions and 74 percent in smaller jurisdictions reported that obtaining the cooperation of witnesses was a significant problem. Prosecutors said witnesses were afraid to cooperate because of possible retaliation, a neighborhood culture that frowned on informers, or personal connection with the gang member(s) in question. Some prosecutors' offices ask the police to videotape witness statements in case witnesses should change their minds later, "forget" what they saw, or be murdered. Many witnesses are also afraid of and do not trust the police; because of personal experiences, these witnesses often protect each other and their neighbors.

Few judges have developed special approaches to dealing

with gang youth. Those who have not tend to emphasize a get-tough approach, often based on community desires, trying many youths as adults. Some judges have developed a community-oriented approach, taking into account social aspects of each case. Many communities look for a get-tough approach; they don't want to see violent gang youth treated leniently.

Spergel and his associates (1994) believe that gang members should be tried in juvenile court, rather than being transferred to adult court and treated as adults, especially in cases where rehabilitation may be successful. Judges should consider all aspects of a gang member's life and behavior, including such factors as his age, his position in the gang, history of criminal behavior, and the gang's reputation. Juvenile court codes and legislation should also be developed.

Most probation offices do not have special programs or officers to deal with gang members, but some cities have developed special units for working with gang members placed on parole. In California, Los Angeles, San Jose, San Diego, and Orange County have instituted special units that provide intense supervision and often work closely with local community social-service agencies. Some programs also work with other agencies to provide group counseling, remedial education, employment training, and job-placement services.

Prison officials attempt to suppress all gang activity within the prison system. They may move gang leaders from one facility to another in attempts to prevent them from associating with one another. Some youth correctional systems will coordinate activities with local law-enforcement and community agencies as well as provide employment training and work programs.

The Role of Schools in Preventing Gang Activity

Schools often experience problems with gang members, especially those who bring their rivalries and attitudes to school with them. Members of a specific gang may claim school buildings as their territory and control this territory by intimidating and fighting with students. Other gang members drop out of school because they are bored, they don't care about education, or they prefer the freedom and excitement out on the street to the many rules and regulations at school.

Although school officials can't solve the larger societal problems that contribute to participation in gang activities, they may be able to control gang members' behavior while they are in school. The first step is to identify gang activities as soon as possible. A school gang code can be developed, providing guidelines for appropriate responses from teachers and staff to different types of gang behavior. Staff and teachers can apply these rules and regulations in an open manner, asking parents and the community for help or support when necessary. Parents need to be involved in group activities, monitoring school activities, and assisting teachers and staff in class activities. Gang awareness classes can be developed. Schools also can work with local law-enforcement and social-service agencies to help prevent and intervene in gang activities. They can take the lead in organizing community meetings to help bring awareness of gang activities to the community (Arthur 1992; California Attorney General's Office 1994; Chesney-Lind et al. 1995; Spergel and Alexander 1991; Trump 1993).

Intervention and Prevention

The National Crime Prevention Council asserts that parents can do four things to keep their children out of gangs: (1) develop positive alternative activities for their children to engage in; (2) talk with other parents; (3) work with police and other community agencies to understand the reasons children join gangs; and (4) organize other parents, neighbors, and local community agencies to help stem the growth of gangs in their neighborhoods.

Irving Spergel and David Curry (1990) also discuss four types of intervention-program strategies to keep children out of gangs. Community organization activities focus primarily on involving residents of local neighborhoods in prevention programs and anti-gang activities. Social intervention programs, including outreach and counseling programs, focus on preventing gang participation and attempt to guide youth toward other, more promising activities. Opportunity activities include job training, locating employment opportunities, and educational programs. Suppression activities focus on snuffing out gang activity and include arrests, incarceration, and supervision of gang members.

Communities can do many things to help create successful intervention and prevention programs. The extent of the gang problem within the community must be assessed; local representatives of concerned agencies should provide information for the assessment effort; and factors contributing to gang activities should be discussed. An effective organizational system must be implemented to coordinate activities among all participating agencies. Policies and strategies have to be developed with input from all concerned agencies. Gang members need to be held responsible for their behavior, but the community also has to provide opportunities to help them change their behavior. Staff members must be well trained in all aspects of gang behavior and current research findings in the field.

Why Youths Leave Gangs

Some individuals are able to walk away from gang activity on their own, without the help of outside intervention. There are various reasons for this. As a youth gets older, he may lose interest in the gang, in large part because he is maturing and sees the gang as a dead end (literally or figuratively) for himself. Or a youth may find other activities or interests that become more important than the gang. Others decide that they do not like or support violent activities. A youth may join a gang for specific reasons; once in the gang, however, he discovers that gang life does not meet his expectations, so he quits. Some gang members may discover that they are being used or exploited by the leadership and decide that they want to be needed, not used. In some cases, the home environment may improve, reducing the need for a youth to join a gang to feel part of a family. Some youths may realize that the benefits of being in a gang are not worth the increased likelihood of being incarcerated for gang activity.

Positive Functions of Gangs

For the most part, young people are hurt by gang membership; they may get shot at or killed, they may commit criminal acts, they may terrorize a neighborhood, and they may end up in jail or prison. However, Klein (1995) found that there are positive aspects of gangs and gang life. For example, many young people who join gangs gain a measure of self-confidence and self-respect and, in some cases, these young people will eventually see that gangs cannot give them what they want in life and will leave their gangs as better people. In some cases, the skills that gang members learn, such as cooperation, organization, and teamwork, can be used to improve their neighborhoods and their futures, if applied in the right way. Finally, gangs may have a stabilizing effect on the communities in which they are found, providing activities for the children and a focus to the neighborhood.

Outlook for the Future

There is no question that gangs are becoming more widespread and more violent; they reflect the society in which they operate. More families today are composed of single mothers or single fathers trying to raise children and work or of two-parent families in which both parents work and do not have the time to spend with their children. Many experts believe that this, combined with living in a society often focused on the accumulation of material goods and individual rights, but not individual responsibility, has led to increases in juvenile delinquency and juvenile crime. The growing trend of violence on television, in movies, and in video games may also have a strong influence on our children. In a materialistic culture such as ours, it is easy to understand why a child from a poor section of town finds it easier and more attractive to join a gang and sell drugs or other high-cost items than to work at the local fast food restaurant or some other place for the minimum wage.

Until American society understands that the behavior of the children reflect the attitudes and standards of the society in which they are brought up, levels of violence and the growth of gangs will most likely continue. Gangs provide their members with a sense of belonging, a sense of family and identity that so many children today do not find at home or at school. Programs must be put into place that help children develop these values outside of gang membership. Families must be supported in the search to find positive alternatives to gang participation. Government agencies, private organizations, and community members must work together to find positive alternatives to the negative aspects of gang life.

References

Abadinsky, H. 1979. *Social Service in Criminal Justice*. Englewood Cliffs, NJ: Prentice-Hall.

Akers, R. L. 1985. *Deviant Behavior*. Belmont, CA: Wadsworth.

Alexander, F., and W. Healy. 1935. *Roots of Crime.* New York: Knopf.

Arbuthnot, J., and D. A. Gordon. 1987. "Personality." In *Handbook of Juvenile Delinquency,* ed. H. C. Quay. New York: Wiley.

Arthur, R. 1992. *Gangs and Schools.* Holmes Beach, FL: Learning Publications.

Bandura, A. 1973. *Aggression: A Social Learning Analysis.* Englewood Cliffs, NJ: Prentice-Hall.

Berkowitz, L. No date. *When the Trigger Pulls the Finger.* Washington, DC: American Psychological Association.

Bjerregaard, Beth, and Carolyn Smith. 1993. "Gender Differences in Gang Participation, Delinquency, and Substance Use." *Journal of Quantitative Criminology* 9 (4): 329–355.

Block, Carolyn R., and Richard Block. 1993. "Street Gang Crime in Chicago." *Research in Brief.* Washington, DC: National Institute of Justice, Office of Justice Programs, U.S. Department of Justice.

Bobrowski, Lawrence. 1988. *Collecting, Organizing, and Reporting Street Gang Crime.* Chicago: Chicago Police Department, Special Functions Group.

Bowlby, J. 1949. *Why Delinquency? Report of the Conference on the Scientific Study of Juvenile Delinquency.* London: National Association for Mental Health.

Bureau of Justice Statistics. 1995. *Crime Data Brief.* Washington, DC: U.S. Department of Justice (November).

Burgess, R. L., and R. L. Akers. 1966. "A Differential Association-Reinforcement Theory of Criminal Behavior." *Social Problems* 14: 128–147.

California Attorney General's Office. 1994. *Gangs: A Community Response.* Sacramento: California Attorney General's Office.

California Office of Criminal Justice Planning. 1987. *Report of the State Task Force on Youth Gang Violence.* Sacramento, CA.

Campbell, Anne. 1984. *The Girls in the Gang: A Report from New York City.* Oxford: Basil Blackwell.

———. 1987. "Self-Definition by Rejection: The Case of Gang Girls." *Social Problems* 34: 451–466.

———. 1993. *Men, Women, and Aggression.* New York: Basic Books.

Cartwright, Desmond S., Barbara Thomson, and Hershey Schwartz, eds. 1975. *Gang Delinquency.* Monterey, CA: Brooks/Cole.

Chein, I., D. L. Gerard, R. S. Lee, and E. Rosenfeld. 1964. *The Road to H: Narcotics, Delinquency, and Social Policy.* New York: Basic Books.

Chesney-Lind, Meda, et al. 1995. *Crime, Delinquency, and Gangs in Hawaii: Evaluation of Hawaii's Youth Gang Response System.* Honolulu: University of Hawaii at Manoa Center for Youth Research.

Chin, Ko-Lin. 1990. *Chinese Subculture and Criminality: Non-traditional Crime Groups in America*. New York: Greenwood Press.

Cloward, Richard A., and Lloyd E. Ohlin. 1960. *Delinquency and Opportunity: A Theory of Delinquent Gangs*. Glencoe, IL: Free Press.

Cohen, Albert K. 1955. *Delinquent Boys: The Culture of the Gang*. Glencoe, IL: Free Press.

Conger, J. J., and W. C. Miller. 1966. *Personality, Social Class, and Delinquency*. New York: Wiley.

Cooper, Barry M. 1987. "Motor City Breakdown." *Village Voice*, 1 December: 23–35.

Cortes, J. B., and F. M. Gatti. 1972. *Delinquency and Crime*. New York: Seminar.

Covey, Herbert C., Scott Menard, and Robert J. Franzese. 1992. *Juvenile Gangs*. Springfield, IL: Charles C. Thomas.

Dolan, Edward F., and Shan Finney. 1984. *Youth Gangs*. New York: Simon and Schuster.

Dugdale, R. L. 1942. *The Jukes: A Study in Crime, Pauperism, Disease, and Heredity*. New York: Putnam.

Dunston, Leonard G. 1990. *Reaffirming Prevention. Report of the Task Force on Juvenile Gangs*. Albany, NY: New York State Division for Youth.

Ellis, L. 1987. "Neurohormonal Bases of Varying Tendencies to Learn Delinquent and Criminal Behavior." In *Behavioral Approaches to Crime and Delinquency*, ed. E. K. Morris and C. J. Braukmann. New York: Plenum.

Fagan, Jeffrey. 1988. *The Social Organization of Drug Use and Drug Dealing among Urban Gangs*. New York: Criminal Justice Center, John Jay College of Criminal Justice.

———. 1989. "The Social Organization of Drug Use and Drug Dealing among Urban Gangs." *Criminology* 27(4):633–669.

Feldman, M. P. 1977. *Criminal Behavior: A Psychological Analysis*. London: Wiley.

Freud, Sigmund. 1961. *The Complete Works of Sigmund Freud*. London: Hogarth.

Gardner, S. 1983. *Street Gangs*. New York: Franklin Watts.

General Accounting Office. 1989. *Non-Traditional Organized Crime*. Report to the Chairman, Permanent Subcommittee on Investigations, Committee on Governmental Affairs, U.S. Senate.

Gibbens, T. C. 1963. *Psychiatric Studies of Borstal Lads*. London: Oxford University Press.

Glueck, Sheldon, and Eleanor T. Glueck. 1950. *Unraveling Juvenile Delinquency*. Cambridge, MA: Harvard University Press.

Goddard, H. H. 1916. *The Kallikak Family: A Study in the Heredity of Feeble-mindedness.* New York: Macmillan.

Goldstein, Arnold P. 1983. "United States." In *Aggression in Global Perspective,* ed. Arnold P. Goldstein and M. H. Segall. Elmsford, NY: Pergamon.

————. 1991. *Delinquent Gangs: A Psychological Perspective.* Champaign, IL: Research Press.

Hamm, Mark S. 1993. *American Skinheads: The Criminology and Control of Hate Crime.* Westport, CT: Praeger.

Hawkins, J. D., and J. G. Weis. 1985. "The Social Development Model: An Integrated Approach to Delinquency Prevention." *Journal of Primary Prevention* 6: 73–97.

Hirschi, Travis. 1969. *Causes of Delinquency.* Berkeley, CA: University of California Press.

Illinois State Police. 1989. *Criminal Intelligence Bulletin* 42 (January). Springfield, IL.

Institute for Law and Justice. 1994. *Gang Prosecution in the United States.* Washington, DC: National Institute of Justice, Office of Justice Programs, U.S. Department of Justice.

Johnson, A. M., and S. A. Szurek. 1952. "The Genesis of Anti-Social Acting Out in Children and Adults." *Psychoanalytic Quarterly* 21: 323–343.

Johnson, Claire, Barbara Webster, and Edward Connors. 1995. "Prosecuting Gangs: A National Assessment." *Research in Brief.* Washington, DC: National Institute of Justice.

Johnson, R. E. 1979. *Juvenile Delinquency and Its Origins.* Cambridge: Cambridge University Press.

Klein, Malcolm W. 1971. *Street Gangs and Street Workers.* Englewood Cliffs, NJ: Prentice-Hall.

————. 1995. *The American Street Gang: Its Nature, Prevalence, and Control.* New York: Oxford University Press.

Klein, Malcolm W., Cheryl L. Maxson, and Lea C. Cunningham. 1988. 'Gang Involvement in Cocaine 'Rock' Trafficking." Project Summary/Final Report, Center for Research on Crime and Social Control, Social Science Research Institute, University of Southern California, Los Angeles.

Knox, George W. 1993. *An Introduction to Gangs.* Buchanan, MI: Vande Vere Publishing Ltd.

Korem, Dan. 1994. *Suburban Gangs: The Affluent Rebels.* Richardson, Texas: International Focus Press.

Lombroso, Cesare. 1911. *Crime: Its Causes and Remedies.* Boston: Little, Brown.

Mead, George Herbert. 1934. *Mind, Self and Society*. Chicago: University of Chicago Press.

Mednick, S. A. 1977. "A Biosocial Theory of the Learning of Law-Abiding Behavior." In *Biosocial Bases of Criminal Behavior*, ed. S. A. Mednick and K. O. Christiansen. New York: Wiley.

Meier, R. 1976. "The New Criminology: Continuity in Criminological Theory." *Journal of Criminal Law and Criminology* 67: 461–469.

Mieczkowski, Thomas. 1986. "Geeking Down and Throwing Down: Heroin Street Life in Detroit." *Criminology* 24: 645–666.

Miller, Walter B. 1958. "Lower Class Culture as a Generating Milieu of Gang Delinquency." *Journal of Social Issues* 14 (3): 5–19.

———. 1980. "Gangs, Groups, and Serious Youth Crime." In *Critical Issues in Juvenile Delinquency*, ed. D. Shichor and D. Kelly. Lexington, MA: Lexington Books.

Mirande, Alfredo. 1981. "The Chicano and the Law." *Pacific Sociological Review* 24 (1): 65–86.

Moore, Joan. 1991. *Going Down to the Barrio*. Philadelphia: Temple University Press.

National Crime Prevention Council. 1993. *Helping Youth with Gang Prevention*. Washington, DC: National Crime Prevention Council.

Ostrow, Ronald J. 1992. "FBI Takes Aim at Car Jackers." *Chicago Sun-Times*, 16 September: 28.

Padilla, Felix M. 1992. *The Gang as an American Enterprise*. New Brunswick, NJ: Rutgers University Press.

Patterson, G. R. 1982. *Coercive Family Process*. Eugene, OR: Castalia.

Philibosian, Robert H. 1989. *Gang Violence and Control*. Testimony presented to the Subcommittee on Juvenile Justice of the Senate Committee on the Judiciary. 98th Congress, 1st session hearings, February 7, 9. Sacramento, CA.

Pollock, V., S. A. Mednick, and W. F. Gabrielli. 1983. "Crime Causation: Biological Theories." In *Encyclopedia of Crime and Justice* (Vol. 1), ed. S. H. Kadish. New York: Free Press.

Prothrow-Stith, Deborah. 1991. *Deadly Consequences: How Violence Is Destroying Our Teenage Population and a Plan To Begin Solving the Problem*. New York: HarperCollins.

Quinney, R. 1974. *Critique of Legal Order: Crime Control in Capitalist Society*. Boston: Little, Brown.

Reiner, Ira. 1992. *Gangs, Crime, and Violence in Los Angeles*. Los Angeles: Office of the District Attorney of the County of Los Angeles.

Rodriguez, Luis. 1993. *Always Running: La Vida Loca: Gang Days in L.A.* Willimantic, CT: Curbstone Press.

Rutter, Michael, and Henri Giller. 1983. *Juvenile Delinquency: Trends and Perspectives.* New York: Guilford.

Schuessler, K. F., and D. R. Cressey. 1950. "Personality Characteristics of Criminals." *American Journal of Sociology* 55: 476–484.

Shaw, Clifford R., and Henry D. McKay. 1942. *Juvenile Delinquency and Urban Areas.* Chicago: University of Chicago Press.

Sheldon, William H. 1949. *Varieties of Delinquent Youth.* New York: Harper.

Snyder, J. J., and G. R. Patterson. 1987. "Family Interaction and Delinquent Behavior." In *Handbook of Juvenile Delinquency,* ed. H. C. Quay. New York: John Wiley.

Spergel, Irving A. 1964. *Slumtown, Racketville, Haulburg.* Chicago: University of Chicago Press.

———. 1993. *Gang Suppression and Intervention: An Assessment.* Chicago: University of Chicago, School of Social Service Administration.

———. 1995. *The Youth Gang Problem: A Community Approach.* New York: Oxford University Press.

Spergel, Irving A., et al. 1994. *Gang Suppression and Intervention: Problem and Response.* Chicago: University of Chicago, School of Social Service Administration.

Spergel, Irving A., and Alba Alexander. 1991. *School-Based Model.* Chicago: University of Chicago, School of Social Service Administration.

Spergel, Irving A., and G. David Curry. 1990. "Strategies and Perceived Effectiveness in Dealing with the Youth Gang Problem." In *Gangs in America,* ed. C. Ronald Huff. Newbury Park, CA: Sage.

Spergel, Irving A., and G. David Curry, with Ruth E. Ross and Ron L. Chance. 1990. *Survey of Youth Gang Problems and Programs in 45 Cities and 6 Sites.* Chicago: University of Chicago, School of Social Service Administration.

Sutherland, Edwin H. 1947. *Principles of Criminology.* Philadelphia: Lippincott.

Taylor, Carl S. 1990. *Dangerous Society.* East Lansing, MI: Michigan State University Press.

Thrasher, Frederic. 1927. *The Gang.* Chicago: University of Chicago Press.

Trump, K. S. 1993. "Knowing No Boundaries." *School Safety* (Winter): 8–11.

Vernon, Robert L. 1993. *L.A. Justice.* Colorado Springs, CO: Focus on the Family Publishing.

Vigil, James Diego. 1988. *Barrio Gangs: Street Life and Identity in Southern California.* Austin: University of Texas Press.

Wilson, James Q., and Richard J. Herrnstein. 1985. *Crime and Human Nature*. New York: Simon and Schuster.

Yablonsky, Lewis. 1970. *The Violent Gang*. Rev. ed. Baltimore: Penguin.

Chronology 2

1791	People living in Philadelphia complain about the problems created by young hooligans who travel around together and drink, fight, read sexually oriented material, experiment with sex, and steal.
1820s	The first immigrants from Ireland start moving into the Five Points district of Manhattan, New York. Before this time, Five Points had been a relatively quiet and poor residential area. Gangs, composed primarily of young adults or older teenagers, start forming as a result of the poverty, dirty living conditions, and prejudice that these immigrants face. Each gang has its own colors, style of dress, and distinctive name, and each one uses a variety of weapons, including pistols, knives, brass knuckles, ice picks, and brickbats, in its wars with rival gangs.

1840s   Young women such as Hell-Cat Maggie and Battle Annie have a reputation for fighting in New York City.

1854   The New York Children's Aid Society issues its first annual report that discusses crime committed by juveniles in the city. The report notes that juvenile crime is increasing, that juveniles are well organized, and that they have their own signs, their own language, special places where they gather, their own special guards, and members who help entice or divert potential victims to their area.

1870s   In New York City, residents and members of the press are worried about the growth of juvenile gangs who prowl around, terrorize local citizens, and commit various crimes. Going by such names as the Nineteenth Street Gang and the Short Boys, these groups are affiliated with political parties and local saloons. The gangs help get their favorite politicians elected by using strong-arm tactics. Adults often lead juvenile gangs.

1898   Henry D. Sheldon, writing in the *American Journal of Psychology*, classifies gangs according to their primary purpose for organizing: secret clubs, predatory organizations, social clubs, industrial associations, philanthropic associations, athletic clubs, and literary, artistic, and musical organizations. Athletic clubs are the most popular, with predatory organizations a distant second.

1900   Jewish and Chinese gangs are moving into and establishing their own territories in New York City.

1912   In his book *The Boy and His Gang*, J. Adams Puffer reports on his study of 66 clubs and gangs. He finds that the two types of groups are quite similar to each other; in fact, he uses the two terms almost interchangeably. All clubs and gangs have a specific purpose, such as to cause trouble, to play games, to seek adventure, to steal, or to fight against other gangs. Most gangs have their own territory, which might be a street corner, a club room, or a little building in the woods. He also believes that most boys have a deep need to join a group and that gangs are a normal outgrowth of adolescence.

1926   Paul Furfey examines gangs and their basic characteristics; the gangs he studies are usually composed of juveniles between the ages of 10 and 14 years, are organized by local neighborhood, and are loosely structured. He finds that gangs composed of lower-class members are better integrated than other gangs and stay together as a gang longer. He concludes that most boys join gangs for economic reasons—that is, to make or get money.

1927   Frederic Thrasher, a leading authority on gang activity, writes *The Gang*, based on research he has conducted on 1,313 gangs in Chicago. Thrasher finds that the local community plays a significant role in shaping gang behavior and that members of gangs are able to bond together even though they have no particular purpose or goal. He believes that of the 1,313 gangs, 530 are delinquent, 609 may be delinquent, and 52 are not delinquent. All gangs have three levels of membership: the core group composed of the leader and his closest lieutenants, the general rank-and-file members, and those who are marginal members. He believes that the formation of gangs is a normal result of living in urban slums and that people should not be surprised that these gangs exist.

1931   Clifford Shaw directs the Chicago Area Project, a community-development effort that begins in three inner-city areas. The project involves community residents in planning, supporting, and operating programs and developing their own leadership. Residents of these communities are able to organize themselves to promote their own interests.

The 42 Gang of Chicago is considered one of the most menacing juvenile gangs in the United States. Shaw and fellow University of Chicago sociologist Henry

1931 *cont.*   McKay study this gang, whose 42 tough juvenile members are known to murder police officers, stool pigeons, and robbery victims; strip cars; hold up nightclubs; and kill horses. They are described as a typical scavenger gang. Many members graduate into the Capone mob. Shaw and McKay discover that a gang member achieves high status by being sent to the reformatory.

Shaw and McKay write *Social Factors in Juvenile Delinquency: Report on the Causes of Crime*, a monograph on juvenile delinquency and gangs. They discuss the social forces that lead young people to join gangs. For instance, they say, youths who become delinquent or join gangs are excluded from the normal social order and are told that they are not important in the greater scheme of things. The authors assert that family, school, church, the economy, and the government are not functioning for these children. Gang members are motivated by the same forces as nondelinquents—a desire for recognition and admiration by their peers, protection, excitement, and companionship.

1939   Frank Tannenbaum writes *Crime and the Community*, in which he describes how early members of Chicago gangs graduate into committing more serious criminal acts. Groups that start off as play gangs with members stealing apples or shoplifting may eventually develop into gangs that steal cars, commit robbery, and sometimes murder. Tannenbaum notes the important role the family plays in whether or not a child becomes delinquent.

1940s   Many researchers begin to study juvenile gangs in New York City, primarily in response to growing concern among local citizens that juveniles are joining gangs in increasing numbers and are becoming more violent than in the past.

1942   Many researchers respond to the increasing concern about juvenile crime and the role that gangs play in this crime. Shaw and McKay publish their theory of cultural transmission as an explanation for juvenile delinquency. They believe that living in disadvantaged environments, the lack of social controls, and one group teaching others about crime lead youngsters to participate in criminal activities.

1943 During World War II, many residents of the Mexican-American neighborhoods of Los Angeles experience prosperity for the first time. These Mexican Americans develop a sense of ethnic pride and, as a result, begin to see the types and extent of discrimination they are faced with because of their ethnicity. Many children of these families join gangs and develop their own style of dress and language; this pachuco style includes wearing flamboyant zoot-suit clothing and using a hybrid English/Spanish slang. Many of these gangs are nonviolent and do not get into trouble with the law. However, the media focus on the zoot suits that many young men are wearing. As racial tensions increase, fights break out between youths and U.S. sailors. For several nights, groups of sailors bent on vengeance drive through the barrios and attack the youths while the police, some say, look the other way. Because the police do not help, the youths feel the need to protect their territory from the sailors by responding to the violence shown on the part of the sailors.

William Foote Whyte studies juveniles in gangs and believes that gang members are searching for prestige, support from others, and reassurance from other gang members that they are accepted and valuable. These needs, he says, result from a lack of economic opportunity for young gang members. Life for many of these young men is hard, with limited opportunities to succeed in the larger society. Whyte believes that juvenile gangs are not as violent as many people believe and that they do conform in large part to the ideas of society.

1946 New York City is overwhelmed by violent street-gang activity such as vicious and apparently sense

1946 *cont.* less murders. In a special effort known as the detached-worker program, youth workers walk the streets with gang members. In a short time, the mayor of New York creates a permanent agency, the New York City Youth Board, to reduce gang crime. The Board produces a series of manuals and books in which it develops a concept of gang and gang behavior that is accepted by many similar programs throughout the country.

Sophia Robison and her colleagues study juvenile gangs in Harlem and find that these juveniles are violent and are hostile toward anyone not in their gang. Not all gang members are involved in delinquent acts, however; usually only a core group of members commit crimes against people not in the gang. Most gang members are between the ages of 10 and 18 years, while the leaders are usually 15 to 20. Gangs fight each other, and they steal, mug, and extort money.

1947 Trained social workers begin to make contact with gang members in New York City, particularly in central Harlem, with the objective of changing the attitudes and behaviors of these youths. Workers are assigned to several gangs to help stop such criminal activities as fighting, stealing, smoking marijuana, and committing sexual offenses. As alternatives, workers organize athletic activities, block parties, camping trips, trips to the movies, and other positive activities. Paul Crawford, Daniel Malamud, and James Dumpson later publish a report on the results of these programs.

1949 W. Bernard studies gangs in New York and finds that most gangs have between 25 and 200 members, are age-graded, and have both core and marginal members. Roles of individual gang members are clearly spelled out. Most gang members carry weapons but spend much of their time just hanging out with other members, not fighting other gangs. Bernard also studies female gang members in New York and notes that female membership in gangs

has increased. He finds that most girl gangs are affiliated with male gangs. Initiation rites usually require new members to have sex with male gang
members.

In his study on gangs and gang behavior, Leonard
Dunston finds that Harlem gangs are loosely structured, with the largest having no more than 100
members (Dunston 1990).

1950s   Public awareness of gang activity has grown. Researchers report that several of the larger gangs,
such as the Blackstone Rangers of Chicago and the
Latin Kings, have started organizing gang activity
in smaller cities throughout the Midwest. Issues of
territory, masculinity, and fighting ability become
more important. Some gangs start using heroin,
and the use of heroin increases in gangs whose
members already use it.

Gangs start engaging in big fights, called rumbles,
with their own set of rules. War councils meet to
determine time, place, and weapons to be used for
each rumble. Favorite weapons are bats, bricks,
clubs, and chains.

1950   The Welfare Council of New York City publishes a
report on its work with male gangs and their female affiliates in Harlem. The Council finds that
most girls who are involved in gangs and gang activities are sisters or friends of the male members,
are sexually promiscuous, and commonly have illegitimate children as a result of their activities. The
male gang members are more likely than the females to engage in illegal behavior, although the females admit to encouraging the males to break the
law. The report depicts the girls as exploited by the
male gang members.

1954   The Boston Delinquency Project is founded in an
attempt to reduce juvenile delinquency and crime
in a lower-class area. The basic objectives of this
program are to shift the focus of street-corner gangs

1954 *cont.*   from criminal behavior to law-abiding behavior, improve the coordination of local social-service agencies, and to strengthen the family system. Agencies involved in these activities include the local government, police department, courts, public schools, recreation department, the state youth corrections division, medical clinics, social-work agencies, churches, universities, and a variety of special-cause groups. Field workers establish contact with almost 400 youths who are members of 21 street gangs. As a result of this project, coordination among community agencies is improved, although an evaluation of the project concludes that the law-abiding behavior of gang members does not increase significantly.

The movie *The Wild One*, starring Marlon Brando and Lee Marvin, debuts. Featuring an outlaw motorcycle gang, this movie is based on an actual incident in which a motorcycle gang terrorized and vandalized the town of Hollister, California, in 1947. In the movie, the Black Rebel Motorcycle Club enters the town of Carbonville, disrupts a legitimate motorcycle race, steals the race trophy, and moves on to another town, where it settles in. Another gang, the Beetles, once affiliated with the Rebels but now their bitter rivals, arrives in town. The movie creates a major controversy. In the United States, there are distribution problems because some people believe that young viewers will imitate the violence; in England, the movie is banned.

1955   Albert Cohen writes *Delinquent Boys: The Culture of the Gang*, one of the first scholarly monographs to focus on delinquency and gangs. Cohen discusses what juvenile delinquency is, where it can be found, and the conditions within American society that lead to it. He does not see gang behavior as different from general delinquent behavior and examines delinquency within the context of social forces that shape behavior.

The movie *Blackboard Jungle* depicts the difficult life of a high school teacher in a large metropolitan city.

It stars Glenn Ford, Anne Francis, Sidney Poitier, Vic Morrow, Margaret Hayes, and Richard Kiley. The plot focuses on one of several gangs at an all-boys vocational school and the battles between delinquent boys and their teachers.

The movie *Rebel without a Cause*, starring James Dean focuses on troubled and often delinquent youth. The movie depicts 24 hours in the life of Dean's character Jim Stark, who has just started at a new high school. He encounters a hostile group of students, has a knife fight with the leader of the group, and gets involved in a "chickie run" (two guys drive stolen cars at fast speed toward a cliff, and the winner is the last one to jump out).

1957 The Youth for Service program in San Francisco begins. It is one of the city's first "detached-worker" or "gang worker" programs, in which the worker is literally detached from his desk and office and sent out in the streets to work with gangs. This particular program also employs gang members as workers in a variety of community-service projects throughout the city, including cleanup and repair projects.

1958 Most researchers believe that the Vice Lords have now organized in the Lawndale area of Chicago. Various stories suggest that a group of boys residing at the Illinois State Training School for Boys have dropped their various gang affiliations and banded together to create the Vice Lords, which became one of the toughest gangs in the city.

1960s The Vice Lords incorporate as a nonprofit agency with 8,000 members in 26 divisions. They initiate a variety of economic and community service projects, none of which are successful, according to some sources (Short 1990).

The prevention of delinquency and gangs becomes a national priority, as the press and the general public become more aware of gang activity. The

1960s *cont.* Blackstone Rangers, the Devil's Disciples, and the Vice Lords become well known throughout the country. Many gangs become involved in the civil rights movement and in politics. Some gangs, such as the Vice Lords, the Black Panthers, the Young Lords, and the Black Liberation Army offer a positive alternative to typical gang activity by becoming active in politics and civil rights activities. Toward the end of the decade, several experts note a decline in gang activity; some believe that the increased use of drugs, a growing number of intervention programs, and the increased use of suppression tactics by local police departments have led to this decline. Others believe that gang activity has not declined but that there have been changes in the way people define gangs and identify gang members.

1960 The New York City Youth Board issues a report on the results of a comprehensive study of New York City youth gangs. It examines a variety of youth groups, including street clubs and gangs; all of these groups have different structures and activities. Gang members studied range in age from 12 to 22 years and usually have an antagonistic relationship with the communities in which they live and hang out. They all have their own patterns of behavior and their own language.

The Chicago Youth Development Project is organized by the Chicago Boys Club. The project emphasizes aggressive work on the street and through community organization and focuses on groups rather than individuals. Organizers believe that if dedicated street workers take on youths at risk for a variety of gang and criminal behaviors, the number of youths in trouble with the law will decrease.

Richard Cloward and Lloyd Ohlin write *Delinquency and Opportunity: A Theory of Delinquent Gangs*. They say that legitimate and illegitimate opportunities exist in every community, and when young people believe that legitimate opportunities are not available to them, they turn to illegitimate opportunities for financial and emotional support. The researchers point out that it is difficult being a young person in American society and see job training and job placement as critical elements in helping youths make the transition into adulthood.

1961   The Juvenile Delinquency and Youth Offenses Control Act is passed. The President's Committee on Juvenile Delinquency and Youth Crime is authorized by this act and is charged with controlling various forms of delinquency, including gangs.

The Los Angeles Group Guidance Project is developed under the auspices of the Los Angeles County Probation Department. As a four-year detached-worker project, it emphasizes a group approach to stemming violence, organizing parent clubs and providing group counseling and group activities. The project attempts to change gang members' values, attitudes, and perceptions of gang participation. However, gang activity does not decrease.

The movie *West Side Story* is released. It stars Natalie Wood, Richard Beymer, Russ Tamblyn, Rita Moreno, and George Chakiris. Highlighting the racial and social tensions of street-gang rivalry in New York City, the story pits the Sharks against the Jets. Maria, who is Puerto Rican, arrives in the slums of Manhattan's West Side. Her brother is the leader of the Sharks. Maria falls in love with the former leader of the Jets, a white gang, and their love affair stirs up the racial tension between the two gangs, which plan a 'rumble." In the end, Maria's brother stabs the leader of the Jets to death, then is himself stabbed to death by her boyfriend, who is subsequently cornered and killed by one of the Sharks.

1963   Lewis Yablonsky writes *The Violent Gang*. Along with many other experts, Yablonsky believes that, for the most part, youth who join gangs are not sociopathic or seriously disturbed, but rather a

1963 *cont.*   product of their social status; that is, that most 1963 youth join gangs because of their low social status and their lack of opportunity, including educational, social, and economic opportunity, rather than because they are crazy or unbalanced.

1964   Wah Ching (Youth of China) is the first foreign-born gang organized by Chinese immigrants to protect themselves from American-born Chinese. By recruiting new members among recent immigrants, this gang becomes powerful.

Mobilization for Youth, a project focusing on a 67-block area in the Lower East Side of New York City, begins. It is founded on the premise that delinquent and criminal acts committed by people, including youth, in low-income groups are primarily a result of obstacles they encounter in trying to improve their social and economic situation. Program objectives include "(1) to increase the employability of youths from low-income families, (2) to improve and make more accessible training and work preparation facilities, (3) to help young people achieve employment goals equal to their capacities, (4) to increase employment opportunities for the area's youth, and (5) to help minority group youngsters overcome discrimination in hiring" (Mobilization for Youth 1964, 2). Programs to help these youth reach their goals include a job center, an urban youth service corps, on-the-job training programs, reading clinics, preschool education, and guidance counselors. A staff of lawyers help welfare clients exercise their rights, a housing office collects incidents of landlord violations, and advisors help clients make positive changes in their lives. This program stands out from many others because it helps impoverished residents of low-income areas to help themselves. However, the program worries many people because of its political activities; the FBI investigates those who participate in organized action, newspapers charge the project with subversion, project files are confiscated, and the use and effectiveness of federal as well as local funds are questioned. As Richard Quinney explains, "To provide the poor with services and assistance from above has been the traditional way of doing things. It is regarded as subversive when the poor attempt to change the social pattern of their poverty. Welfare is legitimate oppression, political action by the poor is anarchy" (Quinney 1970, 202).

1965   The United States allows increased Chinese immigration, which adds many Chinese teenagers and their families to the U.S. population. Chinese communities cannot cope with the great influx of immigrants. Newcomers receive little help, and there is an increase in Chinese teenage participation in youth gangs.

1967   The Youth Manpower Project of the Woodlawn Organization in Chicago begins. It is a highly controversial project, costing $1 million, developed by the Community Action Program of the U.S. Office of Economic Opportunity. The project's major goals are to provide job training and referral, reduce gang violence, and reduce the risk of riots in gang areas. The staff includes the leaders of two major gangs: the East Side Disciples and the Blackstone Rangers. Members of each gang staff two training centers; with a professional training staff of only four people and approximately 30 young adults and 600 participating youth, the program is not successful in changing youth attitudes and values. The police, local community agencies, local legislators, national legislators, and the news media choose sides in praising or condemning the project, and it becomes so controversial that the government shuts it down.

1969   David "King David" Barksdale is shot in an ambush. He is the leader and founder of the Black Gangster Disciple Nation. The gang adopts the Jewish Star of David, along with upturned pitchforks, as its symbol. This gang is part of the Folk Nation group of gangs formed in response to the

1969 *cont.*   conglomerate Black P. Stone Nation, a group of gangs who control the Englewood area of Chicago.

1970s   Gang activity and violence appears to subside. Cities find fewer incidences of gang violence and studies of gang organization, characteristics, and activities do not appear with the same frequency as they did in the late 1950s and early 1960s. Many youth agencies refocus their attention on other problems, such as status offenses (which include curfew violations and running away from home) and pay less attention to problems with gangs.

About this time, more studies concerning female participation in gang activities appear. Several researchers begin to rely on female as well as male gang informants. Several studies show that the girls are primarily seen as sexual objects—that is, they are girlfriends of gang members or provide sex to gang members. Females also provide other services to the gang. A girl might lure rival gang members to an area where her gang members can hurt or kill them, or she might carry drugs or weapons for the male gang members because police officers are less likely to search young girls for these objects.

Current prison gangs, unlike prison gangs of earlier years, start forming in response to the number of street gang members in prison rather than because of conditions within the prison. Gangs gain members and integrate their organization into prison life. Gang rivalries and violence increase as gang leaders gain power and control over young inmates. Disciplining gang members becomes more of a problem than disciplining non-gang members.

In the early 1970s, the East Los Angeles Concerned Parents Group forms to combat gang violence. It will become the longest-running grassroots organization as well as one of the most successful in dealing with the youth-gang problem. It starts as a support group for the parents of young gang members who have died in gang-related violence. Brother Modesto Leon, who is a monk in the Claretian Order, works with parents to help them actively communicate with each other no matter what gangs their children are in, to learn how to deal with impending gang fights, and to learn effective ways to control their children. Parents learn to trust people in authority positions, to work with probation officers, and to call the police when they think it is necessary. They also involve themselves in mediation meetings between rival gangs.

1971   The Federation de Barrios Unidos is formed in East Los Angeles. A federation of gangs or barrios, it mediates disputes between rival gangs and gang members, controls gang violence, and works to combat drug use and sales among gang members. The federation forms community improvement associations that use gang members to rehabilitate old buildings, sponsors a boxing program, and mediates rival-gang disputes. Many people declare the program successful in combating gang activity and violence.

1975   Philadelphia develops the Crisis Intervention Network (CIN) as a modified street-worker program. Street workers travel in radio-dispatched cars responding to calls to a crisis-intervention hotline that operates 24 hours a day. They work closely with police to defuse volatile situations, including incidents of gang violence.

1980s   The increased presence of crack cocaine and easy access to guns are believed to be the major factors in the growth of gangs and their institutionalization as major players in the drug trade. Many believe that gang activity has increased and has become more violent and more lethal during this time. Drive-by shootings and gang involvement in the drug trade are increasingly reported in the news.

1980   Los Angeles officials believe that the number of gang homicides are peaking in the city. The gang

1980 *cont.*   unit of the Los Angeles Sheriff's Department doubles in size, the District Attorney's office initiates Operation Hardcore, and Community Youth Gang Services (CYGS) is established. CYGS is one of the largest non-law-enforcement, anti-gang programs in the country. It integrates prevention, intervention, and community mobilization efforts with support from various justice agencies and uses an interactive, multifaceted program called Target Area Strategy (TAS). The Los Angeles County Probation Department authorizes the development of its Specialized Gang Supervision Program, which works with young people who are identified as gang members by themselves or by others, those who participate in gang killings and gang violence, and those on probation who are likely to become involved in gang activity. The primary job of the probation officers is surveillance of gang members.

Teen Angels, a gang-rights magazine, makes its debut. The magazine focuses on the Hispanic market and publishes photographs sent in by gangs, along with any personal messages they want to send. Favorite poses include gang members holding guns, showing gang signs, or displaying drawings of their gang symbols. Reprints of articles by the American Civil Liberties Union (ACLU) often appear in the magazine, emphasizing the rights of individuals and groups and demonstrating to gang members that they do have rights.

1982   At least 83 percent of the largest U.S. cities currently have a gang problem, 27 percent of cities with a population of 100,000 or more, and 13 percent of cities with a population of 10,000 or more, according to Walter B. Miller, who authors the report *Crime by Youth Gangs in the United States* for the U.S. Office of Juvenile Justice and Delinquency Prevention.

1983   Gang observers begin to notice an increase in gangs with an interest in the occult. These gangs are organized around a central theme of gaining occult powers and belief in the power of Satan, and they are primarily composed of affluent white youth.

1984   In Chicago, Clark Reid Martell, 25, founds Romantic Violence, considered to be the first neo-Nazi skinhead gang in the United States. Twelve other young men join Martell in this gang, and six of these members along with Martell are convicted of breaking into a woman's apartment, beating her, and drawing a swastika on the wall with her blood. They commit this act in response to seeing the woman talking with some African-Americans.

1985   Another skinhead gang appears, this time in San Francisco. Robert Heick, 20, changes his name to Bob Blitz, gathers several teenagers together, and forms the American Front. They move into an apartment and call their neighborhood Skinhead Hill. They paint swastikas on the sidewalks in their neighborhood and attack people with long hair, interracial couples, and anyone else they don't like.

Major news media report that the primary elections in the 26th Ward of Chicago involve gang members. Hispanic Alderman Torres is supported by the Democratic party and Gutierrez, the challenger, is supported by the Republican mayor. Both candidates use gang members to help in their campaigns; activities range from hanging election posters to getting out the vote. The former leader of one gang is the coordinator of precinct captains for one candidate.

1987   Many street gangs begin to take on characteristics similar to those of organized crime. They set up systems for laundering money, put murder contracts out on people, and have access to unlimited sources of money.

1988   In response to a new high of 387 gang-related homicides in Los Angeles County in 1987, the city council provides the Los Angeles Police Department with funding to conduct a series of 1,000-officer sweeps through known gang areas to arrest anyone

1988 *cont.*   who dresses like, talks like, or acts like a member of a street gang. The police believe that without these sweeps the number of gang-related homicides will be even higher for this year. So many youths are arrested during these sweeps that the LAPD has to set up mobile booking units at the Los Angeles Coliseum. Some reports indicate that at least half of all those arrested are not gang members.

The California legislature passes the California Street Terrorism Enforcement and Prevention (STEP) Act to help deter serious crime. The act "makes it a crime to engage in criminal gang activity, [but] subjects persons to sentence provision aimed at buildings in which criminal gang activity takes place and permits the prosecution of parents under a parental responsibility theory" (Burrell 1990, 745). "Under the Act, law enforcement officers serve personal notices on gang members, who then become eligible for enhanced sentences. The notice ensures that the gang member has read and understands the Act and that he or she is aware of the gang's illegal activities and its legal status as a criminal street gang" (Reiner 1992, 161).

The police department in Honolulu, Hawaii, estimates that 22 gangs, with 450 members, are active in the city.

1989   Police departments in Ohio (Columbus, Akron, Toledo, and Cincinnati), West Virginia (Wheeling, Charleston), Virginia (Richmond), and Indiana (Indianapolis) begin to notice that crack cocaine has infiltrated their cities. The sale and use of crack cocaine is spreading to smaller cities throughout the United States with the help of large corporate gangs in big cities such as Detroit.

An initiative proposed by the Office of Human Services, U.S. Department of Health and Human Services, is another example of projects using community organization and community mobilization to prevent gang violence. Bringing local neighborhood residents and organizations together to work on solving gang problems is the latest approach believed most likely to stem the violence. This includes local community agency responsibility, inter-agency coordination, grassroots citizen participation, community policing, and youth involvement.

1990 The *New York Times* carries one of the first stories about juvenile gang activity moving to the suburbs: "Not Just the Inner City: Well-to-Do Join Gangs" (April 10, 1990, by Seth Mydan). Some of the cities mentioned as having suburban gangs include Honolulu, Portland, Seattle, Phoenix, Tucson, Dallas, Chicago, Minneapolis, and Omaha.

1992 Officials in Albuquerque, New Mexico, notice an explosion of graffiti, at least some of it created by gang members. The city council addresses this problem by appointing a Task Force on Graffiti Vandalism to study the problems associated with graffiti. As a result of the efforts of the task force, Albuquerque enacts the Graffiti Vandalism Ordinance, which creates an Office of Anti-Graffiti Coordination as well as a city program to cover up the graffiti.

On April 29, a jury in Simi Valley decides that four Los Angeles police officers are not guilty of excessive force against Rodney King. Parts of Los Angeles erupt in riots, and fires destroy several areas of the city. As a result of these riots, attention is drawn to the problem of gangs in the city. Two of the city's major gangs, the Crips and the Bloods, in part as a result of the truce they have in force at the time of the riots, call for a new city to be built. Instead of rebuilding the liquor stores and other businesses, they suggest that all abandoned buildings should be gutted, new parks should be built, local businesses should be encouraged, schools should be rebuilt, and, most importantly, jobs should be created that pay a decent, living wage for the local citizens. The city's plans for the area are different; they include rebuilding the areas and maintaining the status quo without solving the deeper problems.

1993   The police department in Honolulu estimates that 171 gangs with approximately 1,267 members are active in the city.

1994   The Violent Crime Control and Enforcement Act is signed into law by President Clinton. This law puts 100,000 new police officers on the street, pumps nearly $7 billion into prevention programs, and allows 13-year-olds charged with violent crimes (murder, armed robbery, and rape) to be treated as adults. The act allows existing criminal-justice block grants to be used for anti-gang activities and authorizes $1 million for the U.S. attorney general to use in developing a national strategy to help federal law-enforcement agencies coordinate gang-related investigations.

Police in Fort Worth, Texas, having tried every other approach they could think of to reduce gang activity and violence in their city, suggest that six gang leaders should be placed on the police payroll. They believe that these leaders can be trained as mediators in gang disputes and as counselors against violence. City residents complain loudly about paying each of these gang members an estimated $10,000 per year, which they believe will support criminal activity, and the police withdraw their idea.

A *New York Times*/CBS News Poll reports that 18 percent of white youth believe that gangs are a problem in their schools, reflecting a growing belief that gangs are not just a problem in ethnic, primarily African-American and Hispanic, neighborhoods.

References

Asbury, H. 1927. *The Gangs of New York*. New York: Capricorn.

Bernard, W. 1949. *Jailbait*. New York: Greenberg.

Burrell, Susan. 1990. "Gang Evidence: Issues for Criminal Defense." *Santa Clara Law Review* 30 (Summer): 739–790.

Cloward, Richard A., and Lloyd E. Ohlin. 1960. *Delinquency and Opportunity: A Theory of Delinquent Gangs.* Glencoe, IL: Free Press.

Cohen, Albert K. 1955. *Delinquent Boys: The Culture of the Gang.* Glencoe, IL: Free Press.

Dunston, Leonard G. 1990. *Reaffirming Prevention. Report of the Task Force on Juvenile Gangs.* Albany, NY: New York State Division for Youth.

Furfey, Paul Hanley. 1926. *The Gang Age: A Study of the Pre-adolescent Boy and His Recreational Needs.* New York: Macmillan.

Miller, Walter B. 1982. *Crime by Youth Gangs and Groups in the United States,* a report for the National Institute for Juvenile Justice and Delinquency Prevention, U.S. Department of Justice. Washington, DC: Office of Juvenile Justice and Delinquency Prevention.

Mobilization for Youth. 1964. *Action on the Lower East Side, Program Report: July 1962–January 1964.* New York: Mobilization for Youth, Inc.

Puffer, J. Adams. 1912. *The Boy and His Gang.* Boston: Houghton Mifflin Company.

Quinney, Richard. 1970. *The Social Reality of Crime.* Boston: Little, Brown and Company.

Reiner, Ira. 1992. *Gangs, Crime and Violence in Los Angeles.* Los Angeles, CA: Office of the District Attorney of the County of Los Angeles.

Robison, Sophia. 1960. *Juvenile Delinquency: Its Nature and Control.* New York: Holt, Rinehart and Winston.

Shaw, Clifford R., and Henry D. McKay. 1931. *Social Factors in Juvenile Delinquency: Report on the Causes of Crime.* Vol. 2. A Report for the National Commission on Law Observance and Enforcement. Washington, DC: U.S. Government Printing Office.

———. 1942. *Juvenile Delinquency and Urban Areas.* Chicago: University of Chicago Press.

Short, James F. 1990. "New Wine in Old Bottles? Change and Continuity in American Gangs." In *Gangs in America,* ed. C. Ronald Huff. Newbury Park, CA: Sage Publications.

Tannenbaum, Frank. 1939. *Crime and the Community.* Boston: Ginn and Company.

Thrasher, Frederic M. 1927. *The Gang: A Study of 1,313 Gangs in Chicago.* Chicago: University of Chicago Press.

Welfare Council of New York City. 1950. *Working with Teenage Groups: A Report on the Central Harlem Project.* New York: Welfare Council of New York City.

Yablonsky, Lewis. 1970. *The Violent Gang.* Rev. ed. Baltimore: Penguin.

Biographical Sketches 3

This section provides short biographical sketches of individuals who play or have played a key role in working with gangs and conducting research in areas of vital interest to those who are concerned with understanding and working with gangs. People have been chosen based on their prominence in the field of gangs and gang research.

Leon Bing (1950–)

It might seem surprising that Leon Bing, a woman journalist from a rich family in Pasadena, California, would want to write about gang members and would be willing to work to gain the trust of many of these tough young boys. She had written about youth issues and had talked with several youngsters who mentioned gangs and gang activity before she started to focus on gangs herself. Her first contact with gang members occurred in 1986 when she was writing an article for the *L.A. Weekly*. Not knowing how to make contact with them, she asked a ticket-taker at a local movie theater if he knew any gang members or knew where she could find some. He told her that many members of the Bloods met every Sunday afternoon in a certain park in south

Pasadena. Along with Howard Rosenberg, a photo editor from
the *L.A. Weekly*, she went to the park, where they saw plenty of
red, the Bloods' color, worn by teenagers and young men. That
day marked the beginning of her relationship with several gang
members. She wrote *Do or Die*, a book about young gang members and their lives, and for four years she has written articles
about gangs for the *L.A. Weekly*.

Anne Campbell (1951–)

Anne Campbell was one of the first scholars to explore the participation of females in gangs. She is currently a principal lecturer in
the School of Health, Social, and Policy Studies at Teeside University in England and is the author of *The Girls in the Gang* (1984)
and *Girl Delinquents* (1981). Formerly an associate professor in the
School of Criminal Justice at Rutgers University, she has spent
nearly 20 years investigating aggression and violent behavior. She
spent two years as a participant-observer with New York female
gangs and reported the results of this research in *The Girls in the
Gang*. Her current research concerns theories about the similarities and differences in aggressive actions of women and men.

Her research and writing grew out of her frustration with the
lack of information on female delinquency. As a residential social
worker in her first job after graduating from Oxford University in
1972, she worked with delinquent girls. The girls were divided
into two groups. One group was boisterous and aggressive, and,
according to the terminology of the day, they were "acting out";
the girls in the other group were more withdrawn and more complex, displaying self-injurious behavior and other less overt
means of gaining attention. Campbell chose to work with the
boisterous and aggressive group, but found no research in the library that could help her understand the behavior of these girls.
As she struggled to help them she realized that "without some co-
herent conceptual framework with which to approach these girls'
problems" she would not succeed (Campbell 1984, vii).

Campbell returned to Oxford University to work on a doctorate focusing on female delinquency. She became convinced
that delinquent and aggressive behavior expressed by women
was not understood by men. Most men viewed these girls as mal-
adjusted because they seemed to be acting like men. Aggressive
behavior is considered a male characteristic, and women who are
aggressive are seen as unfeminine and not totally sane.

Richard Cloward (1926–)

Richard Cloward received his B.A. from the University of Rochester in 1949, a master's in social work from Columbia University in 1950, and his Ph.D. from Columbia in 1958. He has taught social work at Columbia since 1954. In 1960, along with Lloyd Ohlin, he wrote *Delinquency and Opportunity: A Theory of Delinquent Gangs*, in which they explain their belief that social strain accounts for juvenile and gang delinquency. He was awarded the Dennis Carroll Award by the International Society of Criminology in 1965 because of this book, one of the first to connect social strain and delinquency. He later won the C. Wright Mills Award from the Society for the Study of Social Problems in 1971 for his book *Regulating the Poor*. Other books include *Social Perspectives on Behavior* (1958), *The Politics of Turmoil* (1974), and *Poor People's Movements* (1977).

Albert K. Cohen (1918–)

Cohen received a B.A. from Harvard University in 1939 and his master's degree from Indiana University in 1942. After working for one year at the Indiana Boys School (a state institution for male juvenile delinquents), he returned to Harvard for a year of graduate study in 1946. Cohen joined the sociology department at Indiana University in 1947. He received his Ph.D. in sociology from Harvard in 1951 and, after 17 years at Indiana University, joined the faculty at the University of Connecticut, where he taught for 23 years until his retirement in 1988. His best-known work is *Delinquent Boys: The Culture of the Gang* (1955). Another book, *Deviance and Control* (1966), was one of the first comprehensive textbooks in the field of deviance. His published works have focused primarily on issues relating to the many theories of deviance. He has been a visiting professor at the University of California (Berkeley and Santa Cruz), Cambridge University, John Jay College of Criminal Justice, and the University of Haifa (Israel), and a visiting scholar at Arizona State University and Kansai University in Osaka, Japan. He spent one year at the Center for Advanced Study in the Behavioral Sciences at Stanford. He has contributed articles on gangs and delinquency to several professional journals.

G. David Curry (1948–)

Curry is a professor of criminology at the University of Missouri. He was previously an associate professor in the Crime and Justice Program in the Department of Sociology and Anthropology at West Virginia University. He completed National Institute of Mental Health (NIMH) postdoctoral work with the Methodology Committee in the Department of Behavioral Sciences at the University of Chicago in 1987–1988. He has worked for SPSS Inc., as a statistical writer and as a senior research associate at the University of Chicago for an evaluation of a gang-intervention program targeting minority students in inner-city African-American and Hispanic schools. His publications include *Sunshine Patriots: Punishment and the Vietnam Offender* (1985), "Gang Homicide, Delinquency, and Community," written with Irving A. Spergel and published in *Criminology* in August 1988, and *Survey of Youth Gang Problems and Programs in 45 Cities and 6 Sites* (1990), written with Spergel and others and published by the National Youth Gang Suppression and Intervention Project at the University of Chicago School of Social Service Administration. Curry and Spergel often work together on research concerning youth-gang delinquency. Curry also conducts research on women, violence, and crime.

Jeffrey Fagan

Fagan is director of the Center for Law and Social Policy at the URSA Institute and an associate professor in the School of Criminal Justice at Rutgers University. He has written profiles of violent delinquents, and his research interests and other publications concern youth gangs, the transfer of violent delinquents to adult court, the relationship between drug abuse and criminality, and conflicts and abuse within the family. He is currently principal investigator on a research and development program focusing on the treatment of violent delinquents. He recently completed a study of drug use, drug selling, and other criminality among people who use crack cocaine and other drugs in New York City. Along with Ko-Lin Chin and Robert Kelly, he is conducting research on the patterns of extortion and victimization used by Asian gangs in New York City. He is co-author with Joseph Weis of *Drug Use and Delinquency among Inner City Youths* and is editor of the *Journal of Research in Crime and Delinquency*.

In his research, Fagan has found that substance abuse plays a larger role in a juvenile's participation in gang activities than the degree of integration the juvenile exhibits with his or her family. He has also found that when asked why they joined a gang, many gang members answer that they joined to protect their neighborhood.

Arnold Goldstein

Goldstein joined the Psychology Department at Syracuse University as a professor of clinical psychology in 1963; he taught at Syracuse and directed the university's Psychotherapy Center until 1980. He founded the Center for Research on Aggression in 1981. In 1985, he joined the Division of Special Education at Syracuse. As a researcher and theoretician, he has been interested in working with subjects who are difficult to reach and understand. Since 1980, he has focused most of his research efforts on juvenile offenders and parents who abuse their children. He has developed psychoeducational programs and curricula that are designed to teach prosocial behavior to people who are chronically antisocial. In much of his writing he has focused on young gang members who face more than the normal amount of tension and stress in the process of developing their identity. He believes that many young people join a gang primarily for the status that being a gang member confers on them, rather than for the economic opportunities that the gang provides. In his book *Delinquent Gangs: A Psychological Perspective*, Goldstein explores the characteristics of the contemporary gang and suggests strategies for successful intervention. In *The Gang Intervention Handbook*, Goldstein and Ronald Huff present the work of a group of experts on gang research and intervention strategies.

John Hagedorn (1947–)

Hagedorn is coordinator of the Youth Program in Milwaukee County's Department of Health and Human Services and is affiliated with the University of Wisconsin–Milwaukee Urban Research Center. As a social scientist who also has been a community organizer, journalist, and gang-program director, Hagedorn has broad experience in a variety of situations. Instead of asking the local police department to provide him with the names of gang members to contact for his research, Hagedorn gained access to Milwaukee's gangs through the contacts he made as a gang-program director. He is currently coordinating an effort to reform Milwaukee County's social-welfare system while completing his Ph.D. dissertation on that topic. He is the author (with former gang leader Perry Macon) of *People and Folks: Gangs, Crime, and the Underclass in a Rustbelt City* (1988), published by Lake View Press. The book portrays gang members as racially oppressed minorities and suggests that white sociologists who study gangs offer too much theory and too little fact. His research interests include the relationship of gangs and the people in lower-class and urban neighborhoods, changing public policy toward gangs and the underclass, organizational change in social welfare, and the impact that welfare has on lower-class communities.

Ruth Horowitz (1947–)

Ruth Horowitz, an associate professor of sociology at the University of Delaware, has made important contributions to the scholarly study of gangs. She received her Ph.D. from the University of Chicago and has written several articles on gangs in Chicano communities. Her book *Honor and the American Dream: Culture and Identity in a Chicano Community* was published by Rutgers University Press in 1983. She is currently working with James Inciardi and Anne Pottieger on a study of seriously delinquent and drug-abusing youth and is completing a book on social-service workers and teenage mothers. Horowitz has studied the relationships that develop between gang members and the communities in which they live, and how community residents are able to reconcile their feelings about violent acts committed by gang members and the relationship between themselves and the gang members.

C. Ronald Huff

Huff is currently director of the Criminal Justice Research Center and professor of public policy and management at Ohio State University, where he has taught since 1979. Prior to joining the Ohio State faculty, he taught for five years at the University of California (Irvine) and Purdue University, where he coordinated the applied sociology program and designed the criminology and criminal-justice majors. His previous professional positions have been in correctional, mental health, and children's services agencies and institutions. His publications include more than 40 journal articles and book chapters, numerous research reports and monographs, and six books. He has completed his seventh book, *Convicted but Innocent: Wrongful Conviction and Public Policy* (with Arye Rattner and the late Edward Sagarin). As editor of *Gangs in America* (1990), Huff pulled together other leading experts in the field of gang research and provided important data to researchers and others interested in this field.

Malcolm Klein

As professor of sociology at University of Southern California (USC) and senior research associate with the Social Science Research Institute, USC, Malcolm Klein has conducted research on a variety of topics concerning gangs and gang characteristics. He has been involved in gang research for more than 30 years. From 1962 to 1968, he directed evaluation of and basic research projects on juvenile gangs. Since 1969 his research has focused on comprehensive criminal-justice planning, evaluation of deinstitutionalization programs (that is, programs that focus on getting criminals back into society rather than incarcerating them), and the assessment of the legislative impact on major criminal justice issues. His current research involves police handling of juvenile offenders and police investigation of gang-related homicides.

Klein received the Edwin H. Sutherland Award in 1990 from the American Society of Criminology for his research efforts. He believes that there are no simple solutions to understanding gangs or solving the problems created by gangs. He believes that many criminal-justice agencies wrongly tend to stereotype gang members, blame them for all sorts of problems, and label gang members and other youths in gang neighborhoods as delinquents.

George W. Knox

Knox currently teaches in the Department of Corrections and Criminal Justice, Chicago State University, where he heads the National Gang Crime Research Center. His publications include research on teenage and adult offenders and rehabilitation programs. He is the editor of the *Gang Journal*. His current research efforts focus on the national and international nature of gangs, their characteristics, activities, and patterns of violence. Knox received his B.A. from the University of Minnesota in 1974, his M.A. from the University of Texas at Arlington in 1975, and his Ph.D. from the University of Chicago in 1978.

Cheryl L. Maxson

Maxson is currently a research associate at the Social Science Research Institute at the University of Southern California. Her current research and publication activity focus on the nature of gang violence, gang-identification practices used by police, and police response to gang-related crime. Previous research topics have included predicting legislative change and evaluating the implementation and impact of legislative initiatives.

Walter B. Miller (1920–)

Walter Miller has focused on youth-gang problems since 1954, when he joined the staff of the Special Youth Program in Roxbury, Massachusetts. This program was one of the country's first detached-worker programs, in which social and other youth workers were sent out into the streets to meet with and work with youngsters who were in trouble with the law or at risk of becoming involved in illegal activities. He has published more than 40 papers and books on youth gangs, juvenile delinquency, and lower-class subcultures. One of his papers, "Lower Class Culture as a Generating Milieu of Gang Delinquency" (1958), is the single most frequently cited journal article in the literature on criminology. He retired in 1982 from the Center for Criminal Justice at Harvard Law School and has continued to write, lecture, and consult on youth gangs and related issues.

Joan W. Moore

Joan Moore is a professor in the Department of Sociology at the University of Wisconsin at Milwaukee. She has worked for several years on a series of studies concerning gangs in the East Los Angeles area. These studies have provided material for her two books, *Homeboys* (1978), and *Going Down to the Barrio* (1991). She also has been concerned with the relevance to gangs and gang behavior of many of the popular theories of poverty in Latino communities and is co-editing a document focusing on impoverished communities.

Lloyd Ohlin (1918–)

A sociologist, Ohlin received his B.A. from Brown University in 1940, his M.A. from Indiana University in 1942, and his Ph.D. in 1954 from the University of Chicago. He was a sociology instructor at Indiana University, a sociologist and actuary at the Illinois Parole and Pardon Board in Joliet, a supervising research sociologist, and a director at the Center for Education and Research in Corrections at the University of Chicago. In 1960, with Richard Cloward, he wrote *Delinquency and Opportunity: A Theory of Delinquent Gangs*. In this book, they discuss their belief that juvenile and gang delinquency can best be explained by theories of social strain. He joined the faculty at Columbia University as a professor of sociology in 1956 and became director of the Research Center in 1962. He spent one year as a special assistant to the secretary for juvenile delinquency in the Office of the Secretary of the U.S. Department of Health, Education, and Welfare. In 1967 he became the Roscoe Pound professor of criminology at Harvard University. In addition to his teaching duties, he has been a member of the research council of the Division of Youth for the state of New York, associate director of the President's Commission on Law Enforcement and Administration of Justice, chairman of the advisory board of the Massachusetts Department of Youth Services, chairman of the advisory board of the National Institute of Law Enforcement and Criminal Justice, and a consultant to the Ford Foundation, the National Institute of Mental Health, and the American Bar Foundation. Two books edited by him are *Combating Crime* (1967), and *Prisoners in America: Perspectives on Our Correctional System* (1973).

Luis J. Rodriguez (1954–)

Rodriguez grew up in South Central Los Angeles and was 11 years old when the 1965 Watts riots erupted in his old neighborhood. In 1970, when he was 16 years old, he was beaten and arrested during the Chicano Moratorium Against the War, known to many as the East L.A. Riot. The riot resulted when sheriff's officers and police attacked demonstrators, leaving at least three dead and much of Whittier Boulevard in flames. Rodriguez is now an award-winning poet, journalist, and critic whose works have appeared in the *Nation*, *Chicago Reporter*, *Playboy*, and the *Los Angeles Weekly*. He also is the publisher of the Tia Chucha Press, which has published poetry by African-American, Puerto

Rican, Chicano, and Native American writers. *Always Running: La Vida Loca: Gang Days in L.A.*, his poignant book about growing up in Watts and East Los Angeles, was published in 1992.

James F. Short (1924–)

James Short was one of the first scholars to write about gangs. He is a professor of sociology at Washington State University, where he has also served as dean of the graduate school (1964–1968) and director of the Social Research Center (1970–1985). He received his Ph.D. from the University of Chicago in 1951. His books include *Suicide and Homicide* (1951), written with Andrew F. Henry, *Group Process and Gang Delinquency* (1965), written with Fred L. Strodtbeck, and *Delinquency and Society* (1990). He has contributed to many books, including *Juvenile Gangs in America* (1967), edited by Malcolm W. Klein. He is a former editor of the *American Sociological Review* and an associate editor of the *Annual Review of Sociology*. A former president of the Pacific and American Sociological Associations, he has participated as a fellow at the Center for Advanced Study in the Behavior Sciences, the Institute of Criminology at Cambridge University, the Rockefeller Center in Bellagio, and the Centre for Socio-Legal Studies at Oxford. He has received numerous honors, including NIMH and Guggenheim Fellowships, the Edwin H. Sutherland Award from the American Society of Criminology, the Bruce Smith Award from the Academy of Criminal Justice Sciences, and the Paul W. Tappan Award from the Western Society of Criminology. He is the 1990 Beto Chair professor of Criminal Justice at Sam Houston State University.

Irving Spergel (1924–)

One of the major researchers in the field of gang studies, Spergel received his B.S. in 1946 from the City College of the City University of New York, an M.A. from Columbia University, a master's in social work from the University of Illinois in 1952, and a doctorate in social work from Columbia University in 1960. He has been a professor in the School of Social Service Administration at the University of Chicago since 1960 and is a principal investigator for the National Youth Gang Suppression and Intervention Research and Development Program, a long-term evaluation of a gang-intervention program. This program, funded by the Office of Juvenile Justice and Delinquency Prevention of the National Institute of Justice, targets minority students in African-American and Hispanic inner-city schools. As a street-gang worker, supervisor, and court worker in the 1950s in New York City, Spergel learned first-hand about gangs and the problems they cause as well as the problems these youths face while growing up.

His major research interests are youth gangs, community organization, and the evaluation of programs for youth services. He has completed a statewide evaluation of the Comprehensive Community Based Youth Services program of the Illinois Department of Children and Family Services, a diversion program for status offenders, those found guilty of curfew violations or running away from home. This program attempts to keep status offenders from being sent into the juvenile-justice and the child-welfare systems. Spergel has been a consultant for the B'nai Brith Youth Organization; the U.S. Departments of Justice, Labor, and State; the American Social Health Association, and the Illinois Department of Corrections. He has received awards from a variety of organizations and agencies including the National Institute of Mental Health, the Ford Foundation, the President's Committee on Juvenile Delinquency and Youth Development, the Office of Economic Opportunity, the Law Enforcement Assistance Administration, the U.S. Department of Justice, and the Illinois Law Enforcement Commission. His major publications include *Street Gang Work* (1966), *Community Problem Solving: The Delinquency Example* (1969), *Community Organizations: Studies in Constraints* (1972), and *Social Innovation: Politics, Program, Evaluation* (1982). His most recent publication is *The Youth Gang Problem: A Community Approach*, an excellent and comprehensive resource book. He has also contributed to several books and has written many journal articles, organizational publications, and research reports.

Carl S. Taylor (1949–)

After receiving his bachelor's degree at Michigan State University (MSU), Taylor was hired by the MSU Office of Student Affairs to run its Minority Aid Program, which he developed into a successful program that was copied by many other campuses. After earning his master's degree in criminal justice in 1976 at Michigan State, he worked as a manager for a security company in Detroit, where he became interested in gangs and gang behavior. Taylor received his Ph.D. in the administration of higher education in 1980 from MSU. He became director of Criminal Justice Programs at Jackson Community College in Michigan in 1989 and adjunct professor in the School of Criminal Justice at MSU. He is currently professor of criminal justice and clinical professor at Grand Valley State University in Allendale and director of the Youth Culture Studies Center. At the University of Michigan, he was a member of the Public Health Think Tank on Substance Abuse in 1990. He also was an instructor for the National Institute for Corrections, a guest lecturer at the FBI academy, a member of the Black Community Crusade for the Children's Task Force on Violence sponsored by the Children's Defense Fund, a member of the Michigan Governor's Committee on Juvenile Justice, and a consultant to the National Institute of Justice.

He has spent the past 14 years conducting extensive research on the subculture of gangs and their impact on society. He also has lectured throughout the country and has appeared on national television programs discussing urban gangs and prisons, gangs and school environments, youth gangs and law enforcement, and drug abuse and gangs. He wrote about his research on Detroit youth and gangs in *Dangerous Society* (1990). In 1993, he wrote *Girls, Gangs, Women and Drugs*, a provocative study of female gang members and the effects of poverty, teen pregnancy, drugs, and illiteracy. He has contributed to several anthologies and professional journals.

Frederic M. Thrasher (1892–1962)

Thrasher wrote *The Gang: A Study of 1,313 Gangs in Chicago* (1927), one of the earliest studies of gangs. Although the book is not heavily statistical, it provides a natural history of gangs. It traces gang development and includes many photographs that help the reader imagine life in the early 1900s. He learned about gangs from social workers, court records, personal observation, census data, and others who had studied gangs.

James Diego Vigil (1938–)

As a young man growing up in East Los Angeles, Vigil was well acquainted with street gangs. Later, as a high school teacher, he worked closely with many Chicano youth groups, and as an anthropologist he has studied street gangs in the barrios of East Los Angeles. Vigil is currently associate professor of anthropology and director of the Center for Urban Policy and Ethnicity at the

University of Southern California. He received his B.S. in 1962 from California State University, Long Beach, an M.A. in social science from CSU, Sacramento, and an M.A. and a Ph.D. in anthropology from UCLA. Previous to his current position, he was chair of Chicano Studies at the University of Wisconsin at Madison, a professor at UCLA and Chaffey Community College, and has taught part-time at Whittier College and CSU's Sacramento and Los Angeles campuses. He concentrates mainly on urban anthropology, and his interest in youth issues comes from his experience as an educator and counselor. He has often focused his research on street gangs, especially the role of street socialization and the development of gangs. He has conducted fieldwork in a variety of urban, rural, and suburban barrios, and this research is documented in his book *Barrio Gangs* (1988). His other publications include *From Indians to Chicanos: The Dynamics of Mexican American Culture* (1984); contributions to *Violence and Homicide in Hispanic Communities* (1988), edited by Jess Kraus and associates and published by the National Institute of Mental Health; and articles in journals such as *Social Problems, Human Organization, Aztlan*, and *Ethos*. He is currently conducting cross-cultural research on gangs, studying African-American, Asian-American, and Latino-American youth.

Lewis Yablonsky (1924–)

Probably best known for his book *The Violent Gang*, first published in 1962, Yablonsky has also written *Crime and Delinquency* (1974) and *Robopaths: People as Machines* (1972). Along with many other experts, Yablonsky believes that most young people who join gangs are not sociopathic or seriously disturbed, but are a product of their low social status and lack of opportunity.

He received his B.S. from Rutgers in 1948 and his M.A. and Ph.D. from New York University in 1952 and 1957, respectively. His first job, while he was working on his master's degree, was as a supervisor for the Essex County Youth House in Newark, New Jersey. He became a lecturer in sociology at the City College of City University of New York in 1951 and went on to lecture at Columbia University, Harvard, and Smith College. He was an associate professor of sociology at the University of Massachusetts, then at UCLA, and retired as a professor at California State University at Northridge. He was a consultant to the Rockefeller Brothers Organization on Delinquency in 1957 and to Columbia Broadcasting System in 1958.

Facts and Statistics, Documents, and Quotations

4

Facts and Statistics

As with other social problems, statistics on the number of gangs in the United States, the total number of gang members, and the number of crimes they commit annually are difficult to obtain. The major problem is in defining the terms "gang," "gang member," and "gang-related crime." Many researchers agree that estimates of the numbers of gangs and individual gang members are not always reliable or comparable because definitions vary. Gangs may have core members, fringe members, and "wannabes"—those who may claim to be gang members but are not so considered by core members. These distinctions usually are not made in any jurisdiction's statistics on gangs. Law-enforcement personnel usually take either a member-defined or a motive-defined approach to classifying crime as gang crime. Member-defined means that any offense committed by a gang member is gang related. Under motive-defined classification, only those crimes committed in the name of the gang, such as defense of territory, retaliation, or witness intimidation, are considered gang crimes. Because there is little agreement among law-enforcement agencies about how to identify gang-related crime, comparisons of data from different cities and states are difficult. However, some researchers have conducted national surveys in an attempt to estimate the depth and breadth of the gang phenomenon in this country.

Major National Surveys

In 1982, Walter Miller published one of the first studies to examine the extent of gang activity throughout the United States. It was supported by the U.S. Department of Justice's Office of Juvenile Justice and Delinquency Prevention (OJJDP). He identified 12 types of youth groups who violate the law, including three types of youth gangs (turf gangs, gain-oriented gangs, fighting gangs). He examined gang problems in 26 of the largest U.S. cities and later expanded his study to include 36 major metropolitan areas. In 18 of the 36 metropolitan areas, respondents reported having some type of gang problem. Approximately 2,300 gangs with 98,000 members existed during the 1970s, with most of them located in the largest cities, primarily Los Angeles, Chicago, New York, Philadelphia, Detroit, San Diego, San Antonio, Phoenix, San Francisco, and Boston. Gang members ranged in age from 10 to 21 years, and they accounted for approximately 42 percent of arrests for serious and violent crimes (Miller 1982).

Irving Spergel, David Curry, and Ronald Chance conducted the first comprehensive national survey of organized responses to gang problems in the late 1980s. They examined organized agency responses to gang activity in 101 cities thought to have problems with gangs. Police departments in these cities were contacted, and the researchers determined that 74 of the cities indeed had some type of gang problem. Finally, 45 of these cities reported that they had an organized agency or community response to their gang problems, and these cities were studied in depth. The researchers found that those cities with chronic gang problems primarily relied on suppression and community-organization strategies to deal with these problems, while cities with emerging gang problems relied primarily on suppression tactics. As a result of this study, Spergel and his colleagues developed a comprehensive model of gang prevention and intervention (Spergel and Curry 1990).

The Office of Juvenile Justice and Delinquency Prevention's Program of Research on Causes and Correlates of Juvenile Delinquency supported three in-depth studies of high-risk, inner-city youth in Denver, Pittsburgh, and Rochester. In 1993, Esbensen and Huizinga conducted the Denver Youth Survey. Also in 1993, Thornberry, Krohn, Lizotte, and Chard-Wierschem examined gang involvement with their Rochester Youth Development Study. Researchers found no gang activity in Pittsburgh. The Denver study found that 7 percent of the sample group were involved in gangs; male gang members were more involved than non-gang males in all types of delinquent activities; gang members did not remain in the gang for long (67 percent reported staying in the gang for only one year); and almost 75 percent reported that their gang was involved in fights, robberies, assaults, theft, and drug sales. The Rochester study found that 55 percent of the gang members were members for only one year, although 21 percent remained in the gang during the three years the study covered. Thornberry and his colleagues also found that their social facilitation model best explained gang participation; this model suggests that the group processes occurring within the gang leads to high rates of delinquency among gang members.

In 1992, Curry, Fox, Ball, and Stone conducted a National Assessment Survey of law-enforcement agencies in the 79 largest U.S. cities and 43 smaller cities. Survey results suggested that 4,881 gangs with 249,324 members existed in 1991. Law enforcement personnel in 91 percent of the 79 large cities reported the presence of gang problems in their cities, and 27 of the 79 cities reported the existence of female gangs. Sixty-four percent of the police departments reported that they believed suppression activities were the most effective in stemming gang activity, 63 percent thought case management of gang-member files was an effective means of preventing gang activities, 60 percent thought increased enforcement against gang members was effective, and 55 percent thought increased law-enforcement liaison activities were effective in preventing gang activity. Between 1988 and 1992, the percentage of cities reporting gang crime problems increased; in all cities crime rose from 72 percent to 85 percent; in the large cities, 75 percent of the cities in 1988 and 89 percent in 1992 reported gang problems; and in smaller cities, 70 percent in 1988 and 86 percent in 1992 reported problems.

In 1989, a school-crime supplement to the National Crime Victimization Survey was conducted. A nationally representative sample of students between the ages of 12 and 19 were interviewed. In central cities, 25 percent of all students reported gangs in their schools, while 8 percent of students in non-metropolitan areas reported gangs in their schools. In those schools in which gangs were found, 35 percent of the students interviewed said they were afraid of being attacked in school by gang members and 24 percent were afraid of being attacked on their way to or from school (Bastian and Taylor 1991).

Scope of the Problem

Walter Miller's 1982 study established that 83 percent of the largest cities in the United States had a gang problem, along with 27 percent of cities with a population over 100,000 and 13 percent of cities larger than 10,000. In 1983, Needle and Stapleton estimated that 39 percent of cities with populations between 100,000 and 249,999 had a gang problem. In a study of 79 of the largest U.S. cities published in 1992, Curry and his colleagues reported that 72, or 91.1 percent, of these cities had a gang problem, based on information provided by the police departments in each city. They estimated that 4,881 gangs were in existence in 1992 with approximately 249,324 members.

In a 1994 survey of 368 prosecutors' offices, the Institute for Law and Justice studied the extent of gang problems in the United States. The institute surveyed all 175 U.S. counties with populations over 250,000 as well as 193 prosecutors randomly selected from counties with populations between 50,000 and 250,000. Of the 175 largest counties, 84 percent reported gang problems within their counties, while 46 percent of the smaller jurisdictions reported some type of problem with gangs in their areas.

Researchers have found that gangs exist in most areas of the country. According to prosecutors in 12 rural areas of Colorado, Iowa, Michigan, Montana, New Hampshire, South Carolina, Texas, and Washington, gangs are the primary criminal problem in these areas (Justice Research and Statistics Association 1993). In 1989 C. Ronald Huff studied gang activity in Ohio through a survey of Ohio police chiefs. He found that the cities of Cleveland and Columbus had the most gangs, 50 and 20 gangs respectively. These gangs apparently developed from break-dancing and rap groups or street-corner groups as a result of increasing competition among local groups.

In 1993, the California Department of Justice estimated that there could be as many as 95,000 Hispanic gang members, 65,000 African American gang members, 15,000 Asian gang members, and 5,000 white gang members, including 400 skinheads, throughout the state at that time. By the year 2000, the department estimates, there could be as many as 250,000 gang members throughout the state; gang size will range from a few members to more than 1,000 members; gangs will recruit younger and younger children to their gangs, starting at age 10; some gangs will have fourth-generation members.

In Hawaii, an analysis of police data collected through the Gang Reporting Evaluation and Tracking (GREAT) System shows that as of December 1994 there were 192 gangs and 1,900 gang members in the state. The majority of the gang members were Filipino and Polynesian (75 percent), while the remainder were Asian (15 percent), African-American (2 percent), Mexican (1 percent), and from other ethnic groups (7 percent). Gang members range in age from 13 to 30 (Chesney-Lind et al. 1995). According to statistics from the Honolulu Police Department, there were 22 gangs with 450 members in 1988; in 1991 there were 45 gangs with 1,020; and in 1993 there were 171 gangs with 1,267 members (Chesney-Lind et al. 1994).

In 1990, the Los Angeles Police Department reported that 329 (30 percent) of all homicides in the city were gang-related homicides, while in Chicago, the police department reported that 101 (11 percent) of all homicides in the city were gang related (Spergel 1992).

The New Mexico Department of Public Safety collects statistics on gangs and reports that as of July 1994, 201 gangs existed in Albuquerque with a documented total of 3,500 members. Other researchers estimate that Albuquerque has approximately 6,000 gang members (New Mexico State Department of Public Safety 1994).

Demographics

Age

Based on reports in newspapers and on television, most people believe that the age at which children join gangs is getting younger and that most gang members are teenagers. In Frederic Thrasher's 1927 study of gangs, he found that members ranged in age from 6 to 50 years, but most members were between the ages of 11 to 25. In a study of New York gangs in the 1970s, H. Craig Collins (1979) found that the age of gang members ranged from 9 to 30, with many more members at both extremes than were found in earlier years. Using police-department data, Ko-Lin Chin (1990) studied New York gangs in the 1980s and found that the range in age of Chinese gang members was from 13 to 37 years, and the mean age was 22.7 years. In a 1992 study using

Honolulu Police Department figures, Meda Chesney-Lind and her colleagues reported that the police estimated that 77 percent of the 1,020 persons they believed were gang members in 1991 were at least 18 years of age. Walter Miller's 1982 study found that gang members ranged in age from 10 to 21 years with the peak age for membership at 17 years.

Most gang homicides appear to be committed by gang members who are in late adolescence or early adulthood. Maxson, Gordon and Klein (1985) studied gang-homicide statistics in Los Angeles in the 1980s and found that the mean age of gang homicide offenders was 19 years in the city and 20 years in the county. Spergel (1983) studied gang-homicide offender statistics in Chicago from 1978 to 1981 and found that 2.2 percent of these offenders were under the age of 14; 50 percent were between the ages of 15 and 18; 21.7 between the ages of 19 and 20; and 25.9 percent were over 21 years.

In Albuquerque, New Mexico, the police department has documented gang members who are heavily involved in drug activity as young as nine years old and are not surprised when they find children as young as 11 or 12 committing serious and violent crimes in the name of their gang (New Mexico Department of Public Safety 1994).

Sex

Data on females who become gang members is difficult to obtain and may often be unreliable. However, data on females who have committed crimes and who are known to the police as gang members are more available and reliable. In 1975, Miller estimated that 10 percent of all gang members were female. In 1979, Collins estimated that, while males outnumbered females in gangs in New York City by 20 to 1, he believed that approximately one-half of all gangs in the city had some type of female auxiliary. Like Miller, researchers such as Campbell (1984) and Lee (1991) have also estimated female participation at 10 percent of all gang members. Other researchers such as Jeffrey Fagan (1990) and Joan Moore (1991), who primarily use self-reports and observations in the field, estimate that female participation in gangs may be as high as 33 percent.

Police data on the number of females in gangs can only reflect the number of female gang members who have committed some sort of crime. These statistics suggest that females commit a relatively small amount of serious gang crime. Using data from the Chicago Police Department, Spergel (1986) found that males comprised 95 to 98 percent of offenders who were involved in serious gang incidents between 1982 and 1984 in four Chicago police districts. In a more recent study of Chicago police records, Bobrowski (1988) found that 12,602 males and only 685 females were arrested for commission of some type of street-gang crime.

Many researchers believe that female involvement in criminal activity is on the rise, and there is some conclusive evidence that females are joining gangs in increasing numbers and are becoming more involved in violent criminal activity. Statistics from New York City show that the number of girls arrested for committing felonies increased by 48 percent over the four-year period from 1986 to 1990 (7,340 to 10,853). In New Jersey, the number of girls arrested for some type of violent crime increased by 67 percent between the years of 1980 and 1990 (Lee 1991). In 1983, Spergel examined gang homicide statistics and found that only one out of 345 gang homicides in Chicago between 1978 and 1981 was committed by a female.

According to a 1994 report from the New Mexico Department of Public Safety, law-enforcement personnel from around New Mexico reported the existence of female gang activity. In Farmington, police reported that a female gang had recently been organized and had started to paint graffiti all over the town; the gang dissolved shortly after the police dealt with the gang and the graffiti. Sources estimated that gang membership in Farmington ranged from 180 to 220 members and approximately 20 percent of these members were female. Females had joined male gangs in Las Cruces; in Santa Fe between 15 and 20 percent of all gang members were female, and there was one all-female gang; gangs in Roswell were approximately 25 percent female, and there were two small all-female gangs.

Race/Ethnicity

In the first national survey that was conducted by Walter Miller (1975), he estimated that 48 percent of gang members in the six largest cities were black, 36 percent Hispanic, 9 percent white, and 7 percent Asian. A few years later, in a more extensive survey in nine of the largest U.S. cities, Miller (1982) found that 44 percent of all gang members were Hispanic, 43 percent black, 9 percent white, and 4 percent Asian. Based on these statistics, he speculated that illegal Hispanic immigrants may have contributed to the increasing number of gangs in California.

Spergel and Curry studied gang problems in 1989 and 1990 and surveyed programs developed to deal with gang problems in 45 cities and six special jurisdictions. They found that 53 percent of all gang members coming into contact with police were black, while only 28 percent were Hispanics. Curry and Spergel believed that "[l]aw enforcement agencies were defining and contacting blacks more often as gang members than were other justice agencies" (Spergel and Curry 1990, 64). In the same study, Spergel and Curry also found that whites and Asians were among the least-mentioned gang members in police statistics as well as other non-law-enforcement agencies. Whites comprised only 2.2 percent of all gang members in law enforcement agencies' reports, and 1.6 percent of gang members were Asian, while in statistics on gang members from non-law-enforcement agencies, only 14.2 percent were white, and 2.2 percent were Asian.

Documents

State Laws

Many states and cities have recently passed laws to help solve the gang problem. The states include California, Florida, Illinois, Minnesota, Ohio, and Washington. The laws tend to focus on the problems associated with increasing gang membership, gang members selling narcotics on or near school grounds, students using beepers primarily for drug sales and distribution, increasing gang-related violence and graffiti, and the need for more adequate information on gangs. The following subsections provide excerpts from specific statutes related to gang activity.

Street Terrorism Enforcement and Prevention (STEP) Acts

California's STEP Act is well known because of its comprehensive attempt to control and prevent street gangs from committing criminal acts throughout the state. Other states have also enacted STEP Acts or STEP-like acts, including Florida and Illinois. The following are excerpts from the acts in these three states.

Street Terrorism Enforcement and Prevention Act (California, 1988)

186.21 Legislative findings and declaration
    The Legislature hereby finds and declares that it is the right

of every person, regardless of race, color, creed, religion, national origin, sex, age, sexual orientation, or handicap, to be secure and protected from fear, intimidation, and physical harm caused by the activities of violent groups and individuals. It is not the intent of this chapter to interfere with the exercise of the constitutionally protected rights of freedom of expression and association. The Legislature hereby recognizes the constitutional right of every citizen to harbor and express beliefs on any lawful subject whatsoever, to lawfully associate with others who share similar beliefs, to petition lawfully constituted authority for a redress of perceived grievances, and to participate in the electoral process.

The Legislature, however, further finds that the State of California is in a state of crisis which has been caused by violent street gangs whose members threaten, terrorize, and commit a multitude of crimes against the peaceful citizens of their neighborhoods. These activities, both individually and collectively, present a clear and present danger to public order and safety and are not constitutionally protected. The Legislature finds that there are nearly 600 criminal street gangs operating in California, and that the number of gang-related murders is increasing. The Legislature also finds that in Los Angeles County alone there were 328 gang-related murders in 1986, and that gang homicides in 1987 have increased 80 percent over 1986. It is the intent of the Legislature in enacting this chapter to seek the eradication of criminal activity by street gangs by focusing upon patterns of criminal gang activity and upon the organized nature of street gangs, which together, are the chief source of terror created by street gangs. The Legislature further finds that an effective means of punishing and deterring the criminal activities of street gangs is through forfeiture of the profits, proceeds, and instrumentalities acquired, accumulated, or used by street gangs.

186.22. Participation in criminal street gang; punishment; felony conviction; sentence enhancement; commission on or near school grounds; pattern of criminal gang activity.

(a) Any person who actively participates in any criminal street gang with knowledge that its members engage in or have engaged in a pattern of criminal gang activity, and who willfully promotes, furthers, or assists in any felonious criminal conduct by members of that gang, shall be punished by imprisonment in a county jail for a period not to exceed one year, or by imprisonment in the state prison for 16 months, or 2 or 3 years.

(b)(1) Except as provided in paragraph (4), any person who is convicted of a felony committed for the benefit of, at the direction of, or in association with any criminal street gang, with the specific intent to promote, further, or assist in any criminal conduct by gang members, shall, upon conviction of that felony, in addition and consecutive to the punishment prescribed for the felony or attempted felony of which he or she has been convicted, be punished by an additional term of one, two, or three years at the court's discretion.

(2) If the underlying felony described in paragraph (1) is committed on the grounds of, or within 1,000 feet of, a public or private elementary, vocational, junior high, or high school, during hours in which the facility is open for classes or school related programs or when minors are using the facility, the additional term shall be two, three, or four years, at the court's discretion.

(3) The court shall order the imposition of the middle term of the sentence enhancement, unless there are circumstances in aggravation or mitigation. The court shall state the reasons for its choice of sentence enhancements on the record at the time of the sentencing.

(4) Any person who violates this subdivision in the commission of a felony punishable by imprisonment in the state prison for life, shall not be paroled until a minimum of 15 calendar years have been served.

(c) If the court grants probation or suspends the execution of sentence imposed upon the defendant for a violation of subdivision (a), or in cases involving a true finding of the enhancement enumerated in subdivision (b), the court shall require that the defendant serve a minimum of 180 days in a county jail as a condition thereof.

(d) Notwithstanding any other law, the court may strike the additional punishment for the enhancements provided in this section or refuse to impose the minimum jail sentence for misdemeanors in an unusual case where the interests of justice would best be served, if the court specifies on the record and enters in to the minutes the circumstances indicating that the interests of justice would best be served by that disposition.

(e) As used in this chapter, "pattern of criminal gang activity" means the commission, attempted commission, or solicitation of two or more of the following offenses, provided at least one of those offenses occurred after the effective date of this chapter and the last of those offenses occurred within three years after a prior offense, and the offenses are committed on separate occasions, or by two or more persons:

(1) Assault with a deadly weapon or by means of force likely to produce great bodily injury . . .

(2) Robbery, as defined in Chapter 4 . . .

(3) Unlawful homicide or manslaughter . . .

(4) The sale, possession for sale, transportation, manufacture, offer for sale, or offer to manufacture controlled substances . . .

(5) Shooting at an inhabited dwelling or occupied motor vehicle . . .

(6) Discharging or permitting the discharge of a firearm from a motor vehicle . . .

(7) Arson . . .

(8) The intimidation of witnesses and victims . . .

(9) Grand theft . . .

(10) Grand theft of any vehicle, trailer, or vessel . . .

(11) Burglary . . .

(12) Rape . . .

(13) Looting . . .

(14) Moneylaundering . . .

(15) Kidnapping . . .

(16) Mayhem . . .

(17) Aggravated mayhem . . .

(18) Torture . . .

(19) Felony extortion . . .

(20) Felony vandalism . . .

(21) Carjacking . . .

(22) The sale, delivery, or transfer of a firearm . . .

(23) Possession of a pistol, revolver, or other firearm capable of being concealed upon the person . . .

(f) As used in this chapter, "criminal street gang" means any ongoing organization, association, or group of three or more persons, whether formal or informal, having as one of its primary activities the commission of one or more of the criminal acts enumerated in paragraphs (1) to (23), inclusive, of subdivision (e) having a common name or common identifying sign or symbol, and whose members individually or collectively engage in or have engaged in a pattern of criminal gang activity.

(g) This section shall remain in effect only until January 1, 1997, and on that date is repealed.

186.22a. Buildings or places used by criminal street gangs; nuisance; additional remedies; confiscation of firearms or deadly or dangerous weapons owned or possessed by gang members.

(a) Every building or place used by members of a criminal street gang for the purpose of the commission of the offenses listed in subdivision (c) of Section 186.22 or any offense involving dangerous or deadly weapons, burglary, or rape, and every building or place wherein or upon which that criminal conduct by gang members takes place, is a nuisance which shall be enjoined, abated, and prevented, and for which damages may be recovered, whether it is a public or private nuisance.

(b) Any action for injunction or abatement filed pursuant to subdivision (a) shall proceed according to the provisions of Article 3 (commencing with Section 11570) of Chapter 10 of Division 10 of the Health and Safety Code, except that all of the following shall apply:

(1) The court shall not assess a civil penalty against any person unless that person knew or should have known of the unlawful acts.

(2) No order of eviction or closure may be entered.

(3) All injunctions issued shall be limited to those necessary to protect the health and safety of the residents or the public or those necessary to prevent further criminal activity.

(4) Suit may not be filed until 30-day notice of the unlawful use or criminal conduct has been provided to the owner by mail, return receipt requested, postage prepaid, to the last known address.

(c) No nonprofit or charitable organization which is conducting its affairs with ordinary care or skill, and no governmental entity, shall be abated pursuant to subdivisions (a) and (b).

(d) Nothing in this chapter shall preclude any aggrieved person from seeking any other remedy provided by law.

(e)(1) Any firearm, ammunition which may be used with the firearm, or any deadly or dangerous weapon which is owned or possessed by a member of a criminal street gang for the purpose of the commission of any of the offenses listed in subdivision (c) of Section 186.22, or the commission of any burglary or rape, may be confiscated by any law enforcement agency or peace officer.

(2) In those cases where a law enforcement agency believes that the return of the firearm, ammunition, or deadly weapon confiscated pursuant to this subdivision, is or will be used in criminal street gang activity or that the return of the item would be likely to result in endangering the safety of others, the law enforcement agency shall initiate a petition in

the superior court to determine if the item confiscated should be returned or declared a nuisance.

(3) No firearm, ammunition, or deadly weapon shall be sold or destroyed unless reasonable notice is given to its lawful owner if his or her identity and address can be reasonably ascertained. The law enforcement agency shall inform the lawful owner, at that person's last known address by registered mail, that he or she has 30 days from the date of receipt of the notice to respond to the court clerk to confirm his or her desire for a hearing and that the failure to respond shall result in a default order forfeiting the confiscated firearm, ammunition, or deadly weapon as a nuisance.

(4) If the person requests a hearing, the court clerk shall set a hearing no later than 30 days from receipt of that request. The court clerk shall notify the person, the law enforcement agency involved, and the district attorney of the date, time, and place of the hearing.

(5) At the hearing, the burden of proof is upon the law enforcement agency or peace officer to show by a preponderance of the evidence that the seized item is or will be used in criminal street gang activity or that return of the item would be likely to result in endangering the safety of others. All returns of firearms shall be subject to subdivision (d) of Section 12072.

(6) If the person does not request a hearing with 30 days of the notice or the lawful owner cannot be ascertained, the law enforcement agency may file a petition that the confiscated firearm, ammunition, or deadly weapon be declared a nuisance. If the items are declared to be a nuisance, the law enforcement agency shall dispose of the items as provided in Section 12028.

Street Terrorism Enforcement and Prevention of 1990 (Florida)

874.02. Legislative findings and intent.

(1) The Legislature hereby finds that it is the right of every person, regardless of race, color, creed, religion, national origin, sex, age, sexual orientation, or handicap, to be secure and protected from fear, intimidation, and physical harm caused by the activities of violent groups and individuals. It is not the intent of this chapter to interfere with the exercise of the constitutionally protected rights of freedom of expression and association. The Legislature recognizes the constitutional right of every citizen to

harbor and express beliefs on any lawful subject whatsoever, to lawfully associate with others who share similar beliefs, to petition lawfully constituted authority for a redress of perceived grievances, and to participate in the electoral process.

(2) The Legislature finds, however, that the state is facing a mounting crisis caused by criminal street gangs whose members threaten and terrorize peaceful citizens and commit a multitude of crimes. These activities, both individually and collectively, present a clear and present danger to public order and safety and are not constitutionally protected.

(3) It is the intent of the Legislature to eradicate the terror created by criminal street gangs by providing enhanced penalties and by eliminating the patterns, profits, proceeds, and instrumentalities of criminal street gang activity.

874.03. Definitions.

As used in this chapter:

(1) "Criminal street gang" means a formal or informal ongoing organization, association, or group of three or more persons who:

(a) Have a common name or common identifying signs, colors, or symbols;

(b) Have members or associates who, individually or collectively, engage in or have engaged in a pattern of criminal street gang activity.

(2) "Criminal street gang member" is a person who engages in a pattern of criminal street gang activity and meets two or more of the following criteria:

(a) Admits to criminal street gang membership.

(b) Is a youth under the age of 21 years who is identified as a criminal street gang member by a parent or guardian.

(c) Is identified as a criminal street gang member by a documented reliable informant.

(d) Resides in or frequents a particular criminal street gang's area and adopts their style of dress, their use of hand signs, or their tattoos, and associates with known criminal street gang members.

(e) Is identified as a criminal street gang member by an informant of previously untested reliability and such identification is corroborated by independent information.

(f) Has been arrested more than once in the company of identified criminal street gang members for offenses which are consistent with usual criminal street gang activity.

(g) Is identified as a criminal street gang member by physical evidence such as photographs or other documentation.

(h) Has been stopped in the company of known criminal street gang members four or more times.

(3) "Pattern of criminal street gang activity" means the commission, attempted commission, or solicitation, by any member or members of a criminal street gang, of two or more felony or violent misdemeanor offenses, or two or more delinquent acts or violations of law which would be felonies or violent misdemeanors if committed by an adult, on separate occasions within a 3-year period.

874.04. Pattern of criminal street gang activity; reclassified penalties

The penalty for any felony or violent misdemeanor, or any delinquent act or violation of law which would be a felony or violent misdemeanor if committed by an adult, shall be reclassified if the offender was a member of a criminal street gang at the time of the commission of such offense that meets the criteria of a pattern of criminal street gang activity.

(1) A misdemeanor of the second degree shall be punishable as if it were a misdemeanor of the first degree.

(2) A misdemeanor of the first degree shall be punishable as if it were a felony of the third degree.

(3) A felony of the third degree shall be punishable as if it were a felony of the second degree.

(4) A felony of the second degree shall be punishable as if it were a felony of the first degree.

(5) A felony of the first degree shall be punishable as if it were a life felony.

874.06. Civil cause of action

Any person or organization which establishes by clear and convincing evidence that it has been coerced, intimidated, threatened, or otherwise harmed in violation of this chapter shall have a civil cause of action for treble damages, an injunction, or any other appropriate relief in law or equity. Upon prevailing in such civil action, the plaintiff may recover reasonable attorney's fees and costs.

874.08. Profits, proceeds, and instrumentalities of criminal street gangs; forfeiture

Any profits, proceeds or instrumentalities of criminal activity of any criminal street gang shall be subject to seizure and forfeiture under the Florida Contraband Forfeiture Act under s. 932.704.

Illinois Streetgang Terrorism Omnibus Prevention Act [Act 147] (1993)

147/5 Legislative findings.

(a) The General Assembly hereby finds and declares that it is the right of every person, regardless of race, color, creed, religion, national origin, sex, age, or disability, to be secure and protected from fear, intimidation, and physical harm caused by the activities of violent groups and individuals. It is not the intent of this Act to interfere with the exercise of the constitutionally protected rights of freedom of expression and association. The General Assembly hereby recognizes the constitutional right of every citizen to harbor and express beliefs on any lawful subject whatsoever, to lawfully associate with others who share similar beliefs, to petition lawfully constituted authority for a redress of perceived grievances, and to participate in the electoral process.

(b) The General Assembly finds, however, that urban, suburban, and rural communities, neighborhoods and schools throughout the State are being terrorized and plundered by streetgangs. The General Assembly finds that there are now several hundred streetgangs operating in Illinois, and that while their terrorism is most widespread in urban areas, streetgangs are spreading into suburban and rural areas of Illinois.

(c) The General Assembly further finds that streetgangs are often controlled by criminally sophisticated adults who take advantage of our youth by intimidating and coercing them into membership by employing them as drug couriers and runners, and by using them to commit brutal crimes against persons and property to further the financial benefit to and dominance of the streetgang.

(d) These streetgangs' activities present a clear and present danger to public order and safety and are not constitutionally protected. No society is or should be required to endure such activities without redress. Accordingly, it is the intent of the General Assembly in enacting this Act to create a civil remedy against streetgangs and their members that focuses upon patterns of criminal gang activity and upon the organized nature of streetgangs, which together have been the chief source of their success.

147/10 Definitions.

"Course or pattern of criminal activity" means 2 or more gang-related criminal offenses committed in whole or in part within this State when:

(1) at least one such offense was committed after the effective date of this Act;

(2) both offenses were committed within 5 years of each other; and

(3) at least one offense involved the solicitation to commit, conspiracy to commit, attempt to commit, or commission of any offense defined as a felony or forcible felony under the Criminal Code of 1961.

"Designee of State's Attorney" or "designee" means any attorney for a public authority who has received written permission from the State's Attorney to file or join in a civil action authorized by this Act.

"Public authority" means any unit of local government or school district created or established under the Constitution or laws of this State.

"States' Attorney" means the State's Attorney of any county where an offense constituting a part of a course or pattern of gang-related criminal activity has occurred or has been committed.

"Streetgang" or "gang" or "organized gang" or "criminal street gang" means any combination, confederation, alliance, network, conspiracy, understanding, or other similar conjoining, in law or in fact, of 3 or more persons with an established hierarchy that, through its membership or through the agency of any member engages in a course or pattern of criminal activity.

For purposes of this Act, it shall not be necessary to show that a particular conspiracy, combination, or conjoining of persons possesses, acknowledges, or is known by any common name, insignia, flag, means of recognition, secret signal or code, creed, belief, structure, leadership or command structure, method of operation or criminal enterprise, concentration or specialty, membership, age, or other qualifications, initiation rites, geographical or territorial situs or boundary or location, or other unifying mark, manner, protocol or method of expressing or indicating membership when the conspiracy's existence, in law or in fact, can be demonstrated by a preponderance of other competent existence. However, any evidence reasonably tending to show or demonstrate, in law or in fact, the existence of or membership in any conspiracy, confederation, or other association described herein, or probative of the existence of or membership in any such association, shall be admissible in any action or proceeding brought under this Act.

"Streetgang member" or "gang member" means any person who actually and in fact belongs to a gang, and any person who knowingly acts in the capacity of an agent for or accessory to, or is legally accountable for, or voluntarily associates himself with a course or pattern of gang-related criminal activity, whether in a preparatory, executory, or cover-up phase of any activity, or who knowingly performs, aids, or abets any such activity.

"Streetgang related" or "gang-related" means any criminal activity, enterprise, pursuit, or undertaking directed by, ordered by, authorized by, consented to, agreed to, requested by, acquiesced in, or ratified by any gang leader, officer, or governing or policy-making person or authority, or by any agent, representative, or deputy of any such officer, person or authority:

(1) with the intent to increase the gang's size, membership, prestige, dominance, or control in any geographical area; or

(2) with the intent to provide the gang with any advantage in, or any control or dominance over any criminal market sector, including but not limited to, the manufacture, delivery, or sale of controlled substances or cannabis; arson or arson-for-hire; traffic in stolen property or stolen credit cards; traffic in prostitution, obscenity, or pornography; or that involves robbery, burglary, or theft; or

(3) with the intent to exact revenge or retribution for the gang or any member of the gang; or

(4) with the intent to obstruct justice, or intimidate or eliminate any witness against the gang or any member of the gang; or

(5) with the intent to otherwise directly or indirectly cause any benefit, aggrandizement, gain, profit, or other advantage whatsoever to or for the gang, its reputation, influence, or membership.

147/15. Creation of civil cause of action.

(a) A civil cause of action is hereby created in favor of any public authority expending money, allocating or reallocating police, firefighting, emergency or other personnel or resources, or otherwise incurring any loss, deprivation, or injury, or sustaining any damage, impairment, or harm whatsoever, proximately caused by any course or pattern of criminal activity.

(b) The cause of action created by this Act shall lie against:

(1) any streetgang in whose name, for whose benefit, on

whose behalf, or under whose direction the act was committed; and

(2) any gang officer or director who causes, orders, suggests, authorizes, consents to, agrees to, requests, acquiesces in, or ratifies any such act; and

(3) any gang member who, in the furtherance of or in connection with, any gang-related activity, commits any such act; and

(4) any gang officer, director, leader, or member. . . .

147/35. Injunctive relief, damages, costs, and fees.

(a) In any action brought under this Act, and upon the verified application of the State's Attorney or his designee, the circuit court may at any time enter such restraining orders, injunctions, or other prohibitions, or order such other relief as it deems proper, including but not limited to ordering any person to divest himself of any involvement or interest, direct or indirect, in any illegal streetgang activity and imposing other reasonable restrictions on the future illegal activities of any defendant.

(b) A final judgement in favor of a public authority under this Act shall entitle it to recover compensatory damages for all damages, losses, impairments, or other harm proximately caused, together with the costs of the suit and reasonable attorneys' fees. Punitive damages may be assessed against any streetgang, against any streetgang officer or member found guilty of actual participation in or to be legally accountable for a course or pattern of criminal activity under this Act.

General Statutes

Washington, like many other states, has experienced increased youth-gang activity; in response, its state legislature passed a law concerning youth gangs, prevention and intervention programs, risk prevention, and activities to sensitize personnel who work with gang members to cultural differences. North Dakota and South Dakota also have statutes concerning gangs. The statutes for all three states are excerpted below.

Chapter 43.310: Youth Gangs (Washington, 1993)

43.310.005. Finding

The legislature finds and declares that:

(1) The number of youth who are members and associates of gangs and commit gang violence has significantly increased throughout the entire greater Puget Sound, Spokane, and other areas of the state;

(2) Youth gang violence has caused a tremendous strain on the progress of the communities impacted. The loss of life, property, and positive opportunity for growth caused by youth gang violence has reached intolerable levels. Increased youth gang activity has seriously strained the budgets of many local jurisdictions, as well as threatened the ability of the education system to educate our youth;

(3) Among youth gang members the high school drop-out rate is significantly higher than among nongang members. Since the economic future of our state depends on a highly educated and skilled work force, this high school drop-out rate threatens the economic welfare of our future work force, as well as the future economic growth of our state;

(4) The unemployment rate among youth gang members is higher than that among the general youth population. The unusual unemployment rate, lack of education and skills, and the increased criminal activity could significantly impact our future prison population;

(5) Most youth gangs are subcultural. This implies that gangs provide the nurturing, discipline, and guidance to gang youth and potential gang youth that is generally provided by communities and other social systems. The subcultural designation means that youth gang participation and violence can be effectively reduced in Washington communities and schools through the involvement of community, education, criminal justice, and employment systems working in a unified manner with parents and individuals who have a firsthand knowledge of youth gang and at-risk youth; and

(6) A strong unified effort among parents and community, educational, criminal justice, and employment systems would facilitate; (a) The learning process; (b) the control and reduction of gang violence; (c) the prevention of youth joining negative gangs; and (d) the intervention into youth gangs.

43.310.007. Intent—Prevention and intervention pilot programs

It is the intent of the legislature to cause the development of positive prevention and intervention pilot programs for elementary and secondary age youth through cooperation between individual schools, local organizations, and government. It is also the intent of the legislature that if the prevention and intervention pilot programs are determined to be effective in reducing problems associated with youth gang violence, that other counties in the state be eligible to receive special state funding to establish similar positive prevention and intervention programs.

43.310.010 Definitions

Unless the context otherwise requires, the following definitions shall apply through RCW 43.310.005 through 43.310.040 and sections 5 and 7 through 10, chapter 497, Laws of 1993; sections 1 through 11 of this act:

(1) "School" means any public school within a school district any portion of which is in a county with a population of over one hundred ninety thousand.

(2) "Community organization" means any organization recognized by a city or county as such, as well as private, non-profit organizations registered with the secretary of state.

(3) "Gang risk prevention and intervention pilot program" means a community-based positive prevention and intervention program for gang members, potential gang members, at-risk youth, and elementary through high school-aged youth directed at all of the following:

(a) Reducing the probability of youth involvement in gang activities and consequent violence.

(b) Establishing ties, at an early age, between youth and community organizations.

(c) Committing local business and community resources to positive programming for youth.

(d) Committing state resources to assist in creating the gang risk prevention and intervention pilot program.

(4) "Cultural awareness retreat" means a program that temporarily relocates at-risk youth or gang members and their parents from their usual social environment to a different social environment, with the specific purpose of having them performing activities which will enhance or increase their positive behavior and potential life successes.

43.310.020 Gang risk prevention and intervention pilot programs—request for proposals

(1) The department of community, trade, and economic development may recommend existing programs or contract with either school districts or community organizations, or both, through a request for proposal process for the development,

administration, and implementation in the county of community-based gang risk prevention and intervention pilot programs.

(2) Proposals by the school district for gang risk prevention and intervention pilot program grant funding shall begin with school years no sooner than the 1994-95 session, and last for a duration of two years.

(3) The school district or community organization proposal shall include:

(a) A description of the program goals, activities, and curriculum. The description of the program goals shall include a list of measurable objectives for the purpose of evaluation by the department of community, trade, and economic development. To the extent possible, proposals shall contain empirical data on current problems, such as drop-out rates and occurrences of violence on and off campus by school-age individuals.

(b) A description of the individual school or schools and the geographic area to be affected by the program.

(c) A demonstration of broad-based support for the program from business and community organizations.

(d) A clear description of the experience, expertise, and other qualifications of the community organizations to conduct an effective prevention and intervention program in cooperation with a school or a group of schools.

(e) A proposed budget for expenditure of the grant.

(4) Grants awarded under this section may not be used for the administrative costs of the school district or the individual school.

43.310.030. Gang risk prevention and intervention pilot programs—scope

Gang risk prevention and intervention pilot programs shall include, but are not limited to:

(1) Counseling for targeted at-risk students, parents, and families, individually and collectively.

(2) Exposure to positive sports and cultural activities, promoting affiliations between youth and the local community.

(3) Job training, which may include apprentice programs in coordination with local businesses, job skills development at the school, or information about vocational opportunities in the community.

(4) Positive interaction with local law enforcement personnel.

(5) The use of local organizations to provide job search training skills.

(6) Cultural awareness retreats.

(7) The use of specified state resources, as requested.

(8) Full service schools under section 9 of this act.

(9) Community services such as volunteerism and citizenship.

43.310.040. Cultural awareness retreats

Cultural awareness retreats shall include but are not limited to the following programs:

(1) To develop positive attitudes and self-esteem.

(2) To develop youth decision-making ability.

(3) To assist with career development and educational development.

(4) To help develop respect for the community, and ethnic origin.

Chapter 12.1-06.2: Criminal Street Gangs (North Dakota, 1995)

12.1-06.2-01. Definitions. As used in this chapter the term:

1. "Crime of pecuniary gain" means any violation of state law that directly results or was intended to result in the defendant alone, or in association with others, receiving income, benefit, property, money, or anything of value.

2. "Crime of violence" means any violation of state law where a person purposely or knowingly causes or threatens to cause death or physical bodily injury to another person or persons.

3. "Criminal street gang" means any ongoing organization or group of three or more persons, whether formal or informal, that acts in concert or agrees to act in concert with a purpose that any of those persons alone or in any combination commit or will commit two or more predicate gang crimes one of which occurs after August 1, 1995, and the last of which occurred within five years after the commission of a prior predicate gang crime.

4. "Participate in a criminal street gang" means to act in concert with a criminal street gang with intent to commit or with the intent that any other person associated with the criminal street gang will commit one or more predicate gang crimes.

5. "Predicate gang crime" means the commission, attempted commission, or solicitation of any felony, misdemeanor crime of violence, or misdemeanor crime of pecuniary gain.

12.1-06.2-02. Criminal street gang crime—Penalty. Any person who commits a felony or class A misdemeanor crime of violence or crime of pecuniary gain for the benefit of, at the direction of, or in association with any criminal street gang, with the intent to promote, further, or assist in the affairs of a criminal gang, or obtain membership into a criminal gang, is guilty of a class C felony.

12.1-06.2-04. Local ordinances not preempted. Nothing in this chapter may be construed as preventing a local governing body from adopting and enforcing ordinances relating to gangs and gang-related violence.

Chapter 22-10. Riot and Unlawful Assembly (South Dakota, 1992)

22-10-14. Definitions. Terms used in §§ 22-10-14 to 22-10-16, inclusive, mean:

(1) "Street gang," a formal or informal ongoing organization, association or group of three or more persons who have a common name or common identifying signs, colors or symbols and have members or associates who, individually or collectively, engage in or have engaged in a pattern of street gang activity;

(2) "Street gang member," a person who engages in a pattern of street gang activity and who meets two or more of the following criteria:

(a) Admits to gang membership;

(b) Is identified as a gang member by a documented reliable informant;

(c) Resides in or frequents a particular gang's area and adopts its style of dress, its use of hand signs or its tattoos and associates with known gang members;

(d) Is identified as a gang member by an informant of previously untested reliability if such identification is corroborated by independent information;

(e) Has been arrested more than once in the company of identified gang members for offenses which are consistent with usual gang activity;

(f) Is identified as a gang member by physical evidence, such as photographs or other documentation; or

(g) Has been stopped in the company of known gang members four or more times; and

(3) "Pattern of street gang activity," the commission, attempted commission or solicitation by any member or members of a street gang of two or more felony or violent misdemeanor offenses on separate occasions within a three-year period for the purpose of furthering gang activity.

22-10-15. Reclassification of felony or violent misdemeanor charge if part of street gang activity. The penalty for conviction of any felony or violent misdemeanor charge shall be reclassified as follows if the commission of such felony or misdemeanor is part of a pattern of street gang activity:

(1) A Class 2 misdemeanor shall be punishable as if it were a Class 1 misdemeanor;

(2) A Class 1 misdemeanor shall be punishable as if it were a Class 6 felony; and

(3) The penalty for any felony shall be enhanced by changing the class of the felony to the next class which is more severe.

Gang Suppression Activities

In addition to its STEP Act, California has enacted a statute on gang-violence suppression. While other states may, to some extent, suppress gang activities, the California statute shows that officials there are willing to go to great lengths to eradicate gang activity. Excerpts from that statute are provided below.

Chapter 3.5 Gang Violence Suppression (1992)

13826.1 Establishment of program; administration, allocation and award of funds; guidelines and procedures; annual report; criteria for funding; composition of advisory committee; participation of rural jurisdictions; operative date of section.

(a) There is hereby established in the Office of Criminal Justice Planning, the Gang Violence Suppression Program, a program of financial and technical assistance for district attorneys' offices, local law enforcement agencies, county probation departments, school districts, county offices of education, or any consortium thereof, and community-based organizations which are primarily engaged in the suppression of gang violence. All funds appropriated to the Office of Criminal Justice Planning for the purposes of this chapter shall be administered and disbursed by the executive director of the office in consultation with the California Council on Criminal Justice, and shall to the greatest extent feasible be coordinated or consolidated with federal funds that may be made available for these purposes.

(b) The executive director is authorized to allocate and award funds to cities, counties, school districts, county offices of education, or any consortium thereof, and community-based organizations in which gang violence suppression programs are established in substantial compliance with the policies and criteria set forth in this chapter.

(c) The allocation and award of funds shall be made on the application of the district attorney, chief law enforcement officer, or chief probation officer of the applicant unit of government and approved by the legislative body, on the application of school districts, county offices of education, or any consortium thereof, or on the application of the chief executive of a community-based organization. . . .

(d) The executive director shall prepare and issue written program and administrative guidelines and procedures for the Gang Violence Suppression Program, consistent with this chapter. These guidelines shall set forth the terms and conditions upon which the Office of Criminal Justice Planning is prepared to offer grants of funds pursuant to statutory authority. . . .

(e) Annually . . . the executive director shall prepare a report to the Legislature describing in detail the operation of the statewide program and the results obtained by district attorneys' offices, local law enforcement agencies, county probation departments, school districts, county offices of education, or any consortium thereof, and community-based organizations receiving funds under this chapter and under comparable federally financed awards.

(f) Criteria for selection of district attorneys' offices, local law enforcement agencies, county probation departments, school districts, county offices of education, or any consortium thereof, and community-based organizations to receive gang violence suppression funding shall be developed in consultation with the Gang Violence Suppression Advisory Committee whose members shall be appointed by the Executive Director of the Office of Criminal Justice Planning, unless otherwise designated.

(g) The Gang Violence Suppression Advisory Committee shall be composed of five district attorneys; two chief probation officers; two representatives of community-based organizations; three attorneys primarily engaged in the practice of juvenile criminal defense; three law enforcement officials with expertise in gang-related investigations; one member from the California

Youth Authority Gang Task Force nominated by the Director of the California Youth Authority; one member of the Department of Corrections Law Enforcement Liaison Unit nominated by the Director of the Department of Corrections; one member from the Department of Justice nominated by the Attorney General; the Superintendent of Public Instruction, or his or her designee; one member of the California School Boards Association; and one representative of a school program specializing in the education of the target population identified in this chapter.

Five members of the Gang Violence Suppression Advisory Committee appointed by the Executive Director of the Office of Criminal Justice Planning shall be from rural or predominately suburban counties and shall be designated by the Executive Director as comprising the Rural Gang Task Force Subcommittee.

The Rural Gang Task Force Subcommittee, in coordination with the Gang Violence Suppression Advisory Committee and the Office of Criminal Justice Planning, shall review the Gang Violence Suppression Program participation requirements and recommend changes in the requirements which recognize the unique conditions and constraints that exist in small rural jurisdictions and enhance the ability of small rural jurisdictions to participate in the Gang Violence Suppression Program.

(h) The Director of the Office of Criminal Justice Planning shall designate a staff member in the Gang Violence Suppression Program to act as the Rural Gang Prevention Coordinator and to provide technical assistance and outreach to rural jurisdictions with emerging gang activities. It is the intent of the Legislature that compliance with this subdivision not necessitate an additional staff person.

13826.15 Legislative findings and declarations; applicants for new grant awards; priority; special considerations for rural and suburban counties.

(a) The Legislature hereby finds and declares that the implementation of the Gang Violence Suppression Program, as provided in this chapter, has made a positive impact in the battle against crimes committed by gang members in California.

The Legislature further finds and declares that the program, when it was originally created in 1981, provided financial and technical assistance only for district attorneys' offices. Since that time, however, the provisions of the program have been amended by the Legislature to enable additional public entities and community-based organizations to participate in the program. In this respect, the Office of Criminal Justice Planning, pursuant to Section 13826.1, administers funding for the program by awarding grants to worthy applicants. Therefore, it is the intent of the Legislature in enacting this measure to assist the Office of Criminal Justice Planning in setting forth guidelines for this funding.

(b) The Office of Criminal Justice Planning may give priority for new grant awards . . .

(c) The Office of Criminal Justice Planning shall consider the unique needs of, and circumstances of jurisdiction in, rural and suburban counties when awarding new grant funds.

Juvenile Justice Boards

Florida has enacted legislation creating district juvenile justice boards. This legislation is excerpted below.

39.025 District Juvenile Justice Boards (1990)

(1) Short title.—This section may be cited as the "Community Juvenile Justice System Act."

(2) Findings.—The Legislature finds that the number of children suspended or expelled from school is growing at an alarming rate; that juvenile crime is growing at an alarming rate; and that there is a direct relationship between the increasing number of children suspended or expelled from school and the rising crime rate. The Legislature further finds that the problem of school safety cannot be solved solely by suspending or expelling students, nor can the public be protected from juvenile crime merely by incarcerating juvenile delinquents, but that school and law enforcement authorities must work in cooperation with the Department of Juvenile Justice, the Department of Health and Rehabilitation Services, and other community representatives in a partnership that coordinates goals, strategies, resources, and evaluation of outcomes. The Legislature finds that where such partnerships exist, the participants believe that such efforts are beneficial to the community and should be encouraged elsewhere.

(3) Intent.—The Legislature recognizes that, despite the large investment of resources committed to address the needs of the criminal justice system of this state, the crime rate continues to increase, overcrowding the state's juvenile detention centers, jails, and prisons and placing the state in jeopardy of being unable to effectively manage these facilities. The economic cost of

crime to the state continues to drain existing resources, and the cost to victims, both economic and psychological, is traumatic and tragic. The Legislature further recognizes that many adults in the criminal justice system were once delinquents in the juvenile justice system. The Legislature also recognizes that the most effective juvenile delinquency programs are programs that not only prevent children from entering the juvenile justice system, but also meet local community needs and have substantial community involvement and support. Therefore, it is the belief of the Legislature that one of the best investments of the scarce resources available to combat crime is in the prevention of delinquency, including prevention of criminal activity by youth gangs, with special emphasis on structured and well-supervised alternative education programs for children suspended or expelled from school. It is the intent of the Legislature to authorize and encourage each of the counties of the state to establish a comprehensive juvenile justice plan based upon the input of representatives of every affected public or private entity, organization, or group. It is the further intent of the Legislature that representatives of school systems, the judiciary, law enforcement, and the Department of Juvenile Justice acquire a thorough understanding of the role and responsibility that each has in addressing juvenile crime in the community, that the county juvenile justice plan reflect an understanding of the legal and fiscal limits within which the plan must be implemented, and that willingness of the parties to cooperate and collaborate in implementing the plan be explicitly stated. It is the further intent of the Legislature that county juvenile justice plans form the basis of and be integrated into district juvenile justice plans and that the prevention and treatment resources at the county, district, and regional levels be utilized to the maximum extent possible to implement and further the goals of their respective plans.

(4) Definitions.—As used in this section:

(a) "Juvenile justice continuum" includes, but is not limited to, delinquency prevention programs and services designed for the purpose of preventing or reducing delinquent acts, including criminal activity by youth gangs, and juvenile arrests, as well as programs and services targeted at children who have committed delinquent acts, and children who have previously been committed to residential treatment programs for delinquents. The term includes children-in-need-of-services and families-in-need-of-services programs; aftercare and reentry services; substance abuse and mental health programs; educational and vocational programs; recreational programs; community services programs; community service work programs; and alternative dispute resolution programs serving children at risk of delinquency and their families, whether offered or delivered by state or local governmental entities, public or private for profit or not-for-profit organizations, or religious or charitable organizations.

(5) County juvenile justice councils.—

(a) A county juvenile justice council is authorized in each county for the purpose of encouraging the initiation of, or supporting ongoing, interagency cooperation and collaboration in addressing juvenile crime.

A juvenile delinquency and gang prevention council or any other group or organization that currently exists in any county, and that is composed of and open to representatives of the classes of members described in this section, may notify the district juvenile justice manager of its desire to be designated as the county juvenile justice council.

(b) The purpose of a county juvenile justice council is to provide a forum for the development of a community-based interagency assessment of the local juvenile justice system, to develop a county juvenile justice plan for more effectively preventing juvenile delinquency, and to make recommendations for more effectively utilizing existing community resources in dealing with juveniles who are truant or have been suspended or expelled from school, or who are found to be involved in crime. The county juvenile justice plan shall include relevant portions of local crime prevention and public safety plans, school improvement and school safety plans, and the plans or initiatives of other public and private entities within the county that are concerned with dropout prevention, school safety, the prevention of juvenile crime and criminal activity by youth gangs, and alternatives to suspension, expulsion, and detention for children found in contempt of court.

(c) The duties and responsibilities of a county juvenile justice council include, but are not limited to:

1. Developing a county juvenile justice plan based upon utilization of the resources of law enforcement, the school system, the Department of Juvenile Justice, the Department of Health and Rehabilitative Services, and others in a cooperative and collaborative manner to prevent or discourage juvenile crime and develop meaningful alternatives to school suspensions and expulsions.

2. Entering into a written county interagency agreement specifying the nature and extent of contributions each signatory agency will make in achieving the goals of the county juvenile justice plan and their commitment to the sharing of information useful in carrying out the goals of the interagency agreement to the extent authorized by law.

3. Applying for and receiving public or private grants, to be administered by one of the community partners, that support one or more components of the county juvenile justice plan.

4. Designating the county representatives to the district juvenile justice board pursuant to subsection (6).

5. Providing a forum for the presentation of interagency recommendations and the resolution of disagreements relating to the contents of the county interagency agreement or the performance by the parties of their respective obligations under the agreement.

6. Assisting and directing the efforts of local community support organizations and volunteer groups in providing enrichment programs and other support services for clients of local juvenile detention center.

7. Providing an annual report and recommendations to the district juvenile justice board, the Juvenile Justice Advisory Board, and the district juvenile justice manager.

(6) District juvenile justice boards.—

(a) There is created a district juvenile justice board within each district to be composed of representatives of county juvenile justice councils within the district . . .

(d) A district juvenile justice board has the purpose, power, and duty to:

1. Advise and assist the district juvenile justice manager and the district administrator on the need for and the availability of juvenile justice programs and services in the district.

2. Develop a district juvenile justice plan that is based upon the juvenile justice plans developed by each county within the district, and that addresses the needs of each county within the district.

3. Develop a district interagency cooperation and information-sharing agreement that supplements county agreements and expands the scope to include appropriate circuit and district officials and groups.

4. Coordinate the efforts of the district juvenile justice board with the activities of the Governor's Juvenile Justice

and Delinquency Prevention Advisory Committee and other public and private entities.

5. Advise and assist the district juvenile justice manager in the provision of optional, innovative delinquency services in the district to meet the unique needs of delinquent children and their families.

6. Develop, in consultation with the district juvenile justice manager, funding sources external to the Department of Juvenile Justice for the provision and maintenance of additional delinquency programs and services. The board may, either independently or in partnership with one or more county juvenile justice councils or other public or private entities, apply for and receive funds, under contract or other funding arrangement, from federal, state, county, city, and other public agencies, and from public and private foundations, agencies, and charities for the purpose of funding optional innovative prevention, diversion, or treatment services in the district for delinquent children and children at risk of delinquency, and their families. To aid in this process, the department shall provide fiscal agency services for the councils.

7. Educate the community about and assist in the community juvenile justice partnership grant program administered by the Department of Juvenile Justice.

8. Advise the district health and human services board, the district juvenile justice manager, and the Secretary of Juvenile Justice regarding the development of the legislative budget request for juvenile justice programs and services in the district and the commitment region, and, in coordination with the district health and human services board, make recommendations, develop programs, and provide funding for prevention and early intervention programs and services designed to serve children in need of services, families in need of services, and children who are at risk of delinquency within the district or region.

9. Assist the district juvenile justice manager in collecting information and statistical data useful in assessing the need for prevention programs and services within the juvenile justice continuum program in the district.

10. Make recommendations with respect to, and monitor the effectiveness of, the judicial administrative plan for each circuit pursuant to Rule 2.050, Florida Rules of Judicial Administration.

11. Provide periodic reports to the health and human services board in the appropriate district of the Department of Health and Rehabilitative Services. These reports must contain,

at a minimum, data about the clients served by the juvenile justice programs and services in the district, as well as data concerning the unmet needs of juveniles with the district.

12. Provide a written annual report on the activities of the board to the district administrator, the Secretary of Juvenile Justice, and the Juvenile Justice Advisory Board. The report should include an assessment of the effectiveness of juvenile justice continuum programs and services within the district, recommendations for elimination, modification, or expansion of existing programs, and suggestions for new programs or services in the juvenile justice continuum that would meet identified needs of children and families in the district.

(7) District juvenile justice plan; programs.—

(a) A district juvenile justice plan is authorized in each district or any subdivision of the district authorized by the district juvenile justice board for the purpose of reducing delinquent acts, juvenile arrests, and gang activity. Juvenile justice programs under such plan may be administered by the Department of Juvenile Justice, the district school board; a local law enforcement agency; or any other public or private entity, in cooperation with appropriate state or local governmental entities and public and private agencies. A juvenile justice program under this section may be planned, implemented, and conducted in any district pursuant to a proposal developed and approved as specified in subsection 10.

(b) District juvenile justice plans shall be developed by district juvenile justice boards in close cooperation with the schools, the courts, the state attorney, law enforcement, state agencies, and community organizations and groups. It is the intent of the Legislature that representatives of all elements of the community acquire a thorough understanding of the role and responsibility that each has in addressing juvenile crime in the community, and that the district juvenile justice plan reflect an understanding of the legal and fiscal limits within which the plan must be implemented.

(c) The district juvenile justice board may use public hearings and other appropriate processes to solicit input regarding the development and updating of the district juvenile justice plan. Input may be provided by parties which include, but are not limited to:

1. Local level public and private services providers, advocacy organizations, and other organizations working with delinquent children.

2. County and municipal governments.

3. State agencies that provide services to children and their families.

4. University youth centers.

5. Judges, state attorneys, public defenders, and the Florida Bar.

6. Victims of crimes committed by children.

7. Law enforcement.

8. Delinquent children and their families and caregivers.

The district juvenile justice board must develop its district juvenile justice plan in close cooperation with the appropriate health and human services board of the Department of Health and Rehabilitative Services, local school districts, local law enforcement agencies, and other community groups and must update the plan annually. To aid the planning process, the Department of Juvenile Justice shall provide to district juvenile justice boards routinely collected ethnicity data. The Department of Law Enforcement shall include ethnicity as a field in the Florida Intelligence Center database, and shall collect the data routinely and make it available to district juvenile justice boards.

Councils and Boards

Recognizing the related problems of gangs and drugs, Arizona passed a law to establish a Drug and Gang Policy Council. Wisconsin has established a Gang Violence Prevention Council. The following paragraphs provide excerpts from the Arizona and Wisconsin laws.

Article 9. Drug and Gang Policy Council (Arizona, 1994)

41-617. Arizona drug and gang policy council; duties

A. An Arizona drug and gang policy council is established which shall consist of members as follows:

1. The governor, who shall serve as chairman.

2. The attorney general.

3. The director of the department of public safety.

4. The director of the department of health services.

5. The director of the department of economic security.

6. The director of the department of corrections.

7. The state superintendent of public instruction.

8. A representative from the Arizona board of regents, appointed by its president.

9. A representative from the state board of directors for community colleges appointed by its chairman.

10. A member of the criminal justice commission appointed by its chairman.

11. A member of the drug enforcement task force appointed by the governor.

12. A representative from the business community appointed by the governor.

13. A representative from the league of Arizona cities and towns appointed by the governor.

14. The administrative director of the courts.

15. The director of the Arizona health care cost containment system administration.

16. The director of the department of juvenile corrections.

17. A representative, appointed by the governor, from a local community group or neighborhood group that is actively involved in community substance abuse issues.

B. The council shall meet and organize by electing from among its members such other officers as are deemed necessary or advisable. The council shall meet at least once during each calendar quarter and additionally as the chairman deems necessary. Staff and support services as are needed for the administration of the council's activities will be supplied from those state agencies represented on the council at the direction of the governor.

C. The objective of the council is to foster cooperation among all state and local governmental entities, neighborhood groups, community organizations and private groups to ensure the optimal delivery of educational, treatment and prevention programs that will reduce the incidences of substance abuse or participation in criminal street gangs as defined in § 13-105 by children, youth and families.

D. The Arizona drug and gang policy council shall:

1. Recommend the basis for effective coordination of all state programs and expenditures, including federal monies, for education, prevention and treatment relating to alcohol and drug abuse and participation in criminal street gangs as defined in § 13-105.

2. Provide a liaison to community groups and private sector programs involved in substance abuse and gangs education, prevention and treatment.

3. Conduct an annual inventory of publicly supported education, prevention and treatment programs related to substance abuse in operation in this state to be submitted by October 31 of each year to the governor, the president of the senate and the speaker of the house of representatives to be made available to the general public through the Arizona prevention resource center. The report shall include:

(a) The name, the location and a description of each program.

(b) The amount and sources of funding for each program.

(c) The agency that administers each program.

(d) The type of substance abuse addressed by each program.

(e) The gender of clientele served by each program and whether the program serves children or adults, or both.

4. Evaluate the results achieved by publicly supported education, treatment and prevention programs and make recommendations to the governor and the legislature for revising programs or redirecting expenditures to achieve better use of public resources.

5. Evaluate the results achieved by publicly supported education, prevention and treatment programs that are related to drug related gang activity in this state and make recommendations to the governor and the legislature for revising programs or redirecting expenditures to achieve better use of public resources.

6. Oversee the operation of the Arizona prevention resource center which shall be established and maintained at the direction of the Arizona drug and gang policy council for the collection, storage and distribution of information relating to substance abuse and gang education and prevention and treatment programs and which shall serve as a referral agency for law enforcement activities.

7. Communicate regularly with the statewide chemical abuse prevention interagency committee and the council on children's behavioral health to collect statewide lay and professional recommendations for prevention, education and treatment programs.

8. Communicate regularly with the Arizona criminal justice commission so that programs for education, treatment and prevention are coordinated with enforcement and related efforts undertaken within the criminal justice system.

E. The Arizona prevention resource center shall be operated with the full cooperation of all agencies and entities involved in the organization and maintenance of publicly supported education, prevention and treatment programs related to substance abuse and gangs.

46.027 Gang Violence Prevention (Wisconsin)

The gang violence prevention council shall conduct public hearings and surveys to solicit the opinions and recommendations of citizens and public officials regarding strategies and programs to prevent children from becoming influenced by and involved with gangs and based on those opinions and recommendations, submit an annual report to the appropriate standing committees of the legislature under s. 13.172(3), the cochairpersons of the joint committee on finances and the secretary, and otherwise provide information and recommendations to interested persons, on ways to improve those existing strategies and programs and ways to establish new strategies and programs to prevent children from becoming influenced by and involved with gangs.

Gang Clothing

Tennessee is one of a few states that has a statute concerning the wearing of gang clothing. It is cited below.

49-6-4215 Wearing Clothing Denoting Gang Membership or Affiliation (1994)

The local and county boards of education in this state are hereby authorized to promulgate and adopt rules and regulations to prohibit sixth through twelfth grade students from wearing, while on school property, any type of clothing, apparel or accessory, including that which denotes such student's membership in or affiliation with any gang associated with criminal activities. The local law enforcement agency shall advise the local board, upon request, of gangs which are associated with criminal activities.

Drive-By Shootings

Several states have enacted statutes to cope with the growing numbers of drive-by shootings committed by gang members, usually against members of other gangs. The Colorado statute, which allows for confiscation of any car and other items used in a drive-by shooting, is excerpted below.

Abatement of Public Nuisance (1987)

16-13-301. Definitions. (2.2) "Drive-by crime" means a first degree assault as defined in section 18-3-202, C.R.S., second degree assault as defined in section 18-3-203, C.R.S., attempted first degree or second degree assault, felony menacing as defined in section 18-3-206, C.R.S., or illegal discharge of a firearm as defined in section 18-12-107.5, C.R.S., any of which is committed while utilizing a vehicle for means of concealment or transportation.

(2.3) "Public nuisance act" means any of the crimes, offenses, or violations set forth in section 16-13-303 (1)(a) to (1)(m), regardless of the location where the act occurred.

(2.7) "Seizing agency" means any agency which is charged with the enforcement of the laws of this state, of any other state, or of the United States and which has participated in a seizure or has been substantially involved in effecting a forfeiture through the development of evidence underlying the claim for forfeiture or through legal representation pursuant to this part 3. The department of corrections shall be deemed to be included under this definition.

16-13-302. Public nuisances—policy. (1) It is the policy of the general assembly that every public nuisance shall be restrained, prevented, abated, and perpetually enjoined. It is the duty of the district attorney in each judicial district of this state to bring and maintain an action, pursuant to the provisions of this part 3, to restrain, prevent, abate, and perpetually enjoin any such public nuisance and to seek the forfeiture of property as provided in this part 3. The general assembly intends that proceedings under this part 3 be remedial and equitable in nature. Nothing contained in this part 3 shall be construed as an amendment or repeal of any of the criminal laws of this state, but the provisions of this part 3, insofar as they relate to those laws, shall be considered a cumulative right of the people in the enforcement of such laws, The provision of this part 3 shall not be construed to limit or preempt the powers of any court or political subdivision to abate or control nuisances.

(2) It is also the policy of the general assembly that asset

forfeiture pursuant to this part 3 shall be carried out pursuant to the following:

(a) Generation of revenue shall not be the primary purpose of asset forfeiture.

(b) No prosecutor's or law enforcement officer's employment or level of salary shall depend upon the frequency of seizures or forfeitures which such person achieves.

(c) All seizures of real property pursuant to this part 3 shall be made pursuant to a temporary restraining order or injunction based upon a judicial finding of probable cause.

(d) Each seizing agency shall have policies and procedures for the expeditious release of seized property which is not subject to forfeiture pursuant to this part 3, when such release is appropriate.

(e) Each seizing agency retaining forfeited property for official law enforcement use shall ensure that the property is subject to controls consistent with controls which are applicable to property acquired through the normal appropriations process.

(f) Each seizing agency which receives forfeiture proceeds shall conform with reporting, audit, and disposition procedures enumerated in this article.

(g) Each seizing agency shall prohibit its employees from purchasing forfeited property.

Other Public Nuisances

A Florida statute considers the premises used by gang members to be a problem and deals with this property as described below.

893.138. Local Administrative Action To Abate Drug-related or Prostitution-related Public Nuisances and Youth and Street Gang Activity (1987)

(1) Any place or premises that has been used on more than two occasions, within a 6-month period:

(a) As the site of a violation of s. 796.07;

(b) As the site of the unlawful sale, delivery, manufacture, or cultivation of any controlled substance;

(c) On one occasion as the site of the unlawful possession of a controlled substance, where such possession constitutes a felony, and that has been previously used on more than one occasion as the site of the unlawful sale, delivery, manufacture, or cultivation of any controlled substance; or

(d) Any place or building used by a youth and street gang for the purpose of conducting a pattern of youth and street gang activity may be declared to be a public nuisance, and such nuisance may be abated pursuant to the procedures provided in this section.

(2) Any county or municipality may, by ordinance, create an administrative board to hear complaints regarding the nuisances described in subsection (1). Any employee, officer, or resident of the county or municipality may bring a complaint before the board after giving not less than 3 days' written notice of such complaint to the owner of the place or premises at his last known address. After a hearing in which the board may consider any evidence, including evidence of the general reputation of the place or premises, and at which the owner of the premises shall have an opportunity to present evidence in his defense, the board may declare the place or premises to be a public nuisance as described in subsection (1).

(3) If the board declares a place or premises to be a public nuisance, it may enter an order requiring the owner of such place or premises to adopt such procedure as may be appropriate under the circumstances to abate any such nuisance or it may enter an order immediately prohibiting:

(a) The maintaining of the nuisance;

(b) The operating or maintaining of the place or premises, including the closure of the place or premises or any part thereof; or

(c) The conduct, operation, or maintenance of any business or activity on the premises which is conducive to such nuisance.

(4) An order entered under subsection (3) shall expire after 1 year or at such earlier time as stated in the order.

(5) An order entered under subsection (3) may be enforced pursuant to the procedures contained in s. 120.69. This subsection does not subject a municipality that creates a board under this section, or the board so created, to any other provision of chapter 120.

(6) The board may bring a complaint under s. 60.05 seeking temporary and permanent injunctive relief against any nuisance described in subsection (1).

(7) This section does not restrict the right of any person to proceed under s. 60.05 against any public nuisance.

(8) As used in this section, the term "controlled substance" includes any substance sold in lieu of a controlled substance in violation of s. 817.563 or any imitation controlled substance defined in s. 817.564.

Federal Initiatives

Public Law 103-322, the Violent Crime and Law Enforcement Act of 1994, Subchapter V, Criminal Street Gangs, contains two sections pertaining to gangs and gang activities. These sections are excerpted below.

§ 14061. Juvenile Anti-Drug and Anti-Gang Grants in Federally Assisted Low-Income Housing

Grants authorized in this Act to reduce or prevent juvenile drug and gang-related activity in "public housing" may be used for such purposes in federally assisted, low-income housing.

§ 14062. Gang investigation coordination and information collection.

(a) Coordination

The Attorney General (or the Attorney General's designee), in consultation with the Secretary of the Treasury (or the Secretary's designee), shall develop a national strategy to coordinate gang-related investigations by Federal law enforcement agencies.

(b) Data Collection

The Director of the Federal Bureau of Investigation shall acquire and collect information on incidents of gang violence for inclusion in an annual uniform crime report.

(c) Report

The Attorney General shall prepare a report on national gang violence outlining the strategy developed under subsection (a) of this section to be submitted to the President and Congress by January 1, 1996.

(d) Authorization of Appropriations

There are authorized to be appropriated to carry out this section $1,000,000 for fiscal year 1996.

The Office of Human Development Services in the Administration for Children, Youth, and Families, within the U.S. Department of Health and Human Services, has developed a Youth

Gang Drug-Prevention Program. The agency believes that a comprehensive approach is needed at the community level to reduce the recruitment of new gang members and the involvement of at-risk youth in gangs. Initial awards have been given to a variety of state, county, and city government offices as well as nonprofit agencies.

The Juvenile Justice and Delinquency Prevention Reauthorization Act of 1992, Public Law 93-415, focuses on juvenile justice and delinquency prevention, runaway and homeless youth services, and missing children's assistance. Among its provisions are two new discretionary grant programs, one focusing on gang-free schools and communities and the other on community-based gang-intervention activities. The administrator of these programs is directed to provide grants for both programs, to prevent and reduce the participation of juveniles in gangs, to develop new approaches within the courts and juvenile detention centers to the problems of young people convicted of serious gang-related offenses, to encourage law-abiding activities within communities that are plagued by gang-related crime, to provide treatment to gang members and to those at risk of joining a gang, and to provide treatment to youths involved in drug-abuse activities.

The Gang-Free Schools grants focus on gang prevention and gang control activities in public elementary and secondary schools. Activities covered may include youth education, social services, crisis-intervention activities, activities to keep children from joining gangs, adult training, school security, information dissemination, and making schools safe havens from gang activity. The Community-based Gang Intervention grants focus on coordination at the community level; organizations and personnel include state and local juvenile-justice personnel, law-enforcement officials, health and social service agencies, employment agencies, schools, and private non-profit organizations. Grants can be used for the development of regional task forces, the coordination of gang-related enforcement and treatment activities, and to provide help to community-based agencies in their efforts to reduce and prevent gang activity.

Quotations

What the Experts Say about Gangs

This section offers comments made by experts and researchers in the field of gang research, providing a different perspective from the information in Chapter 1 and in the beginning of this chapter.

Leon Bing, who conducted gang research in Los Angeles, reflects on the gang problem:

> Whatever intellectuals are out there, you can bet the ranch they're not pondering the gang problem. And maybe there aren't any answers. Building more jails isn't an answer, or mobilizing the National Guard. Underfunded community projects that nobody pays much attention to aren't an answer, either. And as long as African-American gang members kill each other in African-American neighborhoods, the gang problem will continue to be a twenty-second shudder on the eleven o'clock news . . . (Bing 1991, 270–271)

> It's not so hard to understand their feelings. I'd go down to South Central and talk to those youngsters, conduct my little interviews, step into their chaos, and then I'd go home to my well-ordered bookcases and . . . an enclosed courtyard. I'd sit at my typewriter, and the only sounds I'd hear from outside would be the plash of the fountain and the sounds of birds in the trees. I didn't have to worry about a bullet coming in my window, or a sixteen-year-old son going out into the streets to kill some other kid before they killed him (Bing 1991, 271).

Anne Campbell, who has been studying girls and gangs, reflects on the societal influences that lead to the creation of gangs and the experiences of girls within gangs:

> The sense of differentness experienced by the girls is fragmented and diffuse—as indeed it must be since they do not fully embrace an oppositional deviant identity. They do not buy into a countercultural role that is well-articulated and wholly coherent. Rather they reject bits and pieces of the conventional lifestyle that is expected of them in the local community. Inevitably, the girl finds herself in a contradictory and vulnerable position as she attempts to retain her integrity within her shifting self definition. She is Puerto Rican but neither provincial nor unAmerican. She may be poor but her life is neither drab nor criminal. She enjoys her femininity but rejects passivity and suffering.

My evidence suggests that much can be learned from examining how we vilify the traits and actions of others. Much of our social life is spent in talk, and a significant portion of it is concerned not with our own behavior but with that of others. The terms of condemnation in gossip reveal a good deal about our own preoccupations and values. When we criticize others' behavior we assure the listener and ourselves that we are exempt from similar accusations—we set ourselves apart from the object of our derision. Sometimes we level our criticism at figures beyond our acquaintance such as media personalities or politicians; but the most salient reference point for our self definition are those individuals or groups whose social niche we share. This is particularly true for disadvantaged groups who are caught in a restricted social environment with little hope of mobility (Campbell 1987, 464).

Joan Moore, in studying the role that isolation and stigmatization play in the development of Chicano youth gangs, explains:

It is often argued that we should not look at the processes within minority communities for the answers to their problems. Many researchers feel the answers obviously lie elsewhere. This argument is particularly persuasive in the late 1980s, when we try to disentangle the twin effects of drastic shifts in the economy and changes in the political support structures. But this view implies that these communities are passive victims of external social conditions, and this is not entirely true. If an underclass is developing in poor minority communities, respectable members of these communities will react. Exactly how they react depends both on the cues from the larger society and on their own location within the community social structure. In the history just sketched, a major indirect effect of ascriptive labeling of minority youth has been to exacerbate cleavages within minority communities. In the 1940s diffuse racist sentiments became focused, with media and institutional targeting on the youth; what was "just another riot"—a seven-days' wonder—to the press had devastating impacts on the communities involved. In the scramble to establish that there were "good" Mexican kids and that "race" wasn't the issue, respectable Hispanics stigmatized and isolated the "bad" kids—the then comparatively innocuous gang kids and their almost totally innocent families. Then, during the 1960s and the politics of entitlement, the community was reminded that race is the stigma, and the achieved deviants and their families were reintegrated both symbolically and structurally. Once again, this alliance has disintegrated, as have the policies and programs that helped to promote it (Moore 1985, 10).

Meda Chesney-Lind and her colleagues, in examining gang delinquency and police reports in Honolulu, Hawaii, found some disturbing trends. For example, their study found that youth identified as gang members by the Honolulu Police Department do not conform to the image of gang youth suggested by some of the literature as well as the public stereotypes of gang youth.

Specifically, arrests for crimes of violence were infrequent among these youth as were arrests for drug abuse and weapons violations. Moreover, the criminal acts committed by youth labeled by law enforcement as gang members did not differ significantly from delinquent youth who share the gang members' ethnicity, gender and age (Chesney-Lind et al. 1994, 222). . .

Several policy shifts are suggested by this research. At a minimum, computerized databases to track suspected youth should be the subject of external audits to assure that they are accurate, up-to-date, and well documented. Absent these checks, the systems run the risk of inflating the dimensions of the problem and ratifying the particular prejudices of those who enter the data.

Programs directed at preventing and intervening in gang behavior should recognize that, in many parts of the United States, youth involved in gangs may be indistinguishable, in terms of their criminal behavior, from other forms of chronically delinquent youth. It may be that the search for gang-specific forms of intervention are not as necessary as has been assumed. Finally, these data suggest that images of gang activity which stress violence and serious criminal behavior are inaccurate and, in a society where gang has become a code word for race, racist. Instead, these findings direct researchers interested in the phenomenon of gangs to seek to understand and document the complex and multi-faceted nature of these groups rather than simply totalize gang youth as amoral, hardened criminals (Chesney-Lind et al. 1994, 222–223).

As Malcolm Klein explains,

Street gangs are an amalgam of racism, of urban underclass poverty, of minority and youth cultures, of fatalism in the face of rampant deprivation, of political insensitivity, and the gross ignorance of inner-city (and inner-town) America on the part of most of us who don't have to survive there. I've lived there, but I've never had to survive there. Street gangs are understandable once one has some understanding of the ignored sectors of our society (Klein 1995, 234).

Irving Spergel writes about how to help prevent gang involvement:

An important institution for the development of youth gangs is the organization of crime opportunities in particular communities. Variable cultural and population settlement patterns influence gang connections to organized crime. Access to criminal opportunities—or to legitimate labor market opportunities—depends largely on factors of race or ethnic status and location. These variations in opportunities must be addressed in policies and programs that try to stop older gang youths from turning to crime as a career. Cultural sensitivity and structural understanding therefore provide an important basis for developing appropriate community-oriented intervention strategies that control the link between youth gang and adult crime activities (Spergel 1995, 129).

Spergel goes on to explain why he believes that traditional programs developed to end gang violence are not successful.
In sum, traditional social intervention programs,

whether agency-based, outreach or street work, or crisis intervention, have shown little effect or may even have worsened the youth gang problem. Such programs seem somewhat more effective and produce some positive results when they are designed as part of a comprehensive or mixed set of strategies. Multiple-agency service approaches—including value-transformation, deterrence, and opportunity provision strategies, closely integrated with local citizen involvement but fashioned in different ways in different communities for targeted younger and older gang youths—may be promising. Newer approaches or techniques and contexts for dealing with the gang problem must take past experience and insight into consideration (Spergel 1995, 256).

More specifically, Spergel and his colleagues at the University of Chicago, in a report for the National Institute of Justice, write about deterrence, rehabilitation, and prevention policies. They believe that

[p]olicies of deterrence, prevention, or rehabilitation in themselves are insufficient to confront youth gang problems. Operational strategies and methods of carrying them out must be systematically integrated, inasmuch as the youth gang problem has different but interrelated elements. The gang problem is organic, particularly in communities with chronic gang activities. It affects different sectors of a population, such as older and younger gang members, their families, victims, and innocent bystanders in different but reciprocal and interrelated or systemic terms. It may not be realistic to deal only with preadolescents if adolescent and young adult gang members exercise great influence. It may be necessary not only to protect normal, conforming youth but to socialize disruptive youth gang members (Spergel et al. 1994, 3).

Felix Padilla studied a group of second-generation Puerto Rican youth belonging to a Chicago street gang and concludes that

these young men are convinced that conventional society is unlikely to deliver the goods necessary for a better life. Because of this perception, they have turned inward, appropriating social and cultural elements of their Puerto Rican ethnicity and barrio life creatively in a way that enables them to experience gang participation and activities as superior to the roles traditionally forced upon youngsters of their backgrounds by the dominant culture. This sense of cultural resistance and superiority constitutes a critical "vision," an understanding about their chances of getting ahead given the limited amount of resources and opportunities available to ethnic and racial minority youngsters in U.S. society today (Padilla 1992, 5).

According to Robert Vernon,

Valuing material things and money above people is one of the true root causes of our culture's destruction. When the material is apprised more than people, people lose self-esteem and regard for others.

Many young people today lack a healthy sense of self-worth. The intensity of the problem varies from person to person, but at the extreme end of the continuum are those who hate themselves. They see no value in themselves. Their lives are miserable. And if they're just a bunch of garbage waiting to decay, so is everyone else.

Those who have reached this extreme are very dangerous. They're angry and bitter. Life for them is a grievous, sour joke, something to dull with drugs and sex until it mercifully ends. Since that's their view, it's easy to end the "worthless" life of another. When self-respect is nonexistent, so is respect for others (Vernon 1993, 190–191).

What Gang Members Say about Gangs

When we read the accounts of gang members or former gang members as they describe their perspective on gangs, we can see a slightly different view than from the experts in the field. This section offers the words of gang members and their feelings and attitudes about being in a gang, their reasons for joining a gang, and their perspective on society.

Sanyika Shakur, a former gang member known as Monster Kody, explains the futility of attempts to prevent gang activities:

With each new generation of Crip and Blood bangers comes a more complex system, which is now reaching institutional proportions. It is precisely because of this type of participation in the development and expansion of these groups' mores, customs, and philosophies that gangbanging will never be stopped from without. The notion of the "war on gangs" being successful is as realistic as the People's Republic of China telling Americans to stop being American. When gang members stop their wars and find that there is no longer a need for their sets to exist, banging will cease. But until then, all attempts by law enforcement to seriously curtail its forward motion will be in vain (Shakur 1993, 79).

He goes on to say:

And that's what we all were, children. Children gone wild in a concrete jungle of poverty and rage. Armed and dangerous, prowling the concrete jungle in search of ourselves, we were children who had grown up quickly in a city that cared too little about its young. Males, females, dogs, and cats were all targets (Shakur 1993, 111).

As a former gang member, Luis Rodriguez believes that

[g]angs flourish when there's a lack of social recreation, decent education or employment. Today, many young people will never know what it is to work. They can only satisfy their needs through collective strength—against the police, who hold the power of life and death, against poverty, against idleness, against their impotence in society (Rodriguez 1993, 250).

Rodriguez describes the situation in Los Angeles after the riots spurred by the Rodney King verdicts in 1992. He describes how two of the city's largest gangs, the Crips and the Bloods, had been working together on a truce and cooperative projects such as building parks and community centers. Gang-related violent incidents declined. However, Rodriguez describes the activities of the police during this time:

In the months after the uprising [riots after the Rodney King verdicts], police broke up as many gang "unity" rallies as they could, arresting truce leaders, and inflaming the ire of housing project residents in which many of the rallies were being held. The LAPD told the media they feared the gangs were going to turn on them, possibly ambush them. Yet no police officer has been killed or severely hurt since the King verdicts—even during the uprising, although instances have emerged of police shooting several people, some in the back, during and since the riots.

Then several hundred FBI agents were sent in to "break up the gangs" involved in the April/May violence—the largest investigation of its kind. Although there were some 600 Los Angeles youth killed in 1991 from gang and drug-related incidents, the federal government never before provided the commitment or resources that they have since the Crips and Bloods declared peace.

At the same time, the immigration authorities terrorized Mexican and Central American immigrants, placing the largely Salvadoran Pico-Union community under a virtual state of siege (this area was one of the hardest hit in the fires) (Rodriguez 1993, 248–249).

References

Bastian, L., and B. Taylor. 1991. *School Crime: A National Crime Victimization Survey Report*. Washington, DC: Bureau of Justice Statistics.

Bobrowski, Lawrence. 1988. *Collecting, Organizing, and Reporting Street Gang Crime*. Chicago: Chicago Police Department, Special Functions Group.

California Department of Justice. 1993. *Gangs 2000: A Call To Action. The Attorney General's Report on the Impact of Criminal Street Gangs on Crime and Violence in California by the Year 2000*. Sacramento, CA: California Department of Justice.

Campbell, Anne. 1984. *The Girls in the Gang: A Report from New York City*. Oxford: Basil Blackwell.

Chesney-Lind, Meda, et al. 1992. *Gangs and Delinquency in Hawaii*. Manoa: Center for Youth Research, Social Science Research Institute, University of Hawaii at Manoa.

Chesney-Lind, Meda, et al. 1995. *Crime, Delinquency and Gangs in Hawaii*. Manoa: Center for Youth Research, Social Science Research Institute, University of Hawaii at Manoa.

Chesney-Lind, Meda, Anna Rockhill, Nancy Marker, and Howard Reyes. 1994. "Gangs and Delinquency: Exploring Police Estimates of Gang Membership." *Crime, Law and Social Change* 21: 201–228.

Chin, Ko-Lin. 1990. *Chinese Subculture and Criminality: Non-traditional Crime Groups in America.* New York: Greenwood Press.

Collins, H. Craig. 1979. *Street Gangs: Profiles for Police.* New York: New York City Police Department.

Curry, G. David, Robert J. Fox, Richard A. Ball, and Darryl Stone. 1992. *National Assessment of Law Enforcement Anti-Gang Information Resources.* Draft Report to the U.S. Department of Justice, National Institute of Justice.

———. 1993. *National Assessment of Law Enforcement Anti-Gang Information Resources.* Report to the U.S. Department of Justice, National Institute of Justice.

Esbensen, Finn-Aage, and David Huizinga. 1993. "Gangs, Drugs, and Delinquency in a Survey of Urban Youth." *Criminology* 31: 565–589.

Fagan, Jeffrey. 1990. "Social Processes of Delinquency and Drug Use Among Urban Gangs." In *Gangs in America,* ed. C. Ronald Huff. Newbury Park, CA: Sage Publications.

Huff, C. Ronald. 1989. "Youth Gangs and Public Policy." *Crime and Delinquency* 35: 524–537.

Institute for Law and Justice. 1994. *Gang Prosecution in the United States.* Washington, DC: National Institute of Justice, Office of Justice Programs, U.S. Department of Justice.

Justice Research and Statistics Association. 1993. *Violent Crime and Drug Abuse in Rural Areas: Issues, Concerns, and Problems.* Washington, DC: Bureau of Justice Assistance, Office of Justice Programs, U.S. Department of Justice.

Lee, Felicia R. 1991. "For Gold Earrings and Protection, More Girls Take Violence." *New York Times,* November 11, pp. A1, 16.

Maxson, Cheryl L., Margaret A. Gordon, and Malcolm W. Klein. 1985. "Differences Between Gang and Nongang Homicides." *Criminology* 23: 209–222.

Miller, Walter B. 1975. *Violence by Youth Gangs and Youth Groups as a Crime Problem in Major American Cities.* A report for the National Institute for Juvenile Justice and Delinquency Prevention, Office of Juvenile Justice and Delinquency Prevention. Washington, DC: Government Printing Office.

———. 1982. *Crime by Youth Gangs and Groups in the United States.* Washington, DC: National Institute for Juvenile Justice and Delinquency Prevention, Office of Juvenile Justice and Delinquency Prevention.

Moore, Joan. 1991. *Going Down to the Barrio.* Philadelphia: Temple University Press.

Needle, Jerome A., and William Vaughn Stapleton. 1983. *Police Handling of Youth Gangs*. Washington DC: U.S. Department of Justice, Office of Juvenile Justice and Delinquency Prevention.

New Mexico State Department of Public Safety. 1994. *New Mexico Street Gangs: 1994 Update*. Albuquerque: New Mexico Department of Public Safety.

Spergel, Irving A. 1983. *Violent Gangs in Chicago: Segmentation and Integration*. Chicago: University of Chicago, School of Social Service Administration.

———. 1986. "The Violent Gang in Chicago: A Local Community Approach." *Social Service Review* 60: 94–131.

———. 1992. "Youth Gangs: An Essay Review." *Social Service Review* 66: 121–140.

———. 1993. *Gang Suppression and Intervention: An Assessment*. Chicago: University of Chicago, School of Social Service Administration.

Spergel, Irving A., and G. David Curry, with Ruth E. Ross and Ron L. Chance. 1990. *Survey of Youth Gang Problems and Programs in 45 Cities and 6 Sites*. Chicago: University of Chicago, School of Social Service Administration.

Thornberry, Terrence P., Marvin D. Krohn, Alan J. Lizotte, and Deborah Chard-Wierschem. 1993. "The Role of Juvenile Gangs in Facilitating Delinquency Behavior." *Journal of Research in Crime and Delinquency* 30: 55–87.

Thrasher, Frederic M. 1927. *The Gang: A Study of 1,313 Gangs in Chicago*. Chicago: University of Chicago Press.

Directory of Organizations 5

This chapter describes organizations, listed alphabetically, that work in a variety of ways with gangs and gang members as well as local community agencies that focus on stopping or preventing gang activity. They may be research oriented, prevention oriented, or service oriented. These organizations represent the types of services offered by programs throughout the country, but are only a sampling of the many organizations now dealing with gangs and gang violence. Check with local agencies and police departments for area-specific programs, for information about specific police department gang units, and for midnight basketball and other recreation programs. The federal government also operates several grant programs for local community agencies to help them solve problems with gangs, other delinquents, and crime in their communities. These are described at the end of the chapter.

Private, State, and Local Government Organizations

Activism 2000 Project
P.O. Box E
Kensington, MD 20895
(301) 929-8808

(800) KID-POWER
Fax: (301) 929-8907

The Activism 2000 Project is a resource center that was founded to help encourage young people to participate in shaping public policies concerning a wide range of social and political issues. For example, several girls have started organizations to stop domestic violence, sixth-graders have worked with local police personnel to reduce tensions and violence in their community, and high school students in Los Angeles have put together a public service announcement on the prevention of gang violence.

Publications: *Violence in America Info-Starter*, a document designed to provide young people with basic information about a variety of violence issues including gun violence, street violence and gangs, school violence, race and hate-related violence, family violence, and violence in entertainment. It identifies more than 150 federal government agencies, congressional committees, national organizations, and clearinghouses; 24 toll-free numbers; online bulletin board phone numbers; more than 100 publications concerning violence; and educational videotapes. *No Kidding Around* is a 260-page book of true stories about young people who have successfully implemented their ideas for improving their communities. It describes strategies to help young people develop ideas and offers them resources to help address problems in schools, neighborhoods, and communities.

Adelphoi Village
354 Main St.
Latrobe, PA 15650-1558
(412) 537-3052
Fax: (412) 539-7060

Adelphoi Village is a child-care agency that offers specialized programs for young people involved in gangs and satanic cults. These programs include assessments, weekly group counseling, and family counseling and consultation. The program endeavors to educate youth on the major consequences of joining gangs; to provide an open, nonjudgmental forum for youth to discuss problems related to their gang activity; and to help them examine their lives and try to improve their situations. It also teaches them to accept responsibility for themselves and their actions, and provides them with a support system to encourage positive behavior. Staff members help them to understand the cycles of drug, sexual, physical, and other criminal abuses connected with gang involvement and help them to face issues surrounding death, injury, and loss resulting from their gang activity. The program also helps young people develop good communication with their families as well as safeguards for a healthier lifestyle.

African-American Males Initiatives
W. K. Kellogg Foundation
1 Michigan Ave. East
Battle Creek, MI 49017-4058
(616) 968-1611

This program provides grants to organizations serving African American men and boys and has established a national advisory task force to provide direction for the effort. Activities focus on delivering multi-layered services to individuals and teaching young men to become leaders in their communities. The program helps grassroots organizations develop well-conceived projects that give African American men and boys opportunities to make positive changes in their lives; create community systems that break barriers that cause young people to feel isolated and poised for failure; improve the leadership skills of community leaders who develop and operate the projects; and establish successful models that can be replicated locally and nationally. Approximately 15,000 youth and 400 adults are expected to be directly affected by the original 15 projects; most are aimed at young people between the ages of 16 and 18 years.

Alternatives to Gang Membership
City of Paramount
16400 Colorado Ave.
Paramount, CA 90723
(310) 220-2140
Fax: (310) 630-2713

This joint venture between the city of Paramount and the Paramount Unified School District attempts to eliminate the source of future gang membership by teaching children the harmful effects of a gang lifestyle and how to choose positive alternatives. The program's approach is based on the belief that interest in gangs begins at an early age, and a successful anti-gang program must emphasize early identification of children at risk. The program has three components: an elementary school anti-gang curriculum, an intermediate school follow-up program, and neighborhood meetings. Lessons in the elementary school curriculum focus on peer pressure, graffiti, the impact of gang activity on family members, drug use and abuse among gang members, and alternative activities. The intermediate school follow-up program reviews the information presented in the elementary school curriculum and also emphasizes self-esteem, the consequences of a criminal lifestyle, the importance of getting a higher education, and career opportunities. Neighborhood meetings, conducted by city staff members, educate parents about gang activity and provide parents with encouragement and assistance in preventing their children from joining gangs.

Anti-Graffiti Program
Lakewood Police Department
Special Enforcement Team
445 S. Allison Parkway
Lakewood, CO 80226-3105
(303) 987-7111
Fax: (303) 987-7359

Timely removal of graffiti is required under the law in the city of Lakewood, Colorado; removal is required within five days of receiving official notification. The city sends to the owner of a defaced building a brochure containing a detachable consent form. By returning the form to the police department the owner indicates that he or she gives permission for volunteers from the city to paint over the graffiti. (If the form is not returned, the owner is responsible for removing the graffiti.) Trained Lakewood police volunteers, who are graduates of the Citizens Police Academy, take graffiti reports, photograph the graffiti, and conduct low-level surveillance of sites vandalized by graffiti. Other volunteers plan and do the removal work. Whenever possible, young people who are convicted of graffiti crimes in the city court are made to remove the graffiti so that they learn that they are responsible for their actions.

Boys' and Girls' Clubs of America
771 First Ave.
New York, NY 10017
(212) 351-5903

Boys' and Girls' Clubs of America encourage and support many individual Boys' and Girls' Clubs throughout the country. Their current approach to juvenile gang prevention emerged from their

Targeted Outreach Delinquency Prevention effort. Between 1990 and 1992, the national Boys' and Girls' Clubs and 33 local clubs developed this prevention effort in order to reach youth at risk for gang involvement; they devised several strategies for reaching and providing services to 2,000 youth living in areas with gang activity throughout the United States. The clubs focus on ways to provide services for these youth and to identify the strategies that have been most successful in treating at-risk youth.

Publications: *Gang Prevention through Targeted Outreach,* a manual to help individual Boys' and Girls' Clubs develop programs to reach at-risk youth before they become deeply involved in gang activity.

Bresee Youth
3401 W. Third St.
Los Angeles, CA 90020
(213) 387-2822
Fax: (213) 385-8482

Since 1987, the staff and volunteers with Bresee Youth have focused on building strong relationships with local juveniles and their families in the mid-Wilshire and South Central neighborhoods of Los Angeles. The program offers a variety of alternative activities for at-risk youth. It operates after-school and school vacation programs for more than 600 youths, as well as literacy programs. Its MacLab provides kids with the opportunity to learn computer skills to strengthen their education. Its Youth Employment Services (YES) program provides part-time jobs for students while they are in school and helps them to develop a sense of responsibility; YES also provides referrals to local businesses and individuals in need of part-time help. Because Los Angeles does not have many parks or recreation facilities for inner-city youth, Bresee Youth also offers a recreation area and full-size gym as well as basketball and volleyball leagues that work to keep many students off the streets and out of trouble with the law. An outdoor wilderness program offers camping trips and retreats from urban life, as well as outdoor adventure trips with activities such as backpacking, rock climbing, rappelling, fishing, and white-water rafting. The program is also planning a print shop/copy center and silk screening business to train and employ many youth, another youth center in South Central Los Angeles, and a scholarship program for ninth and tenth graders to motivate them to do well in school.

California Wellness Foundation
Violence Prevention Initiative
6320 Canoga Ave., Suite 1700
Woodland Hills, CA 91367-7111
(818) 593-6600

This foundation was created as an independent, private organization to improve the health of California residents. It designs, develops, and evaluates health-promotion and disease-prevention programs and encourages individuals and communities to adopt healthy lifestyles. Through the Violence Prevention Initiative, the foundation hopes to develop and evaluate a comprehensive multidisciplinary approach to combating youth violence and gangs throughout California. This initiative has four components: a leadership program, a community action program, a policy program, and a research program. The leadership program promotes the importance of leadership in preventing acts of violence. The community action program provides resources and technical assistance to various communities to reduce youth violence through health-promotion programs. The policy program advocates changes in public policy that might help reduce gang violence. The research program seeks to expand current knowledge about causes and prevention of youth violence; it will examine the relationships between violence and alcohol and other drugs, firearms and gang involvement, socioeconomic factors, and public health conditions.

The foundation has also established community-action grants to provide resources and technical assistance to communities that want to reduce youth violence through pilot collaborative health-promotion programs.

Center for the Study and Prevention of Violence
Institute of Behavioral Science
University of Colorado
910 28th Street
Campus Box 442
Boulder, CO 80309-0442
(303) 492-1032
Fax: (303) 443-3297

The primary purpose of the center, founded in 1992, is to provide information and assistance to groups and individuals studying the causes of violence and ways of preventing it, especially youth violence and gang activity. The center's Information House gathers research literature relating to violence and offers bibliographic searches on requested topics via its online database, which contains abstracts and references to research papers, programs, curricula, videos, books and journal articles, and other sources of information about causes of violence and prevention strategies. Reviews of literature are conducted and currently include topics such as evaluating juvenile violence prevention, violence and the schools, the effects of the mass media on violence, the family and juvenile violence, gangs, guns and violence, and alcohol and drugs and their influence on juvenile violence. These reviews combine an evaluation of the scientific literature and comments from current practitioners and policymakers. The center provides technical assistance to individuals and groups developing or evaluating programs that focus on violence prevention. The Center also has a research component that analyzes data and develops and conducts studies to understand the causes of violence.

CHOICES Youth Program
San Bernardino County Sheriff's Department
P.O. Box 569
San Bernardino, CA 92402
(909) 387-3700

This program was developed by the San Bernardino County Sheriff's Department to help young people develop a positive self-image. The program emphasizes academic success and positive home lives and counters negative influences that many at-risk children face without the knowledge or training to help deal with these influences. As a comprehensive prevention and intervention program, CHOICES offers a series of one-hour group sessions, held twice a week over 17 weeks, that bring together at-risk youth in grades 6 through 8 to explore new ways to deal with old problems. Five sections or steps are offered; the first section provides 34 hours of training in conflict resolution, anger management, coping skills, positive family and peer relations, academic success strategies, and peer mediation. During a one-day field trip and a two-day wilderness camp, youths practice what they have learned in the classroom sessions in a more stressful but controlled situation. A tutoring program brings volunteer mentors from the local community together with students for two hours per week to help the students with their studies and to act as strong positive role models for them. Parents also participate in classes to help improve family communication. In the final section, local community organizations provide after-school and weekend activities to reinforce the lessons the students learned in earlier sessions. Some of the participating organizations include Campfire Boys and Girls, Boys' and Girls' Clubs, and the YMCA. Organizers believe that CHOICES is successful in large part because of the multidisciplinary approach that involves law-enforcement personnel, area schools, local community groups, and parents.

Community Action Problem Solving
16030 N. 56th St.
Scottsdale, AZ 85254
(602) 495-5006

The Community Action Problem Solving (CAPS) program works to reduce gang activity and violent crime in local neighborhoods. Police opened a storefront office in Scottsdale (a community within Phoenix) and several police units came together to work on solving community problems. Community Action Officers are assigned to a specific geographic location and organize neighborhood block watches, respond to radio calls, and work with the appropriate agencies to solve zoning problems and deal with abandoned houses. They also coordinate services with the departments of parks and recreation, human resources, and zoning, as well as child protective services and the drug enforcement bureau. The Proactive Directed Patrol Squad (PDPS) conducts surveillance or undercover investigations to control drug and crime problems, including gang activities. The Bike Patrol Unit conducts neighborhood surveillance and talks with local residents. A juvenile activity coordinator counsels students, plans academic and recreational activities, and refers students to other community agencies for needed services.

Community Services
San Mateo Police Department
2000 S. Delaware St.
San Mateo, CA 94403
(415) 377-4545

This program works to build partnerships between the police department and residents, community organizations, and other city government departments in San Mateo. Community police officers are assigned to specific neighborhoods within the metropolitan area and act as a liaison between local residents and the city. They identify problems and develop long-range solutions. One cooperative program, the Street Gang Mediation Process, combines the efforts of the juvenile court, county probation offices, conflict resolution center, and the police to work with local gangs. The program has facilitated a truce between two local gangs and is working with other gangs to achieve peace. The Graffiti Removal Program uses citizen volunteers and donated materials to remove graffiti. Juveniles who have been arrested for painting graffiti on walls and buildings are made to help in this effort.

Community Youth Gang Services
144 South Fetterly Avenue
Los Angeles, CA 90022
(213) 266-4264

Community Youth Gang Services (CYGS) is one of the largest non–law enforcement anti-gang programs in the country. It integrates prevention, intervention, and community mobilization efforts with support from various justice agencies through an interactive, multifaceted program called Target Area Strategy (TAS). TAS is a dual-recovery plan aimed at reclaiming physical locations controlled by gangs as well as those youth affected by gangs. It has six major components: crisis intervention, community mobilization, prevention, parent-teacher education, job development, and graffiti removal. CYGS's Career Paths Program, a 15-week course presented in elementary schools, teaches kids about the negative aspects of gangs and promotes positive alternatives. Its Star Parenting Program provides parents with the tools to address the complexities of parenthood and gang prevention.

Publications: a general information guide and pamphlets on *Levels of Individual Involvement, Gang Development and Behavior,* and *Common Gang Lifestyle Characteristics.* The booklet *Gang Education, Assessment and Planning System,* describes the experiences of several communities in East and Central Los Angeles in combating gang activity and provides a model for other communities to follow.

Direction Sports
600 Wilshire Blvd., Suite 320
Los Angeles, CA 90017
(213) 627-9861

Direction Sports is a nonprofit organization that attempts to serve the emotional, educational, and recreational needs of disadvantaged youth. It attacks educational deficiency problems at the roots by working to change attitudes and increase motivation and by using team sports as the magnet for involvement. Its primary interest has been the development and refinement of peer-run programs. Employing inner-city teenagers to work as coaches and teachers for area youths, Direction Sports provides viable alternatives to the gang, drug, and cruising culture of the streets. It aims to design programs that support the educational system and enhance youths' self-esteem.

Gang Violence Reduction Program
Research and Development Division
Chicago Police Department
1121 South State St.
Chicago, IL 60605
(312) 747-6207

This program was developed to reduce street-gang-related violence in the 10th police district on Chicago's West Side. Up to 200 known, hard-core gang members are identified and targeted in an attempt to change their behavior. The police, probation and pretrial-services staff, former gang members from the community, researchers, and a neighborhood council cooperate to mediate and defuse conflicts among the major street gangs in the area. Outreach and crisis-intervention services are provided along with individual referrals for training, education, and job opportunities in an effort to provide alternatives to gang membership. The probation department manages the caseloads of gang members and provides them with intensive supervision, including frequent home visits, curfew checks, drug testing and treatment, and other services such as counseling, classes, and referrals for community service. The University of Chicago's School of Social Service Administration plans and coordinates the gang-outreach services. A community advisory group includes representatives from local agencies, community organizations, and residents and provides advice and other help to the project staff.

Georgia Department of Children and Youth Services
2 Peachtree St.
Atlanta, GA 30303-3139
(404) 657-2410
Fax: (404) 657-2479

The department funds a number of delinquency prevention programs that incorporate violence reduction strategies; several are provided through contracted services with private agencies.

These contractors provide services to help youth who are at risk for ending up in the juvenile justice system to withstand pressure to join gangs. One of these programs is the Family Connection Program, which teaches job-readiness skills and behavior management and provides family counseling, violence-prevention education, training in youth leadership and conflict resolution, summer school activities, and parent education. These programs are offered in the city of Decatur, as well as Dawson, Gordon, Houston, Richmond, and Sumter Counties.

The department offers several prevention projects in metropolitan Atlanta through contracts with private organizations. The Boys' and Girls' Clubs provide tutorial, job-readiness, and cultural enrichment services. Clark-Atlanta University offers tutoring, counseling, and supervision for youth referrals from DeKalb Juvenile Court. The Southwest YMCA provides drug-abuse awareness, violence prevention, intramural sports competition, other recreational activities, and tutorial services. Youth Enhancement Services works with school-age youth and offers tutorial, cultural enrichment and job-readiness skills training. Youth on probation and youth from the Fulton Multi-Service Center receive help from Youth Enhancement Services in obtaining their high school equivalency diplomas. Project IMPACT, a comprehensive juvenile diversion program, provides delinquency-prevention services to pre-delinquent and delinquent youths and their families who live in or near DeKalb County. The Wholistic Stress Control Institute provides training in stress management and violence prevention for students, parents, teachers, and other interested professionals.

Guardian Angels
982 East 89th St.
Brooklyn, NY 11236
(718) 649-2607

In 1979 the Guardian Angels began as an anti-crime patrol on the subways of New York City. As criminal acts have escalated over the years, the Guardian Angels' role has expanded as well. They are now asked to do more and more in communities trying to combat crime, such as organize patrols and assist residents in their fight against crime. The Guardian Angels are an international, multicultural, and multi-ethnic network of more than 5,000 young men and women volunteers, with more than 40 chapters throughout the United States as well as Canada, Australia, England,

France, Germany, Italy, Russia, and Sweden. Patrolling in groups of four, they are well-trained in what to do when they see a crime in progress, how to protect themselves and the victims, how to make a citizen's arrest, and how to work effectively with the police to put criminals in jail. Members are taught discipline, responsibility, respect, loyalty, and self-esteem. They escort senior citizens to appointments and to other activities, assist the handicapped, provide self-defense demonstrations and training courses, and distribute food to the hungry and homeless. Guardian Angels also speak at elementary, junior, and senior high schools and colleges about their program and how to prevent crime, as well as about the dangers of drugs, gangs, substance abuse, peer pressure, and the importance of staying in school. Members are trained extensively in self-defense, first aid and CPR, and ways to communicate effectively with people.

Juvenile Justice Clearinghouse
Office of Juvenile Justice and Delinquency Prevention
National Institute of Justice
U.S. Department of Justice
P.O. Box 6000
Rockville, MD 20849-6000
(800) 638-8736
Internet: http://www.ncjrs.com

The Office of Juvenile Justice and Delinquency Prevention (OJJDP) established the Juvenile Justice Clearinghouse as a component of the National Criminal Justice Reference Service (NCJRS) in 1979. The clearinghouse is a comprehensive resource for information on a variety of juvenile-justice topics, including gangs and gang-related information. Juvenile-justice professionals and anyone else seeking information can speak with an information specialist about specific areas of inquiry. The clearinghouse coordinates the distribution of OJJDP publications and disseminates information about research sponsored by OJJDP, training projects, and program initiatives. It also provides access to the NCJRS library, which is one of the world's most comprehensive sources of criminal-justice and juvenile-justice literature. The NCJRS also has an electronic bulletin board on the Internet that provides timely information on a variety of topics of interest to juvenile justice professionals.

Publications: *Gang Suppression and Intervention: Community Models* provides a framework for creating promising approaches to reducing the problems created by juvenile gangs. *OJJDP and Boys and Girls Clubs of America: Public Housing and High-Risk Youth* describes successful delinquency-prevention initiatives. Topical searches and topical bibliographies also are available on the subject of juvenile gangs.

Lansing City Gang Strategy Program
124 West Michigan Ave.
Lansing, MI 48933
(517) 483-4141
Fax: (517) 483-6066

For the past three years, the city of Lansing has been working on a comprehensive strategy to combat gang activity in the city, and it has developed several plans and programs to help minimize the gang presence. It has decentralized the police department, believing that police officers should be closer to the neighborhoods they patrol; community policing has been instituted throughout the city. Lansing has expanded its programs to provide all human services in all wards of the city; the Lansing school district has offered to provide space for these programs in middle and high schools. The Mobile Police Headquarters travels to area schools and park sites to provide an opportunity for local citizens to ask questions of city officials, and activities are provided for children. Approximately 135 active Neighborhood Watch programs are in effect. The Police Department developed a gang handbook, which is distributed to all Neighborhood Watch coordinators, and there are workshops for Neighborhood Watch coordinators and police officers. The city has contracted with the Black Child and Family Institute to develop Teens Against Graffiti (TAG) teams to help paint over any reported graffiti. A gang hotline responds within 24 hours to all calls. The city council has passed a curfew ordinance and has established a family assessment program to identify troubled families and offer follow-up intervention. The city has also established summer teen programs, including Project Play, to establish new playgrounds throughout the city; Brotherhood Against Drugs, which is a night basketball and counseling program for both boys and girls; Youth Program Pilots, looking for innovative new youth programs; camp programs; middle-school sports programs; the Police Athletic League, which has more than 500 youth participating in soccer, basketball, and baseball programs; and a recreational skating program, which has a mobile skating rink available for use throughout the city for both in-line and roller-skating activities. The city also has three special youth programs, including a youth and family task force that is examining ways to expand after-school activities in high-risk neighborhoods; a drug-free youth task force, which is an interagency group focusing on prevention and intervention; and a violence prevention program.

Los Angeles County Probation Department
Gang Alternative and Prevention Program
3221 Torrance Blvd.
Torrance, CA 90503
(310) 222-2666

The Gang Alternative and Prevention Program (GAPP) focuses on pre-delinquent and at-risk youth living in neighborhoods with a high rate of crime, violent gang activity, and heavy use of drugs. The program's primary attention is given to elementary and junior-high youths who are either identified as at-risk for serious gang activity or who already display signs of participating in gang-related activity. These signs may include writing graffiti, using gang slang, wearing gang clothes, intimidating others, or associating with known gang members. Seven geographical areas are served, including Antelope Valley, Centinela, East Los Angeles, Long Beach, Rio Hondo, the San Gabriel Valley, and the San Fernando Valley. Youths are provided with several ongoing services, including individual and group counseling, use of prevention resources, bicultural and bilingual services, special programs such as tutoring and parent education, and recreational, educational, and cultural experiences. The objectives of each GAPP program include ensuring long-term community protection, reducing drug use and gang participation, intervening with first-time offenders, offering positive alternatives and enhanced self-esteem for youth before they become involved in drug or gang activities, networking with community groups working in the field of drug and gang prevention, providing intensive supervision, and ensuring the imposition of appropriate penalties for youth who are on probation or under GAPP supervision.

Los Angeles County Probation Department
School Crime Suppression Program
3221 Torrance Blvd.
Torrance, CA 90503
(310) 222-2665

The purpose of the School Crime Suppression Program (SCSP) is to address serious problems, including violence, gang activity, vandalism, and truancy, that disrupt school activities throughout Los Angeles County. The Los Angeles County Probation Department has placed deputy probation officers at more than 20 high schools to allow greater supervision and other support services to juveniles on probation. Areas included within this program include Antelope Valley, Centinela, Crenshaw, East Los Angeles, Long Beach, and the San Gabriel Valley. The program has several objectives: to reduce campus violence committed by juveniles on probation, improve the attendance record of these juveniles, provide positive alternatives and enhanced self-esteem for at-risk youth before they start joining gangs or using drugs, network with community and parent groups concerned with gang and drug prevention, and provide intensive supervision for juveniles who are in school and on probation. Programs are tailored by each SCSP office to the specific juveniles and school it serves. Programs identify students who are on probation and provide them with coordinated supervision services, monitor attendance and report attendance problems and violations to the court, and provide consultation and information to schools. They also help schools and communities develop delinquency-prevention programs; conduct drug testing when necessary; refer students for tutoring, recreation, job training, and cultural experiences; participate in public information and training activities; and refer families to parental education programs.

MAD DADS
2221 North 24th St.
Omaha, NE 68110
(402) 451-3500

MAD (Men Against Destruction) DADS (Defending Against Drugs and Social Disorder) was founded in June 1989 in the basement of the Omaha Pilgrim Baptist Church by a group of men who were fed up with gang violence and the unimpeded flow of illegal drugs in their community. The group encourages all "strong, drug-free men" to act as positive parental role models and, by example, to address city-wide issues concerning youth and their families. It conducts weekend street patrols within troubled areas, reporting crime, drug sales, and other destructive activities to the proper authorities. MAD DADS also offers positive community activities for youth, chaperones community events, and provides street counseling at any time.

There is also a division of MOMS AND KIDS who work with the MAD DADS. They now have chapters in Houston, Denver,

New York City, Baltimore, Columbus, Ohio, Greenville, Mississippi, several cities in Florida, and Council Bluffs, Iowa, as well as Omaha and Lincoln, Nebraska.

Metro Denver Gang Coalition
c/o Channel 9 News
500 Speer Blvd.
Denver, CO 80203
(303) 871-9999

In September 1993, several grassroots community organizations in the Denver metropolitan area met to identify and attempt to resolve issues concerning programs and service delivery for at-risk youth, especially those youth becoming involved in gang-related activities. After many meetings over several months, the coalition was formed in January 1994 to provide an arena for service providers and community members to share information, support program efforts, and create positive changes in youth, families, and communities. Approximately 30 nonprofit agencies, the Denver Public Schools, and a local news organization are members of the coalition. Their goals include the following: to facilitate cooperation among service providers; to curtail gang-related activity and youth violence; to promote healthy relationships between the community and service programs; to act as an advocate for the passage of appropriate laws to curtail gang-related activities; and to work together to provide funding for service providers.

National Association of
Police Athletic Leagues
200 Castlewood Dr.
Suite 400
North Palm Beach, FL 33408-5696
(407) 844-1823
Fax: (407) 863-6120

One of the largest juvenile-crime prevention programs with more than 3 million members, the National Association of Police Athletic Leagues (PAL) provides a forum for sharing information, promotes national training seminars, develops fund-raising programs, initiates public-awareness projects, develops regional and national tournaments, and publishes a national newspaper. It promotes competition for the advancement of sportsmanship and citizenship. Local chapters throughout the nation offer a variety of activities, including sports programs, arts and crafts, dance, music, drama, social services, vocational guidance, remedial reading, gardening, field trips, and other popular youth activities. The organization works with neighborhood youth who are bored, apathetic, lonely, and are dealing with the countless problems of living in the city; the long-term goal is to reach these youths before they become delinquent or involved in gang activities.

**National Clearinghouse on
Satanic Crime in America**
USCCCN International, Inc.
P.O. Box 1185—Nixon Station
Edison, NJ 08818-1185
(908) 549-2599
Fax: (908) 549-2599

This organization primarily serves as an awareness, training, and investigative research organization for crimes and criminal activities that appear to be Satanic, occult, ritualistic, or gang-related. It maintains a database of persons, registered and unregistered groups, and destructive activities related to cult and occult involvement, as well as demographics of criminal acts and timely educational materials. It offers publications, videos, training seminars, and related efforts.

Educational material: *Don't Touch that Gun*, VHS, a two-part program that provides short vignettes instructing children not to touch a gun in any situation and to tell a parent or other adult if someone else is playing with a gun.

**National Consortium on Alternatives
for Youth at Risk, Inc.**
5250 17th St., Suite 107
Sarasota, FL 34235-8247
(813) 378-4793
(800) 245-7133
Fax: (813) 378-9922

Established in 1979 as a result of a national consortium of more than 50 juvenile-justice professionals, this program is a foundation-supported educational group that researches and disseminates information on the needs of youth and on programs that help meet these needs. It started out with an emphasis on using outdoor experiences as an alternative to incarceration and as a significant contribution to the desperate needs of these youngsters;

the program has expanded to include additional alternatives to incarceration. Its five priorities include: (1) to research alternatives for youth-at-risk; (2) to conduct surveys to validate the success of various programs; (3) to determine what factors make a program successful; (4) to acquaint practitioners with alternative programs that are available to at-risk youth; and (5) to disseminate information on the needs of at-risk youth. It relies primarily on donations from individuals for funding, but it is also partially supported by foundation grants.

National Council of Juvenile and Family Court Judges
P.O. Box 8970
Reno, NV 89507
(702) 784-6012
Fax: (702) 784-6628

The National Council of Juvenile and Family Court Judges provides counsel on juvenile and family law to the nation's juvenile and family jurists. It offers continuing education to judges, referees, probation officers, social workers, law-enforcement personnel, and other juvenile-justice professionals. It stays abreast of changes in laws concerning child abuse and neglect, crack babies, foster care, custody issues, school violence, gangs, and serious juvenile crime. It offers programs to address current topics in these areas.

National Council on Crime and Delinquency
685 Market St., Suite 620
San Francisco, CA 94105
(415) 896-6223
Fax: (415) 896-5109

A nonprofit organization, the NCCD focuses its attention on developing and promoting criminal- and juvenile-justice strategies that are fair, humane, effective, and built on a solid economic foundation. It researches critical criminal justice issues, formulates innovative approaches to controlling crime, and implements unique programs. The NCCD has developed standards and guidelines for probation and parole professions, and it currently is developing strategies to help criminal-justice professionals effectively manage corrections systems. It provides studies and policy recommendations for juvenile- and criminal-justice reform. Its goal is to help federal and state officials, criminal-justice professionals, and community organizations develop and implement programs that will improve the criminal-justice system.

National Crime Prevention Council
1700 K St. NW, Second Floor
Washington, DC 20006-3817
(202) 466-6272
Fax: (202) 296-1356

The National Crime Prevention Council is a private, nonprofit organization with a major focus on enabling people to help prevent crime and build safer, more caring communities. It manages a public-service advertising campaign, provides information and referral services and technical assistance, conducts training in crime-prevention skills and techniques, and conducts demonstration programs and research to discover the most effective ways to prevent crime in local communities. Its Youth as Resources project started as a demonstration in three Indiana cities in 1987. This locally based program provides small grants to youths to help them design and carry out projects to meet their community's needs. Youth as Resources is based on the premise that young people, given the opportunity, have the desire and ability to organize and act effectively to help solve some of society's most pressing problems.

Publications: *Helping Youth with Gang Prevention* is a packet of information designed to help crime-prevention professionals identify important concepts and promising strategies, locate resources, and encourage youth to solve their problems peacefully and build safer and more caring communities. *Tools to Involve Parents in Gang Prevention* is a collection of reproducible materials to help parents prevent their children from joining a gang. In addition to information for parents, it includes activity sheets for young children, word games, and three mini-posters. Other publications include the *Catalyst* newsletter covering current news in crime and drug prevention; *Getting Together to Fight Crime;* and *Stop the Violence, Start Something*, which describes steps that individuals and communities can take to prevent violence and crime.

National Resource Center for Youth Services
The University of Oklahoma
College of Continuing Education
202 West 8th St.
Tulsa, OK 74119-1419
(918) 585-2986
Fax: (918) 592-1841

The National Resource Center provides training, technical assistance, publications, conference planning, and information and referral services on a variety of adolescent issues. Its programs focus on a number of serious issues concerning youth, including runaways and homelessness, AIDS/HIV, independent living, substance abuse, residential care, sexual abuse, and cultural diversity. The center provides training materials and services to professionals and agencies who work with at-risk youth. The Managing Aggressive Behavior program provides trainer certification in skills needed to manage the aggressive behavior of children with whom the participants work and offers consultation on how to plan training sessions. Direct training is also provided for recognizing a developing crisis and intervening appropriately.

Publications: *Youth Mediation Resource Guide* and *Conflict Resolution*, two curricula that focus on ways to mediate and resolve conflicts among youth.

National School Safety Center
4165 Thousand Oaks Blvd., Suite 290
Westlake Village, CA 91362
(805) 373-9977
Fax: (805) 373-9277

In 1984 a presidential directive created the National School Safety Center to meet the growing demand by school professionals for additional training and education in the areas of school crime and violence prevention. The center is a partnership of the U.S. Department of Justice, the U.S. Department of Education, and Pepperdine University. Its purpose is to promote safe schools as well as to ensure quality education for all children. Its mandate is to focus national attention on cooperative solutions to problems that disrupt the education of children, with a special emphasis on ways to eliminate crime, violence, and drugs from schools, as well as programs that focus on improving student discipline, attendance, achievement, and school climate. It provides technical assistance, legal and legislative aid, and publications and films, and it conducts training programs and provides technical assistance for education and law-enforcement practitioners, legislators, and other governmental policy makers. Staff members work with governors, attorneys general, school officials, and communities in every state to develop customized and safe school training and planning programs. The center also serves as a clearinghouse for current information on school safety issues and maintains a resource center with more than 50,000 articles, publications, and films.

Publications: The School Safety News Service is a major source of information for school crime and violence prevention planning. *School Safety*, a journal focusing on specific issues related to school safety is published three times a year and distributed to approximately 50,000 school administrators, law-enforcement officers, state and federal legislators, juvenile- and family-court judges, journalists, governors, attorneys general, and school superintendents. *School Safety Update* is a newsletter offering updates on major issues facing school systems today and is published six times each year. The center also issues special reports on topics relating to school safety; for example, *Gangs in Schools: Breaking Up is Hard to Do* (1993) provides information on types of gangs, ways to prevent or reduce gang involvement, and descriptions of more than 20 successful programs.

New Mexico Center for Dispute Resolution
620 Roma NW
Suite B
Albuquerque, NM 87102
(505) 247-0571
Fax: (505) 242-5966

The NMCDR is a nonprofit organization established in 1982 to provide mediation services for a wide range of disputes, develop and implement innovative applications of mediation, and provide mediation and conflict resolution training to other organizations and to individuals. It is nationally known for its innovative conflict-resolution programs for children, youth, and families. Programs include peer mediation in schools, parent/child mediation, victim/juvenile offender mediation, mediation in juvenile corrections and residential facilities, and violence-prevention skills for juvenile offenders and their parents. NMCDR also sponsors national training institutes for professionals throughout the country on topics such as school mediation, parent/child mediation, and mediation and conflict-resolution for gang-involved youth. It sponsors a Violence Intervention Program along with the Juvenile Probation and Parole Office in Bernalillo County, New Mexico. The program provides a cost-effective community option for juvenile offenders likely to be incarcerated for drug-related or violent offenses, promotes public safety by providing surveillance and risk-control strategies for juvenile offenders, and works to improve the cognitive and social skills of juvenile offenders and their parents to enhance their ability to function effectively in interpersonal relationships.

Publications: *Managing Conflict: A Curriculum for Adolescents*, developed in collaboration with the Youth Diagnostic and Development Center, is a 15-lesson curriculum designed to teach communication, problem-solving, and anger-management skills. *Training and Implementation Guide for Student Mediation in Elementary Schools* prepares school staff to implement a school-wide mediation program. The center also has a training guide developed for secondary-school staff. *Mediation and Conflict Resolution for Gang-Involved Youth* is designed as a training or resource manual for those who work with youths.

New Mexico Youth at Risk Foundation, Inc.
2901 Cuervo Drive NE
Albuquerque, NM 87110
(505) 883-7114
Fax: (505) 888-7671

This nonprofit, all-volunteer organization deals with troubled youth throughout New Mexico. Its program goes beyond traditional prevention and intervention models to address issues of human and adolescent development. One component, the Committed Partners for Youth program, works to alter the attitudes and core beliefs that youths have about themselves, others, their circumstances, and life itself. Young people identified by the agency attend a presentation about the program; if they choose to participate, they undergo a comprehensive enrollment process. Staffers of the year-long program work to increase the youths' self-esteem; help them learn to take responsibility for their choices, actions, and past mistakes; get along better with family and friends; communicate more effectively; seek higher education; learn that fighting and violence are not the answer to solving problems; stop selling drugs; refuse to join gangs; and develop long-range goals. The program includes a five-day non-residential intensive course and a 14-month follow-through after-care program.

Omega Boys Club
One Hallidie Plaza, Suite 701
San Francisco, CA 94102
(415) 346-1183
Fax: (415) 346-2055

This organization is for youths and young adults between the ages of 11 and 25 and bases its ideology on the old saying that it takes an entire village to raise a child. The club believes in the extended family and idea that unrelated adults and youths can come together and have an impact on the issues of drugs, gangs, and violence. The club's academic program prepares and assists members who are interested in pursuing a college degree. It provides non–college-bound members with verbal, academic, keyboard, and computer literacy skills to successfully enter the job market and encourages and facilitates the development of entrepreneurial capabilities. The Peer Counseling Program works with incarcerated youths to keep them from returning to delinquent behavior; directors, volunteers, and peer counselors hold weekly meetings with youthful offenders and act as advocates. Omega's violence prevention effort also reaches out to the community at large. Major components include a weekly radio call-in talk show, an annual youth conference in which participants seek solutions to the violence in their communities, and Street Soldier training in which members learn to conduct violence prevention work in other communities.

Prince William County Community Services Board
8033 Ashton Ave.
Suite 107
Manassas, VA 22110
(703) 792-7730
Fax: (703) 792-7704

The Community Services Board co-sponsors and is the contact for the "Turn Off the Violence" campaign, a coalition of more than ten different organizations and individuals working to raise awareness about violence and the ways communities can reduce it. Two problem areas the campaign seeks to address are the media's negative influence on attitudes concerning the acceptability of violence and the lack of information available to young people about positive ways to resolve conflict. People are asked to turn off violence in all its forms, including physical, sexual, domestic, verbal, family, gang, and playground violence; hate crimes; and violence in music. The campaign's volunteers provide a list of positive, safe, legal, and enjoyable alternatives to violence; distribute educational materials to educators, law enforcement personnel, and youth-group leaders; solicit sponsors; produce public-awareness materials; and operate a speakers bureau.

Salt Lake City Gang Project
315 East 200 South
Salt Lake City, UT 84111
(801) 799-GANG

This gang task force works to prevent and suppress gang activity by coordinating services at the local, county, and state levels. Members include police officers, prosecutors, community activists, business leaders, city department directors, and county and state government personnel. These members meet monthly to discuss problems and develop strategies to resolve these problems. The gang unit helps to provide at-risk youth with alternatives to the gang life by working with local business, government, and community leaders to provide work opportunities, including job corps and apprenticeships. Youths are referred to drug rehabilitation and education programs if necessary. Police officers patrol known gang areas, conduct sting operations, and maintain a data base that contains names of gang members, gang crimes committed, and the location at which these crimes were committed. The unit's community coordinator educates neighborhood groups on how to spot, deter, and report gang activity.

Society for Prevention of Violence
3439 West Brainard, Room 102
Woodmere, OH 44122
(216) 591-1876

The Society for Prevention of Violence is dedicated to reducing the prevalence of violent acts and asocial behaviors in children and adults through education. It teaches children and adults skills intended to build their character, help them acquire a strong value system, motivate them to develop their communication skills, and promote positive interpersonal relationships. The society works to help participants integrate social and academic skills in order to develop positive alternatives and reach their full potential. It encourages people to contribute to society by making decisions and solving problems through effective and appropriate means. A variety of workshops, such as "Gangs, Guns, Drugs, and Violence," are aimed at school personnel.

Study Circles Resource Center
P.O. Box 203, Rt. 169
Pomfret, CT 06258

(860) 928-2616
Fax: (860) 928-3713

Study Circles Resource Center is a project of the Topsfield Foundation, a private, nonprofit organization dedicated to improving the quality of public life in the United States. The Foundation promotes the use of small-group, democratic, highly participatory discussions that provide ways for individuals within the community to come together to resolve problems such as crime and the effects of gangs and gang violence. Study Circles promotes an increase in the number of people volunteering to help fight crime and violence, stronger neighborhood watch activities, new mentoring relationships between adults and young people, more effective community policing efforts, and increased youth involvement in violence prevention efforts.

Publications: *Confronting Violence in Our Communities: A Guide for Involving Citizens in Public Dialogue and Problem Solving*, a study focusing on community violence, including gang, drug-related, and domestic violence. Topics covered include the effect that violence has on individual lives, the reasons why violence occurs in our society, what steps neighborhoods can take to prevent violent activities, and what schools can do to prevent or stop violence.

VisionQuest
P.O. Box 12906
Tucson, AZ 85732
(602) 881-3950

VisionQuest was founded in 1973 by a former VISTA (Volunteers in Service to America—the "domestic Peace Corps") volunteer who borrowed the name from the Native American practice of sending a boy entering manhood away for solitary fasting, meditation, and dreaming to pursue a vision from the Great Spirit. The program offers a broad network of responsive program alternatives for youths, many of whom have been referred from the juvenile-justice or mental-health systems. These juveniles range in age from 13 to 21, tend to have trouble developing and maintaining healthy relationships with family members and friends, and may also have trouble adapting to the school environment. Programs offered include impact camps, wagon trains, sailing, biking, backpacking trips, group homes, at-home treatment, alternative schools, and diagnostic and shelter care. As a national organization, it contracts with several government agencies in order to provide specialized services. The goal of the program is to help these youth return to their homes and communities with new self-respect and social survival skills. Staff members develop a program tailored to an individual's behavioral, health, and educational needs. Services provided include educational assessment; behavioral and psychological assessment; evaluation and diagnosis; health assessment and medical referrals; program planning and quarterly review; individualized educational programming; psychological and/or psychiatric counseling; individual and group counseling; parent counseling; family intervention and support; crisis intervention; and recreational activities. The programs focus on breaking down gang affiliations and replacing them with new, positive connections.

Al Wooten Jr. Heritage Center
9106 South Western Ave.
Los Angeles, CA 90047
(213) 756-7203
Fax: (213) 756-9159

This youth center offers after-school and weekend academic and recreational classes for young people in South Central Los Angeles who are between the ages of 8 and 18. Major goals are to offer alternatives to gang involvement, increase basic-skills test scores, reduce the high dropout rate, help youth reconnect with the community, assist in developing career and vocational skills and goals, and to train youths to be leaders and positive role models in their community. The outreach program aims to help young participants build positive self-images and develop maturity while improving academic performance. Staff members offer leadership development, recreational activities, community youth services, cultural activities, and academic training including tutoring, literacy, and remedial courses. A mentoring program pairs successful business and community members with youths who need positive role models.

Federal Government Programs

These federally funded programs offer grants to local agencies and organizations to help finance programs related to gangs and gang violence. Funding levels and telephone numbers for contacting these agencies are provided when available.

Assistance for Delinquent and At-Risk Youth

This program is administered by the Attorney General, supported by the Ounce of Prevention Council. Grants are made to
public or private nonprofit organizations to be used for residential services to youth between the ages of 11 and 19 years who
have come into contact, or are at risk for coming into contact,
with the juvenile-justice system. Services may include programs
to increase self-esteem, improve academic skills, provide vocational and job training skills, and other related tasks. (Contact
phone number: (800) 421-6770.)

Local Crime Prevention Block Grant Programs

This program is administered by the attorney general and provides
funds to local government agencies. Funds may be used for education, training, research, prevention, treatment, diversion, and rehabilitation programs to prevent juvenile gangs and juvenile violence;
programs that prevent young children from joining gangs; programs providing employment opportunities for disadvantaged
teenagers; midnight sports programs; supervised sports and recreation programs; programs focusing on reducing gang participation;
family outreach teams; and multidisciplinary teams, including law-
enforcement agencies, set up to respond to violent incidents. The
funding level is approximately $75 million per year, beginning in
fiscal year 1996. (Contact phone number: (800) 421-6770.)

Gang Resistance Education and Training (GREAT) Projects

This is a classroom program developed to prevent youth violence
and to keep young people out of gangs. Supported by the U.S.
Bureau of Alcohol, Tobacco and Firearms and the Federal Law
Enforcement Training Center, this program was first developed
in Phoenix, Arizona, as a comprehensive and innovative anti-
gang and violence prevention program aimed at teaching young
people the skills necessary to say no to gangs. Law-enforcement
personnel and federal agents teach the GREAT curriculum to students in elementary, junior high, and middle schools. At the time
of this writing, more than 1,300 police officers and special agents
from more than 530 agencies representing 45 states, the District
of Columbia, and military personnel from bases located overseas,

have been trained to present the core curriculum. Approximately 2 million students have participated in the program. The curriculum covers crimes, victims, individual rights, cultural sensitivity, prejudice, conflict resolution, drugs, the responsibilities of various individuals within the community, and the importance of setting goals in life. The skills that students learn are designed to help them avoid the peer pressure to join gangs. Law-enforcement agencies can also supplement the curriculum by setting up a summer recreation and education program. The funding level is $7.2 million for fiscal years 1996 through 2000. (Contact phone number: (202) 927-8500.)

National Community Economic Partnership

This program is administered by the Department and Health and Human Services, Office of Community Services. It provides lines of credit to community-development corporations to develop and operate projects designed to provide employment opportunities for low-income, unemployed, or underemployed individuals. Financial and technical assistance is also available to local community-development corporations. The funding level is $45 million for fiscal year 1996, and $70 million for fiscal years 1997 through 1999. (Contact phone number: (202) 401-9333.)

Ounce of Prevention Grant Program

This program is administered by the Ounce of Prevention Council, which comprises the attorney general, the secretaries of Education, Health and Human Services, Housing and Urban Development, Labor, Agriculture, Treasury, and Interior, and the director of the Office of National Drug Control Policy. The program provides funds for local governments, Indian tribal governments, colleges and universities, and private nonprofit organizations. Community coalitions and programs that focus on multidisciplinary approaches to combat juvenile gangs and substance abuse are emphasized. Programs may focus on education and recreation, tutoring, skills and job training and placement, programs that provide adult role models, and programs that work to reduce teen pregnancy, substance abuse, and child abuse. The funding level is approximately $1.5 million for startup in fiscal year 1995, and $15 to $18 million in succeeding years. (Contact phone number: (202) 307-5911.)

Selected Print Resources

6

This chapter contains descriptions of recently published books, manuals, journal articles, and training guides on issues relating to gangs and gang behavior. Because many such books and journal articles have been published recently, this chapter lists the best-known and more readily available materials on a variety of topics within this field; by no means is it a comprehensive listing of the current literature.

Books

Books on Gangs

Bing, Leon. 1992. *Do or Die.* New York: HarperPerennial. 277 pages. ISBN 0-06-092291-5

As a journalist, Bing offers compelling analysis and first-person accounts of gang life and activity. Female gang members describe their lives and how they became involved in gangs. Bing's talks with staff and gang members in juvenile probation camps reveal what life is like there. Family members tell her about the impact on the family of a child involved in a gang. Bing's poignant narrative provides insight into the motivations of these young people so turned off by society and its rules.

Campbell, Anne. 1991. *The Girls in the Gang*, 2d ed. Cambridge, MA: Basil Blackwell. 295 pages. Notes, index. ISBN 1-55786-120-X.

Campbell focuses on females in gangs and tells the stories of three such girls, Connie, Weeza, and Sun-Africa, as learned from her many conversations with them. Campbell emphasizes "the importance of the relationship and social network in which the individual is located" (page xi), the environment in which the three girls live, and the friendship and support networks that they have developed. She discusses the history of gangs, especially as this history pertains to female members, the changing role of females in gangs, and all-female gangs. She describes living conditions in urban America, how these conditions lead to gang activity, and how the stresses of growing up in this environment can lead a young girl to believe that her best chance for survival is to join a gang. Campbell paints a poignant picture of the three girls' lives, hopes, and dreams.

Cervantes, Richard C., ed. 1992. *Substance Abuse and Gang Violence*. Newbury Park, CA: Sage Publications. Index. ISBN 0-8039-4283-4.

Cervantes presents the writings of a variety of experts on substance abuse and gang violence. Part I focuses on research issues, including a discussion of criminal activity and use of alcohol and cocaine by multi-ethnic gang members. Legal and policy issues are described in Part II, including the impact of drugs on a community and public-policy approaches to alcohol-related problems. Part III features prevention and intervention strategies. Part IV focuses on survivors of gang violence, and the writers discuss the psychological effects of exposure to gang violence, survivors' responses to gang violence, and a working typology of grief among homicide survivors.

Chin, Ko-Lin. 1990. *Chinese Subculture and Criminality: Non-Traditional Crime Groups in America*. Westport, CT: Greenwood Press. 189 pages. Index. ISBN 0-313-27262-X.

Chin provides a history of the Chinese secret societies, known as the triads, as well as the history of tongs and street gangs. Through interviews, participant observation, official reports and documents, and newspaper and magazine articles the author reveals the structure, characteristics, and activities of these gangs. Chin uses subcultural theories to explain the unique characteristics of Chinese criminality.

Covey, Herbert C., Scott Menard, and Robert J. Franzese. 1992. *Juvenile Gangs.* Springfield, IL: Charles C. Thomas. 290 pages. References, index. ISBN 0-398-05798-2.

In recent years, rising interest in juvenile gang activity has spurred the writing of many books on a variety of topics related to gangs. The authors wrote this particular book in response to recent political and social changes that have had an impact on the characteristics of the juvenile gang; these changes have occurred in politics, the economy, and drug use. Public interest in gangs has soared, as has the number of dramatic headlines concerning gang violence in local communities. In this document, the authors attempt to 'provide breadth and generality that may help to put separate studies of gangs in particular times and locations within an appropriate historical, comparative, and theoretical context" (page ix). Chapter 1 offers information on how various authorities have defined a gang, how gangs are structured, characteristics of individual gang members, the extent of gang behavior, and public and mass-media reactions to gangs. Chapter 2 deals with gang violence and includes information on gangs and weapons, gang versus nongang violence, drug use, and drug trafficking. Examining race, ethnicity, and contemporary gangs, Chapter 3 discusses classification and typology issues and presents information on African American, Hispanic, white ethnic, and Asian American gangs, as well as Jamaican 'posses." The subject of female gangs and gang members, including the nature of female participation, gang characteristics, structure and processes, and why females join gangs is discussed in Chapter 4. Chapter 5 provides a historical perspective of gangs in western history. Chapter 6 offers comparative perspectives on juvenile gangs and includes a discussion of methodological problems encountered in conducting comparative studies; information is also presented on the extent of gang activity in Canada, Australia, South America, Europe, and Asia. Typologies are discussed in Chapter 7, and various theories on juvenile gangs are presented in Chapter 8. Theories on gang formation, evolution, membership, and delinquency are offered in Chapter 9. Intervention programs and their characteristics are described in Chapter 10. Finally, Chapter 11 discusses the future of juvenile gangs in America, based on an analysis of past theory, research, and policy.

Cummings, Scott, and Daniel J. Monti, eds. 1993. *Gangs: The Origin and Impact of Contemporary Youth Gangs in the United States.* Albany: State University of New York Press. 355 pages. Bibliography, index. ISBN 0-7914-1326-8.

Cummings and Monti have gathered together several of the foremost experts in the field of juvenile gangs for this collection, including Joan Moore, James Diego Vigil, Felix Padilla, and Jerome Skolnick. The authors attempt to show what impact gangs and their activities have on the different communities in which they are found. Part I describes what is currently known about gangs, including many of the problems faced by gang researchers, and the relationship between gangs and drugs and violence. The behavior and organization of gangs in different settings are described in Part II, including Hispanic street gangs, gang graffiti, working gangs, gang migration, and gangs in more- and less-settled communities. Finally, articles in Part III describe what can be done about gangs, including the response to gangs in California, gangs and civil rights, and public-policy issues.

Dawley, David. 1992. *The Autobiography of the Vice Lords.* 2d ed. Laurel, MD: American Correctional Association. 205 pages. ISBN 0-88133-628-9.

As a former member of the Vice Lords, Dawley tells the gang's story in the first-person, describing how this violent black street gang grew from engaging in street fights to becoming a full-fledged street corporation, its early leadership, and the power that it had in the Lawndale area of Chicago. For social-service personnel, law-enforcement officials, and criminal-justice workers, this book provides a street-level, personal, real-life account of the growth and development of a street gang and demonstrates the effects of major social factors on gang development. In this edition Dawley adds accounts of the gang's activities since 1973.

Goldstein, Arnold P. 1991. *Delinquent Gangs: A Psychological Perspective.* Champaign, IL: Research Press. 313 pages. References. Index. ISBN 0-87822-324-X.

In this book, Goldstein explores the characteristics of the contemporary gang and suggests strategies for successful intervention. He provides his definition of a gang, reviews their history, presents theories of gang behavior, evaluates gangs according to their composition and function, and evaluates them according to their psychological foundations: gangs as aggressors, as delinquents, as hyperadolescents, as groups, and as communities. Goldstein then discusses intervention strategies at various levels of intervention, including individual, group, community, and state intervention approaches. Goldstein argues that researchers often examine the negative aspects of gangs while rarely looking at the positive aspects, that researchers should also look at those gang members or entire gangs that are able to renounce their negative behavior and work to encourage law-abiding behavior from all citizens, including youth who are tempted to join gangs or are already gang members.

Goldstein, Arnold P., and C. Ronald Huff, eds. 1993. *The Gang Intervention Handbook.* Champaign, IL: Research Press. 532 pages. References. Index. ISBN 0-87822-335-5.

Goldstein and Huff have gathered a group of experts in the field of gang research and intervention for this comprehensive review of gang-intervention strategies. This book describes individual approaches to intervening in gang activities as well as public-policy reforms that could be instituted to help reduce gang activity. Contributors are authorities in the fields of psychology, criminology, sociology, criminal justice, counseling and human development, public policy, special education, and law enforcement. Chapters include discussions concerning gangs in the United States; a historical perspective of gang-intervention strategies; cognitive, behavioral, moral, and interpersonal-skills training intervention; interventions developed for the family and school; recreation, employment training, and community change interventions; a description of the National Youth Gang Survey; gangs and the police; the problems encountered when prosecuting gang members; correctional interventions; the role of cultural sensitivity in stopping or preventing gang activities; public-policy and macrolevel interventions; major issues involved in intervening in gang activities; and opportunities available to help youth decide to get out of the gang life.

Hagedorn, John M. 1988. *People and Folks: Gangs, Crime and the Underclass in a Rustbelt Community.* Chicago: Lake View Press. 237 pages. Bibliography, index. ISBN 0-941-702-20-0.

As a sociologist, Hagedorn collaborates with Perry Macon, a former gang member, to investigate characteristics of gangs in Milwaukee, Wisconsin. Hagedorn believes that the gangs are primarily a product of the black urban underclass. This underclass has been abandoned by the flight of middle-class blacks, as they gain economic security, to safer communities. Statistics on economic conditions in Milwaukee illustrate the problems faced by many residents; for example, the number of families living on less than $10,000 in 1985 rose by 25 percent over 1984. Hagedorn suggests that as the poor become poorer, the gangs become more powerful, helped by the growing number of school dropouts and the unemployed. He poignantly illustrates the alienation that many of these gang members feel—from themselves, their neighborhoods, and the larger society.

Huff, C. Ronald, ed. 1990. *Gangs in America.* Newbury Park, CA: Sage Publications. 351 pages. Bibliography, index. ISBN 0-8039-3828-4.

For this book Huff pulled together fellow experts on gang research, including Albert Cohen, David Curry, Ruth Horowitz, Malcolm Klein, Anne Campbell, Jeffrey Fagan, John Hagedorn, Irving Spergel, and Walter Miller, to contribute sociological and anthropological perspectives on gangs and to discuss defining and measuring gang violence, drugs, growing knowledge concerning gangs, and public-policy issues. The major thinkers of the 1950s and 1960s provide a historical perspective on gangs as well as an explanation for the increasing diversity and spread of gangs throughout the United States. Various aspects of different types of gangs, including Asian, Hispanic, Vietnamese, and female gangs are discussed by several contributors. Fagan writes about the relationship between drugs and gangs. The various forms of field research are reviewed. Spergel and Curry write about the relationship between suppression and intervention strategies in the prevention of gangs and gang violence and the results of each strategy. Huff closes by describing ways in which many cities respond to gang problems and reviewing the best intervention approaches.

Jankowski, Martin Sanchez. 1991. *Islands in the Street: Gangs and American Urban Society.* Berkeley: University of California Press. 382 pages. Bibliography, index. ISBN 0-520-07264-2.

In this book Jankowski relates the results of his study of 37 Hispanic, African American, and Irish gangs in Los Angeles, Boston, and New York. He presents gangs as illegal commercial enterprises that have been started by angry young men who see others gain their slice of the American pie and want the same opportunities. Jankowski analyzes gang behavior in social-Darwinist terms, believing that gangs exist in a symbiotic relationship with their community, the police, and the local government. The author has worked with gangs for ten years, and he views gangs as human organizations with individual members who are not evil.

Juvenile Justice and Public Policy: Toward a National Agenda. New York: Macmillan, 1992. 280 pages. References, index. ISBN 0-669-26902-6.

Juvenile-justice scholars and researchers describe some of the major issues facing them in the 1990s. The strengths and weaknesses of several national data bases are discussed, as well as the dynamics of gangs, why children join them, how the composition of gangs has changed over the years, and strategies to address the problems associated with gangs. Other topics include diverting young people from the juvenile-justice system, the future of the juvenile court, new and emerging roles for prosecutors, and coordination of activities among juvenile-justice, child welfare, and children's mental health services. Two chapters examine the costs and benefits of a variety of state and local youth detention and incarceration policies. Issues of race, gender, and ethnicity and how they affect attitudes toward and treatment of juvenile criminal activities are described. Finally, the book addresses the role of the private sector in juvenile corrections, crime-fighting policies, and a national juvenile-justice agenda.

Klein, Malcolm W. 1995. *The American Street Gang: Its Nature, Prevalence, and Control.* New York: Oxford University Press. 270 pages. References, index. ISBN 0-19-509534-0.

Klein, who has been involved in gang research for more than 30 years, provides an excellent resource book on gangs. He focuses on four issues: the various definitions of gangs, their growth and spread throughout the country, the connection between gangs and drugs, and the role of group process in controlling gang behavior. He describes the contemporary street gang, who joins gangs, the different forms that gangs can take, how cities and police departments handle the problems associated with gangs, gang-suppression tactics, ways that schools cope with gang problems, and programs that are operated by corrections systems. Klein believes that gang problems are not going to diminish over time because society's approaches to controlling and preventing gang behavior will not change significantly. Current urban problems in the United States will become more severe, street-gang culture has spread throughout the country, and other countries are beginning to experience gang problems similar to ours as their urban areas experience similar problems to ours. Klein believes that the dynamics of street gangs can be understood once the problems associated with growing up in blighted urban areas are understood.

Knox, George. 1993. *An Introduction to Gangs.* Buchanan, MI.: Vande Vere Publishing. 498 pages. Bibliography, index. ISBN 1-883218-07-1.

Knox teaches at Chicago State University in the Department of Corrections and Criminal Justice and heads the National Gang Crime Research Center. This book serves as a textbook for an introductory-level college course on gangs; it also is a good resource for training professionals who work directly with gang-involved or at-risk youth. It offers a discussion of theories of gang origins, characteristics, and behaviors; research into numerous aspects of gangs and their behavior; and policy issues related to the behavior and treatment of gangs. Other topics include classification factors for gang analysis, class influences in gang membership, gangs as an urban way of life, an organizational approach to analyzing gangs, group theory applied to gangs, gangs and drugs, gang crime and organized crime, the role of law enforcement, juvenile and adult correctional institutions, the family and the gang, and gang prevention and intervention strategies.

Korem, Dan. 1994. *Suburban Gangs: The Affluent Rebels.* Richardson, TX: International Focus Press. 283 pages. Notes, index. ISBN 0-9639103-1-0.

In 1981, Korem began investigating stories concerning criminally and socially dangerous antisocial groups and the reasons they form. Most people believe that gangs form in inner-city, economically depressed areas, but some researchers are discovering that gangs are also forming in other, more prosperous areas. In this book, Korem explores the growth of white, affluent gangs in prosperous communities. He examines the reasons why these gangs form, the payoffs that members expect to receive from the gang, what inspires youth to join these gangs, whether or not a predictable profile of these gang members exists or can be developed, effective strategies to help a youth get out of a gang, and ways to prevent youth from joining these gangs. He covers delinquent gangs, ideological gangs, and gangs focusing on the occult. He relates the stories of several gang members and discusses prevention strategies, including strategies that don't work and several that are promising.

Monti, Daniel J. 1994. *Wannabe Gangs in Suburbs and Schools.* Cambridge, MA: Blackwell Publishers. 174 pages. Index. ISBN 1-55786-614-7.

Monti reports his findings from his research on juvenile gangs in a school district in a midwestern city. He describes his discussions with many students, some gang members and some nonmembers, and reveals that some of the students scare him because they have no feeling, no emotions, no "light." He sheds light on the reality of gangs and gang members, their existence in schools, and the forces that work to entice a child into joining a gang. Many of the children feel that childhood has failed them, that they have grown up too soon into a world they do not like and did not choose. They talk about drugs, money, fighting, sex, and other issues important to them. Gangs in the suburbs and schools that Monti studied are different from inner-city neighborhoods and schools. His intent is to "show you how the world of gangs can be drawn closer to the world that we occupy and need to make more available to their members" (page 133).

Moore, Joan W. 1992. *Going Down to the Barrio: Homeboys and Homegirls in Change.* Philadelphia: Temple University Press. 181 pages. Bibliography, index. ISBN 0-87722-854-X.

Moore interviews two samples of adults who have been members of Hispanic gangs in Los Angeles. These gangs were known as the "White Fence" and "El Hoyo Maravilla" during the late 1940s and early 1950s as well as the 1960s and 1970s. She suggests that the growth of these and other gangs was a direct result of the changing economy in the Los Angeles area, which led to lower-paying and less secure jobs. Gangs have become institutionalized, and gang members have a more difficult time leaving the gang because of fewer opportunities in the larger society. Studying the attitudes of gang members over time has allowed Moore to examine the changing dynamics of gang life and the increasing influence of the news media and law-enforcement personnel in portraying gang members and their problems in a distorted and stereotypical light. She suggests that these gangs changed from social groups to groups involved in crime and drugs as a direct result of reduced economic opportunities.

Padilla, Felix M. 1992. *The Gang as an American Enterprise.* New Brunswick, NJ: Rutgers University Press. 198 pages. References, index. ISBN 0-8135-1805-9.

Many researchers believe that gangs are fully operational businesses, with their own rules and regulations, and that gangs are recognized by their members as the only viable means to surviving in the only world they know. This book is based on the story of a group of second-generation Puerto Rican youth belonging to a Chicago street gang Padilla calls the "Diamonds." Padilla studies a subgroup of this gang, which he calls the "Streeter and Green Avenue boys," for more than 16 months between 1989 and 1990. This gang operates a street-level drug dealing enterprise. To all of its members, the gang is seen as a viable and established business enterprise "within the U.S. economy, with its own culture, logic, and systematic means of transmitting and reinforcing its fundamental business virtues" (page 3). Padilla reviews the early lives of these gang members to help the reader understand their motivations for joining the gang. He takes the reader from the moment these youths join the gang through their school experiences, their relationships with the police, and their eventual (for many of them) exit from the gang in an attempt to rejoin mainstream society. Most of the members interviewed believe that joining the gang is the only recourse available to them, the only way they can challenge current societal beliefs and constraints.

Rodriguez, Luis J. 1993. *Always Running: La Vida Loca: Gang Days in L.A.* Willimantic, CT: Curbstone Press. 260 pages. Glossary. ISBN 1-880684-06-3.

The son of Mexican immigrants, Rodriguez was born in El Paso, Texas, and grew up in Watts and East Los Angeles, where he joined his first gang when he was 11 years old. By the time he turned 18, he was experienced in gang warfare, drug overdoses, and police brutality. He wrote this emotional, gripping book about his own experiences after his son joined a gang in Chicago. Recreating the many experiences and conversations he had at an early age, he helps the reader understand some of the reasons why these children join gangs and why for many of them it is a matter of life and death. He shows how living in poverty in the inner cities of this country saps people's energy and can easily lead to all types of illegal behavior. Working on a more personal level, Rodriguez is able to get at the reasons why gangs develop in a way that few social scientists can.

Sanders, William B. 1994. *Gangbangs and Drive-bys: Grounded Culture and Juvenile Gang Violence.* Hawthorne, NY: Aldine de Gruyter. 111 pages. References, index. ISBN 0-202-30537-6.

Sanders presents data from an examination of hundreds of gang violence incidents over a 12-year period, analyzes the common patterns of gang violence, discusses ways that police departments can develop gang units, and traces the development of one such unit. An overview of patterns and major forms of gang violence includes gangbangs, drive-by shootings, robberies, extortion, assaults, and rape. Sanders notes that gangs differ in their style, organization, and activities, based on whether they are composed of Hispanic, African-American, white, or other racial or ethnic group members. The options open to police departments for dealing with gangs are presented, with the focus being on reactive policies, since police departments typically interact with gangs only when one or more crimes have been committed.

Shakur, Sanyika (a.k.a. Monster Kody Scott). 1993. *Monster: The Autobiography of an L.A. Gang Member.* New York: Atlantic Monthly Press. 383 pages. ISBN 0-87113-535-3.

At the age of 11, Kody Scott used a sawed-off shotgun to pump eight rounds into a group of rival gang members. He had just been initiated into the Crips gang in South Central Los Angeles. He soon became known for the viciousness of his attacks against rival gang members and earned the nickname "Monster." He experienced juvenile hall, probationary camp, and the California Youth Authority and worked his way up the ladder in the gang organization until he became one of the O.G. (old gangsters), a term conferring respect for his devotion to the gang and for the ways he had supported, protected, and furthered the cause of the gang. He wrote this book from his cell in solitary confinement at San Quentin, California's maximum-security prison at Pelican Bay. He relates his experiences growing up in South Central Los Angeles, within the gang environment, and with frequent police harassment of blacks. He describes the gang culture, its organization, the efforts of the police to stop the gang activity, and the role that gang membership plays in growing up in South Central.

He helps the reader understand why kids join gangs and how gangs support their members.

Spergel, Irving A. 1995. *The Youth Gang Problem: A Community Approach.* New York: Oxford University Press. 346 pages. Glossary, references, index. ISBN 0-19-509203-1.

This is an excellent resource book that covers just about every topic concerning gangs, with up-to-date information concerning many aspects of gangs, their formation, and their characteristics. Spergel discusses research limitations in the field, the scope and seriousness of the gang problem, gangs and drugs, gangs and violence, gang member demographics, gang subculture, gang structure, gang members' experiences, and youth gangs and organized crime. In a section on policies and programs to help prevent or stop gang activities and violence, Spergel discusses theoretical perspectives; plans for controlling and reducing gang violence; the role of the police, prosecutors, defense attorneys, and judges; the function of probation, the corrections system, and parole; social intervention strategies; the role of education and jobs in preventing and stopping gang activities; neighborhood mobilization efforts; and evolving national policy relating to gangs.

Taylor, Carl S. 1989. *Dangerous Society.* East Lansing: Michigan State University Press. 150 pages. ISBN 0-87013-277-6.

Taylor has studied Detroit gangs and their evolution, composition, goals, and influence on crime and drugs, and reports on his findings in this book. He conducted his informal study over five years, interviewing more than 200 teenagers, some of whom were members of gangs and some of whom were not. He describes three different types of gangs—scavenger, territorial, and corporate/criminal—and allows many of the gang members to tell their own stories. They cover such topics as working, selling drugs, role models, marriage, sports, prisons, school, violence, females in gangs, and training programs. Taylor describes the subculture of gang life and the community response to gang life and gang violence and draws conclusions about the type of community effort that will be required to solve the problems created by gangs and help prevent children from joining them.

————. 1993. *Girls, Gangs, Women and Drugs.* East Lansing: Michigan State University Press. 217 pages. Glossary. ISBN 0-87013-320-9.

This provocative study of female gang members addresses such topics as poverty, teen pregnancy, drugs, and illiteracy through interviews with subjects who are drug users and distributors in Detroit. The first chapter describes the study methodology and gang typology. Chapter 2 provides a historical perspective on African American female participation in gangs. In Chapter 3, case studies of three females are presented: Dewana is active in a scavenger-type gang that sells narcotics, Erica sells crack, and Mona also sells narcotics. Chapters 4 and 5 include excerpts from interviews with women who use drugs and describe themselves as crack addicts, shedding light on their daily lives. The opinions of several interviewees are presented in Chapter 6, including their thoughts on racism, sexism, education, and current events. Chapter 7 features excerpts of interviews with twin sisters, one attending college and the other a new mother, who both belong to an all-female territorial gang. Stories of women in the criminal-justice system are presented in Chapter 8, including the roles of a female police officer, an attorney, a circuit court judge, a county probate court administrator, a juvenile-court judge, a probation officer, an assistant prosecutor, a warden, a former inmate, and social workers. In the final chapter, Taylor summarizes the female gang experience and draws conclusions on gang typologies, poverty, class issues, and teenage mothers. An appendix contains the field questions, while another presents a glossary of gang slang.

Vigil, James Diego. 1988. *Barrio Gangs: Street Life and Identity in Southern California.* Austin: University of Texas Press. 202 pages. Glossary, references, index. ISBN 0-292-71119-0.

Vigil believes that once the many factors that lead to young people's participation in gangs are understood, an effective plan to stop gang participation can be developed. This book is a step forward in understanding the multiple stresses and pressures that influence barrio gang life. Vigil describes the many factors and ineffective influences of major social institutions that lead many Chicano youth to join gangs for a sense of identity and support. He discusses the ecological and socioeconomic background leading to the development of street gangs; the sociocultural factors, such as being caught between Mexican and American cultures, that lead to the development of the Chicano street style of youth; the gang subculture as a way of life; the notorious side of the gang subculture; and the psychodynamics of gangs. He presents four life histories of young men involved to some extent in gang life.

Wright, Richard. 1994. *Rite of Passage*. New York: Harper-Collins. 151 pages. Bibliography. ISBN 0-06-023419-9.

This novel by the well-known author of *Native Son* (1940) and the 1945 autobiography *Black Boy*, is the never-before published story of Johnny Gibbs' fall from grace. Johnny is growing up in New York City in the late 1940s when he is told that his parents are not his real parents, only foster parents, and that he must leave them to move in with another set of foster parents. Up until this point, Johnny is a happy child who loves his parents, does well in school, and respects his teachers. When he learns this terrible news, his world falls apart and he is drawn into a world of violence. He runs away from home, from all that he knows, and enters a frightening world that he had no idea existed.

Books on Gangs (Young Adult Sources)

Bonham, Frank. 1972. *Cool Cat*. New York: Dell. 189 pages. Young adult. ISBN 0-440-91520-1.

A young boy lives in the ghetto and has friends who hope to earn money as movers. However, their efforts often are thwarted by some other boys who are more interested in faster and easier ways of making money.

Garland, Sherry. 1993. *Shadow of the Dragon*. San Diego: Harcourt Brace. 314 pages. ISBN 0-1527-3520-1.

Danny Vo, as a high school sophomore, tries to resolve the differences between the values of his Vietnamese family and his new life in America.

Greenberg, Keith Elliot. 1992. *Out of the Gang*. Minneapolis: Lerner Publications. 40 pages. Bibliography. ISBN 0-8225-2553-4.

Through the use of stark black and white photographs, Greenberg tells the stories of two young gang members living in New York City. Butch Young grew up in the Bedford Stuyvesant section of Brooklyn, and Gino Mercado grew up in the Williamsburg section. Butch first joined the 21 Junior Blackjacks and later joined the Crazy Homicides, while Gino was a member of a graffiti crew known as the King of Graffiti. At the time of the story, Butch is married, a father, and a member of the Guardian Angels, and Gino has left his gang after watching his fellow gang members beat up a young boy. The photographs show gang members and their weapons, the scar left by a gunshot wound, and other images of the violence of gang life. For grades 5 through 9.

Mowry, Jess. 1990. *Rats in the Trees.* Santa Barbara, CA: J. Daniel and Company. 162 pages. ISBN 0-9367-8481-4.

Thirteen-year-old Robby moves to Oakland, California, with his skateboard, excited about living near the ocean. He becomes friendly with the Animals, a street gang whose interests include skateboarding, beer, rap, slang, and plenty of danger. Mowry describes the world Robby had entered through nine interrelated stories in which his friends play out comic book-style battles of good and evil, experiencing fighting, cruelty, and death.

————. 1992. *Way Past Cool.* New York: Farrar Straus Giroux. 310 pages. ISBN 0-06-097545-8.

This novel about street gangs in Oakland, California, focuses on 13-year-old Gordon, leader of the Friends, a gang of young teenage black boys who are trying to hold on to their territory. They live by a strict code of honor. Their rival gang, the Crew, often have many of the same problems as members of the Friends. Derek, a 16-year-old drug dealer, cruises the neighborhoods of the Friends and the Crew and tries to set the two gangs against each other. The author paints a shocking portrait of gang life.

Myers, Walter Dean. 1988. *Scorpions.* New York: Harper and Row. 218 pages. ISBN-06-024364-3.

Jamal is a member of the Scorpions, a local gang. He is worried about his mama, about his brother, Randy, who needs money to appeal his conviction for robbing a bakery, and about his fellow gang members, who want him to take over as leader of the Scorpions. Randy was the leader, but he thinks that Jamal should take over now that he is in jail. Other gang members have other ideas. Jamal does take over the leadership and gets into trouble with a gun.

Books on Violence and Youth

American Psychological Association. *Violence & Youth; Psychology's Response,* Volume I: Summary Report of the American Psychological Association Commission on Violence and Youth. Washington, DC: American Psychological Association, 96 pages.

The American Psychological Association convened the Commission on Violence and Youth in 1991 to review the vast body of literature and research on violence and youth and to use the knowledge from that literature to help solve the current problems created by violent youth. This summary report presents an overview of the causes of youth violence and suggests ways that research can help create, evaluate, and replicate effective treatment and prevention programs. Influences reviewed here include biological factors, family and child-rearing factors, school and academic achievement, emotional and cognitive development, and social and cultural factors. Societal factors explored include attitudes toward violence in society, poverty and socioeconomic inequality, and prejudice and discrimination. The availability of firearms, alcohol and other drugs, gang involvement, mob violence, violence in the mass media, ethnic minority cultures, and cultural factors in preventing and treating violent youth are all examined. Characteristics of successful intervention programs are described, and recommendations are made for future research.

Ewing, Charles Patrick. 1990. *When Children Kill: The Dynamics of Juvenile Homicide*. Lexington, Mass.: Lexington Books. 173 pages. Notes, index. ISBN 0-669-21883-9.

Ewing, a clinical and forensic psychologist and attorney, studies juveniles who kill their parents or siblings, juveniles who kill while committing other crimes, gang killings, girls who kill, children under age 10 who kill, thrill killings, cult-related killings, and murders committed by disturbed children. He estimates that each year in the United States between 1,000 and 1,500 juveniles are arrested and charged with murder or manslaughter. Society reacts with horror to stories in the news about children committing murder, the debate over how to handle these children (as children or adults) continues, and society's idealized concept of childhood is challenged. Ewing reviews legal and scientific studies and examines the legal system's provisions for dealing with juvenile murderers—all U.S. jurisdictions provide for prosecuting juveniles as adults under certain circumstances. He closes with a review of suggested techniques to reduce juvenile crime.

Hamm, Mark S. 1993. *American Skinheads: The Criminology and Control of Hate Crime*. Westport, CT: Praeger. 245 pages. References, index. ISBN 0-275-94987-7.

The recent growth of the skinhead movement in the United States has drawn increasing attention from reporters and academics alike, and acts of violence by skinheads have made headlines in many daily newspapers. In this timely book, Mark Hamm provides a criminological and sociological analysis of the American skinheads and their organized hate-crime violence. He reviews the history of the skinheads, covering the first generation of skinheads, the second generation of neo-Nazi skinheads, groups such as Romantic Violence and the White Aryan Nation, and Tom Metzger's role in the growth of the skinhead movement. Hamm describes his own study of skinheads begun in 1989. He traveled to various U.S. cities and approached skinheads in their own environment—street corners, bars, record shops, survivalist outlets, and rock concerts—and asked them to participate in his research; sent letters to leaders of 26 organizations on the mailing list of the White Aryan Nation, asking them to call him collect to answer questions he had about them and their movement; and talked with skinheads incarcerated in several states. In all cases, he told the subjects who he was and that he wanted to tell their story with academic objectivity. His findings offer insights into the life and organization of American skinheads. He describes their beliefs, values, and norms and how they use their beliefs to justify violent crimes against people they view as enemies.

Stanton, Marietta. 1990. *Our Children Are Dying: Recognizing the Dangers and Knowing What To Do.* Buffalo, NY: Prometheus Books. 217 pages. Bibliography. ISBN 0-87975-609-8.

Stanton presents a comprehensive overview of the ways and reasons why children die, including accidents, illnesses, child abuse, drug use, violence, and suicide. Her purpose is to explain these causes and help prevent future deaths through individual efforts and community-based programs. When examining children's deaths by homicide, Stanton looks to our violent society as part of the cause, including child abuse and battered wives. She also believes low self-esteem pushes some children into committing dangerous pranks in order to gain approval from friends and peers. Often, children join gangs for the family atmosphere they can provide. She discusses current research and lists resources that are available to parents and other concerned individuals who want to help reduce the incidence of juvenile deaths.

Violence Prevention: A Proactive Approach. 1994. Lexington, MA: D. C. Heath and Co. 26 pages. ISBN 0-669-36103-8.

This document is a result of the collaboration of D. C. Heath and Company and the Community Board Program in San Francisco. From evaluations of the Community Board Program's curriculum, *Conflict Resolution: A Secondary School Curriculum,* evaluators found that many teachers believed that prejudice was a major factor in many of the conflicts involving students. *Violence Prevention* offers ways to improve teacher and student awareness of causes of prejudice. Lessons focus on learning to become aware of conflict, attitudes toward conflict, assessing personal styles of conflict, and ways to resolve conflicts nonviolently. Student activities include role playing and worksheets for identifying and observing conflicts and determining the student's conflict style. Handouts for measuring feelings, active listening, and story scripts are also included. Student sections promote awareness of school-based violence as well as gang, domestic, and sexual violence; assessment; and conflict resolution.

Whyte, William F. 1993. *Street Corner Society: The Social Structure of an Italian Slum,* 4th ed. Chicago: University of Chicago Press. 418 pages. ISBN 0-226-89545-9.

Originally published in 1943, this ethnographic study of street gangs in an Italian-American slum in Boston was one of the first published studies of group or gang behavior. Whyte describes the people who live in an economically deprived Italian community named Cornerville in 1937, their social organization, and the intricate social world of the street gangs and "corner boys." His method and style of studying groups set a standard for many sociologists to follow when portraying real people in real situations. Whyte tells the story of Doc, a member of the Norton gang, and the gang's activities and battles. He describes the characteristics of social clubs, the Mafia-style organized crime, the changing social organization of a voluntary organization, and the leadership traits within these social groups, as well as the organization's role in politics.

Articles, Manuals, and Training Materials

Aiken, Carol, Jeffrey P. Rush, and Jerry Wycoff. 1993. **"Preliminary Inquiry into Alabama Youth Gang Membership."** *Gang Journal* 1 (2): 37–48.

The authors asked 11 juvenile gang members who were incarcerated in county detention facilities in Alabama to complete a questionnaire concerning their reasons for joining a gang. They also gathered demographic information. Most of the interviewees were male and were growing up without a positive male role model in their lives. They joined a gang for economic reasons, primarily because they did not feel that they had any legitimate means to earn money. Many claimed that they did not trust any authority figures and that they did not trust their fellow gang members; however, they remained in the gang because they did not believe they had any alternative means to make money.

Arthur, R. 1992. *Gangs and Schools.* Holmes Beach, FL: Learning Publications.

As a result of growing gang violence, use of weapons, and gang-related crime, schools are seeing an increase in gang-related activities and the number of gang members coming to school. Schools are often the location of drug deals and violent acts. School officials are spending more time policing their areas, protecting their students, and fighting crime, and are therefore spending less time teaching students. Arthur believes that schools should continue to hold out against gang activity and reduce the attractiveness of gangs by encouraging more bonding of students with teachers, classrooms, and their communities. Schools should teach students about the alternatives to gang membership. Suggestions for alternative activities are provided.

Bjerregaard, B., and C. Smith. 1993. **"Gender Differences in Gang Participation, Delinquency, and Substance Use."** *Journal of Quantitative Criminology* 9 (4): 329–355.

The authors examine the rate of and reasons for female membership in gangs. Using data from the Rochester Youth Development Study, the authors compare gang participation and delinquent involvement of both male and female youth. They conducted interviews with 7th and 8th graders in Rochester, New York, public schools and with the students' caretakers. The sample consisted of 262 females and 707 males, and whites comprised 15.5 percent, blacks 67.6, and Hispanics 16.9 percent of the total sample. Variables studied included social disorganization, level of poverty, school expectations, peer delinquency, parental attachment, parental supervision, sexual activity, and level of self-esteem. The study found that gang involvement for both males and females was associated with increased levels of delinquency and substance use. For females, gang involvement was associated with lack of school success. The authors conclude that theory and intervention activities must address female participation in gangs as an important part of today's urban youth problems.

Chance, R. 1992. *Judges: Technical Assistance Manual.* Chicago: University of Chicago School of Social Service Administration.

This is one of a series of training handbooks and manuals developed by the University of Chicago School of Social Service Administration for various professions and organizations. This manual describes the ways to implement a promising court approach to the juvenile-gang problem. Judges within the juvenile-court system are provided with a model for administering gang cases as well as suggestions about how to become involved in local community efforts that are initiated to prevent gang problems. Seven sections provide information on assessing the youth gang problem, setting goals and strategies, implementing organizational development activities, court functions and issues, mobilizing community resources, selecting and training judges, and research and evaluation activities.

Chesney-Lind, Meda, Anna Rockhill, Nancy Marker, and Howard Reyes. 1994. **"Gangs and Delinquency: Exploring Police Estimates of Gang Membership."** *Crime, Law and Social Change* 21: 201–228.

Gathering statistics on the number of gangs in existence, the number of members, and the extent of crimes committed by gang members is difficult. Most of these statistics come from local police departments, which often define "gang," "gang member," and "gang-related crime" in their own terms; these definitions may not always be the same as or similar to definitions from other police departments. In this study Chesney-Lind and her colleagues examine the significance of police estimates of gang membership using statistics gathered by the Honolulu Police Department (HPD). Honolulu, like other major cities throughout the country, has seen the number of gangs and their criminal activities rapidly escalate during the 1980s and 1990s. According to statistics from the HPD, there were 22 gangs with 450 members in 1988; in 1991 there were 45 gangs with 1,020; and in 1993 there were 171 gangs with 1,267 members. The HPD uses the Gang Reporting, Evaluation and Tracking (GREAT) system for measuring gang activity, using certain criteria to determine an individual's membership in a gang. These criteria include the following: the individual admits membership, has gang tattoos or wears gang colors, is arrested in the company of other gang members, hangs out with other known gang members, or is identified by a reliable informant. Chesney-Lind and her colleagues found that youths arrested in Honolulu are not similar in characteristics to gang members as reported in current literature. For example, these youths were not frequently arrested for violent crimes or for drug abuse and weapons violations. Criminal acts committed by those identified as gang members were similar to those committed by non–gang members who were of similar age, ethnicity, and gender. They also found that a 'significant proportion of self-identified gang members reported minimal levels of delinquent activity in the previous twelve months" (page 222). They conclude that additional studies must be conducted to examine current assumptions about gang membership and serious criminal activity and to examine police definitions of gang membership.

Curry, G. David, and Irving A. Spergel. 1988. **"Gang Homicide, Delinquency, and Community."** *Criminology* 26 (3): 381–405.

Using community-level data from the Chicago area, Curry and Spergel examine the relationship between delinquency, poverty, and gang crime. Their research distinguishes patterns of delinquency and gang activity; delinquency is primarily associated with chronic poverty, while gang activity is related to social disorganization that occurs with the resettlement of families and the associated period of cultural isolation. Chronic poverty occurs more for blacks than other ethnic and racial groups in Chicago's communities, while social disorganization impacts Hispanics more than other ethnic groups. The researchers used statistics on gang homicides gathered by the Gang Crime Unit of the Chicago Police Department. Major variables included ethnicity and race, measures of gang-homicide rate, delinquency rate, unemployment rate, the percentage living below the poverty line, and the mortgage investment per dwelling. The results of their analysis indicate that poverty and social disorganization are most strongly associated with delinquency and gang homicides. The strongest predictor of delinquency is poverty. Incidents of gang homicides in Hispanic communities appear to be unrelated to poverty levels. Generally, the patterns of gang homicide and delinquency are quite different, especially in relation to the poverty and ethnic/race variables. The authors see gangs as 'residual social subsystems often characterized by competition for status, and, more recently, income opportunity through drug sales" (page 400). They believe that social opportunity and community organization in combination with activities aimed at suppressing gang activity may be the most effective means of dealing with the problem of gang activity and violence.

———. 1992. **"Gang Involvement and Delinquency among Hispanic and African-American Adolescent Males."** *Journal of Research in Crime and Delinquency* 29 (3): 273–291.

Surveying 139 Hispanic and 300 African American males in the 6th, 7th, and 8th grades in four Chicago inner-city schools, Curry and Spergel measure the relationship between gang involvement and juvenile delinquency. One of their research objectives was to determine whether African American and Hispanic youth differ in their gang socialization experiences; other researchers have found differences in gang structure and activities among various racial and ethnic groups, similar to differences found in the structure and activities of lower-income Hispanic and African American communities. The authors supplemented their survey with data from police department records as well as school disciplinary and other records. The authors found differences between Hispanic and African American youth in their reasons for joining gangs. Hispanic youths tend to join gangs for individual personal reasons, as a result of their frustrations with the educational system, or because joining a gang raises their self-esteem. African American youth were found to join gangs for more social or interpersonal reasons, particularly because they are exposed to gang members in school and at home and want to be part of this group. The authors also found that some youths were involved in delinquent behavior but were not involved in gangs (more African American than Hispanic youth) and that some were involved in gangs but not involved in delinquent behavior. As a result of their study, Curry and Spergel suggest that gang delinquency should be treated as a social, rather than an individual, problem; that procedures for measuring gang involvement should be developed and tested; gang involvement should be distinguished from gang delinquency; nongang delinquency should be distinguished from gang delinquency; and differences in gang delinquency that are associated with specific ethnic and racial groups should be taken into account when developing gang-delinquency prevention programs.

Davis, James. 1993. **"Psychological versus Sociological Explanations for Delinquent Conduct and Gang Formation."** *Journal of Contemporary Criminal Justice* 9 (2): 81–93.

Psychologists and sociologists have their own theories to explain the delinquent behavior of youth and the reasons why youths join gangs. Davis reviews the literature concerning both psychological and sociological theories of delinquent and gang behavior and concludes that little agreement exists between these two fields. While some researchers believe that psychological theories do little to explain the conduct and behavior of gang members, others believe that psychological factors are critically important in explaining behavior. Others contend that sociological theories go farther in explaining why youths join gangs, that sociological factors such as race and poverty are more important than any psychological factors. The importance of the family's role in the occurrence of delinquent behavior is emphasized by some researchers, while others believe that the family has little effect. Most of the research reviewed did find that self-image is a consistent factor explaining participation in delinquent behavior. Davis concludes that sociological and psychological factors, as well as biological factors, must be considered when studying delinquent and gang behavior.

Davisson, S. 1992. **"Juvenile Gang Checkpoints and Their Constitutionality."** *Journal of Juvenile Law* 13: 127–132.

Police departments in some cities, in response to gang activities and violence, have set up vehicle checkpoints to identify juvenile gang members. However, the U.S. Supreme Court has yet to uphold as constitutional a police roadblock designed to promote general law enforcement. In only two contexts has the court allowed suspicionless roadblocks; both situations involved specific government interests, not just general law enforcement. *Galberth v. United States* was a case resulting from a roadblock the District of Columbia had set up under a program called Operation Clean Sweep to control drug trafficking. The roadblock stopped an individual who was arrested and convicted for carrying a pistol without a license, possession of an unregistered firearm, and unlawful possession of ammunition. The District of Columbia Court of Appeals did not find that the government's deterrence interest was substantial enough to outweigh the individual's liberty interest. The court found that the roadblock violated the Fourth Amendment. In time, with more serious consequences of gang violence, the courts may expand police powers and liberalize search-and-seizure rules and uphold gang checkpoints as constitutional.

Ellis, Arthur L. 1992. **"Urban Youth Economic Enterprise Zones: An Intervention Strategy for Reversing the Gang Crisis in American Cities."** *Urban League Review* 15 (2): 29–40.

The author believes that attempts by public-policy makers and intervention strategists must focus on economic development activities for youth in order to keep them from participating in youth gangs and other delinquent activity. Current intervention models focus on one of three areas: prevention, rehabilitation, or suppression. According to Ellis, many of these programs are the source of serious concern to professionals because of their denial of rights to those involved and their similarity to policies of police states. The author suggests that areas in inner cities with street-gang activity should be considered as youth economic enterprise zones, similar to those areas designated by the initiatives developed by U.S. Senator Jack Kemp in which businesses received tax breaks for setting up shop. Objectives of these zones would include increased business activity to increase the number of available jobs to youth in these areas; promoting businesses that youth are interested in; allowing the businesses to enjoy tax and other incentives; encouraging these businesses to be managed by and staffed by area youths; helping underwrite costs for businesses created by youths; and encouraging the development of job-training programs. These activities could help increase literacy and management skills, improve attitudes toward work and responsibility, and improve self-esteem of young people. Ellis also suggests that corporate mentors should be encouraged to participate as role models.

Esbensen, Finn-Aage, David Huizinga, and Anne W. Weiher. 1993. **"Gang and Non-Gang Youth: Differences in Explanatory Factors."** *Journal of Contemporary Criminal Justice* 9 (2): 94–116.

Many people believe that gang members are substantially different from non–gang members even though little research exists to substantiate this belief. While most research has used police gang-unit statistics or case studies, this article reports on a study using data from the Denver Youth Survey, an in-depth study of families. Characteristics of gang members and the extent of differences between gang and non–gang members are examined in this study. Using census data to identify high-risk neighborhoods in Denver, Colorado, and using a probability sample, researchers interviewed 1,527 youth between the ages of 7 and 15 and one of their parents on self-reported participation in gang activities, delinquent activity, and other attitudinal measures.

Fagan, Jeffrey. 1989. **"The Social Organization of Drug Use and Drug Dealing Among Urban Gangs."** *Criminology* 27 (4): 633–667.

For at least 200 years gangs have, in some form, been present in American urban areas. Gangs have often been involved in both group and individual acts of violence and more recently in the use or sale of drugs. In this study, Fagan examines the patterns of crime, drug use, and drug dealing among gangs and gang members in inner-city neighborhoods with high crime rates in South Central Los Angeles, the University Heights section of San Diego, and the West Side of Chicago. He recruited a sample of 151 gang members from all three city areas using intermediaries from neighborhood organizations or referrals from gang members identified by these organizations. Researchers administered questionnaires that included demographic criteria, self-reported delinquency and measures of drug use and sales, gang structure, roles within the gang, perceptions about whether other gang members participate in various gang activities, other area gangs, and the relations between the gang and law-enforcement and other social agencies. Fagan identified four types of gangs: those involved in few delinquent activities and reporting little drug use, basically a social group; those involved primarily in non-drug criminal activities but with a relative high prevalence of drug use, drug sales, and vandalism, basically a party gang; those whose members are serious delinquents, with no extensive involvement in drugs or drug activities; and those whose members are serious delinquents who are extensively involved in drug use and drug sales. The study found a positive relationship between drug involvement and serious gang acts, and these gangs usually had developed rules and procedures to maintain and enforce appropriate behavior. All gangs were involved in drug activity to some degree, but those gangs heavily involved in PCP, heroin, and cocaine were more likely to be heavily involved in drug dealing. Similar gang types were found in all three cities. Members of violent gangs also reported the use of some type of social organization and cohesion to control the behavior of the gang members.

Gang Intervention Handbook. 1993. Champaign, IL: Research Press Company.

This handbook offers information on how to implement a comprehensive gang intervention strategy that can offer specialized services to gang members based on their demographic, structural, and behavioral characteristics. It describes patterns of gang behavior and current preventive efforts as well as psychological intervention activities, interpersonal skills training, and contextual interventions. Intervention activities conducted by the police, prosecutors, and corrections personnel respond to illegal and antisocial behavior of gang members. The importance of cultural sensitivity and public policy is discussed, along with ways to address the macrolevel social and economic factors that leave children at high risk for becoming involved in gang activities.

Hatchell, Billie Sargent. 1990. *Rising above Gangs and Drugs: How To Start a Community Reclamation Project.* Lomita, CA: Community Reclamation Project.

Designed as a model anti-gang/drug program in Los Angeles that could be copied by any community experiencing similar problems, the Community Reclamation Project produced this manual to help others develop a similar program. The goals of the project are described and explained, and each chapter discusses specific aspects of program development and implementation. Topics discussed include assessing the community's needs for this type of program, developing a budget, selecting staff members, suggestions for general office procedures, creating a community identity, producing a newsletter, developing publicity, encouraging corporate sponsorship as well as neighborhood involvement, developing specific community activities, conducting a civil gang abatement effort, and developing school programs and a parent training program. An appendix contains forms for community assessment, a community survey, and other forms helpful for starting a program.

Horowitz, Ruth. 1987. **"Community Tolerance of Gang Violence."** *Social Problems* 34 (5): 437–450.

This is one of the few articles that explores the relationship between community residents and violent gang members and the ways in which the residents tolerate the gangs' violent behavior. The author spent three years studying responses to violent gangs in a Chicago Chicano community as a participant-observer. Horowitz found that community members generally tolerated actions of gangs that most people would consider "senseless acts of violence" (page 437). The ways in which community members avoided knowledge or awareness of violent acts committed by their sons and neighbors are described as well as the ways community members may view these violent acts as a result of "cultural standards of honor" (page 438). Community tolerance is based on a cultural and social order that constantly changes and is negotiated; when that order breaks down, violent gang behavior is no longer tolerated. Horowitz believes that when parents believe that they cannot control their sons' behavior and keep them out of trouble, they find that they must work with the gang members to reach a common understanding. Parents may try to believe that their sons are not participating in violent gang activities, which works as long as the sons are able to offer reasonable explanations of their behavior and don't allow their actions in the gang to interfere with their roles as good sons.

Howell, James C. 1994. **"Recent Gang Research: Program and Policy Implications."** *Crime and Delinquency* 40 (4): 495–515.

Howell examines recent research on youth-gang activities, especially the role of drugs and violence in gang activity and the accuracy of media reports that the number of gangs and gang members is growing. The author believes that current knowledge of street gangs, their activities, and reasons why people join gangs is limited. He reviews studies that have shown that gang members tend to be between the ages of 10 and 21 years, are less likely than other juveniles to be arrested for drug offenses (although they are becoming more involved in the illegal drug market), are more likely to be involved in delinquent behavior than other juveniles, and tend to report being a member of a gang for less than one year. He also reviews studies showing that prevention activities generally consist of community organization programs and suppression activities. Other study topics include gang migration patterns, the increasing numbers of females joining gangs, and the increasing involvement of gangs in the drug market. Howell offers recommendations on ways the Federal government can become more involved in lowering gang membership, preventing children from joining gangs, and stemming the violence associated with youth gangs.

Jackson, Pamela Irving. 1991. **"Crime, Youth Gangs, and Urban Transition: The Social Dislocations of Postindustrial Economic Development."** *Justice Quarterly* 8 (3): 379–397.

Based on a multivariate analysis of quantitative data collected from U.S. cities with populations of more than 25,000 in 1970 and

1980, this article reports the findings of a study concerning crime and young gangs. According to the author, up until the time of this analysis, a national study of the effect of recent economic and social changes on crime rates, types of crimes committed, and the development of youth gangs throughout the United States had not been conducted. This study's central thesis is that changes in demographic and economic conditions in cities have contributed to crime and the appearance of youth gangs. The study controlled for competing explanations, such as "opportunity factors related to the ease and profit of crime, age structure, racial and income heterogeneity, and economic deprivation" (page 380). The impact of regional variations was also examined. Analyses indicated that crime rates in cities are influenced by both long-term and short-term changes in population levels as well as by declining levels of positions available in manufacturing and wholesale/retail fields. The decline of urban areas has contributed to higher rates of crime in these areas and the growth of gang activity.

Keeney, S., M. Smith, and J. Sidwell. 1992. *Mediation and Conflict Resolution for Gang-Involved Youth: A Training and Resource Manual.* Albuquerque: New Mexico Center for Dispute Resolution.

This manual is a guide for individuals and organizations involved in mediation and conflict resolution work with gang members. It offers suggestions for mediating interpersonal conflict situations among gang-involved youth, working with other agencies to mediate gang disputes in schools, teaching communication and conflict resolution skills to youth, and responding with more sensitivity to conflicts involving racial and ethnic issues. The importance of understanding conflict, family conflict and dysfunction, case management, and record keeping and collection is emphasized. Materials for mediation and conflict resolution activities are included.

Klein, Malcolm W., Margaret A. Gordon, and Cheryl L. Maxson. 1986. **"The Impact of Police Investigations on Police-Reported Rates of Gang and Nongang Homicides."** *Criminology* 24 (3): 489–512.

Police departments around the country differ on their definition of gang-related crimes. In some cities, such as Los Angeles, a crime in which a gang member kills someone in a robbery is considered gang-related, while in other cities, such as Chicago or Philadelphia, this crime is not considered gang-related. The authors believe that the ways in which police departments categorize these crimes play an important role in statistics and consideration of gang-related homicides. In order to study this issue, the authors analyzed whether the procedures police use to investigate homicides play a major role in the reported rates of gang-related homicides. Using Los Angeles Police Department and Los Angeles Sheriff's Department statistics from murder investigation files, the authors found that the ways police departments define gang-related homicides has little impact on the investigative process.

Klein, Malcolm W., Cheryl L. Maxson, and Lea C. Cunningham. 1991. **" 'Crack,' Street Gangs, and Violence."** *Criminology* 29 (4): 623–650.

Using data collected from the narcotics investigation files and homicide files of three Los Angeles Police Department precincts and two Los Angeles County Sheriff's Department areas where crack cocaine and gangs were prevalent, this study examines the relationships among street gangs, crack cocaine, and violence. The researchers examined data collected from areas that had the highest combination of arrests for selling cocaine and reported gang activity in South Central Los Angeles between 1983 and 1985—a time when crack cocaine use grew rapidly and became a significant problem in many communities. The research showed a significant increase in sales of crack cocaine during these years, and an increase in the number of gang members involved, although researchers also found that gang members' involvement was declining. Most of the cocaine arrests involved crack, but the researchers reported a low number of suspects and low levels of drugs and cash. While the number of arrests for selling crack cocaine increased, the increase was not dramatic—gang members bring nothing special to the business of selling crack cocaine. The researchers concluded that the distribution of crack cocaine was primarily a phenomenon of regular drug dealers, not street gangs.

Knox, George W., and Edward D. Tromanhauser. 1992. **"Gang Members as a Distinct Health Risk Group in Juvenile Correctional Facilities."** *Prison Journal* 71 (2): 61–66.

Many researchers believe that juvenile gang members are at greater risk for health problems than other juveniles. Knox and

Tromanhauser conducted a study of the health-risk behavior of juveniles confined in juvenile correctional facilities. Staff at 44 facilities administered questionnaires to confined juveniles, and 1,801 surveys were completed and returned to the researchers. Most of the respondents were male (88 percent), the median age was 16 years, and 19 percent were Hispanic, 27 percent were white, 46 percent were African American, and 8 percent were of some other ethnic or racial origin. The authors found that a significant number of respondents (46 percent) reported that they had, at some time, been a member of a gang. The study found that 59 percent of Hispanics had been in a gang, 46 percent of African Americans, and 35 percent of whites. Gang members were confined to these facilities for longer periods of time than non–gang members, and gang members were more likely to be involved in fights and were more likely to be injured in these fights. Gang members also were more likely to smoke cigarettes, drink alcohol, use marijuana, and use cocaine than non–gang members and were likely to have thoughts about committing or to have tried committing suicide. Gang members were also more likely to have unprotected sex, get someone pregnant or become pregnant, and to have a sexually transmitted disease. The authors conclude that juveniles, as well as adults, in the corrections system are at higher risk than others outside of prison. They suggest that additional resources must be made available to lower the at-risk behavior of all juveniles, including those affiliated with gangs.

Lasley, James R. 1992. "Age, Social Context, and Street Gang Membership: Are 'Youth' Gangs Becoming 'Adult' Gangs." *Youth and Society* 23 (4): 434–451.

This study examines the extent to which young gang members in inner cities stay with the gang as they become adults. Gang members were selected from Orange County, California, and Los Angeles to act as a representative sample of gang members among all socio-economic levels. Gang members were interviewed individually. The author found little empirical evidence to support the hypothesis that gangs are increasingly composed of adults. No matter what their socio-economic level, gangs were found to be composed primarily of adolescents.

Lyon, Jean-Marie, Scott Henggeler, and James A. Hall. 1992. **"Family Relations, Peer Relations, and Criminal Activities of Caucasian and Hispanic-American Gang Members."** *Journal of Abnormal Child Psychology* 20 (5): 439–449.

This article reports on the findings of a study of family relations, peer relations, and criminal activities of 131 juvenile offenders who were incarcerated at the time of the study. This group was divided into four groups: white gang members, white non–gang members, Hispanic gang members, and Hispanic non–gang members. The study found that gang members had a higher rate of reported criminal behavior than did non–gang members; white gang members and non–gang members were more likely to report incidents of general delinquency and home delinquency (for example, running away from home or stealing from family members) than Hispanic youth; gang members appeared to be more aggressive and less socially mature than non–gang members; and no relationship was found between being in a gang and having a high level of bonding with friends. A high rate of hard drug use was reported by Hispanic gang members, while Hispanics who were not gang members had low rates of drug use.

Maxson, Cheryl L. 1995. **"Street Gangs and Drug Sales in Two Suburban Cities."** *Research in Brief.* Washington, DC: National Institute of Justice.

This research report describes the results of a study to determine the level of street-gang involvement in drug sales. Arrest records for drug sales were compared in two cities in the Los Angeles area, Pomona and Pasadena, between 1989 and 1991. The author compares these statistics with those from an earlier study of cocaine sales and gang involvement in South Central Los Angeles between 1983 and 1985. The relationship between street gangs, drug sales, and violence was not as strong as the author anticipated. She found that gang members were arrested in 27 percent of cocaine-sale arrests, and gang arrests were more likely to involve rock or crack cocaine than nongang arrests. The report is of interest to law-enforcement personnel, prosecutors, probation officers, city government officials, social-service personnel, and researchers.

National Crime Prevention Council. 1993. *Helping Youth with Gang Prevention.* Washington, DC: National Crime Prevention Council.

The National Crime Prevention Council has developed this packet of information on gang prevention in order to help crime-prevention professionals identify important concepts and promising strategies, locate resources, and emphasize ways to encourage youth to solve their problems peacefully and build safer and more caring communities. A background section offers information on major gang issues, including a summary of the gang problem, gang-prevention strategies, geographic trends, descriptions of types of gangs, who joins gangs, why kids join gangs, how to identify signs of gang-related activity, strategies for gang prevention, and several specific prevention strategies. Another section provides what the authors call reproducibles, materials that can be copied for distribution to the appropriate audiences. Items include a summary of the status of youth today, an activity sheet for elementary-school students to encourage thinking about self-esteem issues that relate to gang involvement, a brochure providing guidelines for peaceful resolution of problems, a discussion of several projects that have been developed by youth with adult assistance, and crime prevention tips. Another section offers descriptions of specific programs set up to help prevent or intervene in gang activity. The final section provides a list of resources available to those involved in preventing or intervening in gang activities in their neighborhoods.

Regulus, Thomas A. 1994. **"Effects of Gangs on Student Performance and Delinquency in Public Schools."** *Journal of Gang Research* 2 (1): 1–13.

This article summarizes the results of a study to determine the relationships among youth gangs, school crime, and the academic performance of students, as well as retention and dropout rates in a large urban public high-school system. The primary research aim was to determine whether or not youth gangs contribute to high levels of crime in schools and if participation in gangs leads to poor student academic performance. Data were collected for two consecutive academic years from 61 high schools to determine whether or not observations made were constant over time. A variety of published and official reports demonstrated that gang activity, school crime, low student achievement levels, and high dropout rates were chronic problems within the entire school system. The study found that the number of gangs evident within each school was not related to high levels of school crime or gang crime, although schools experiencing problems with gangs did have higher levels of school crime. Implications from the results of this study are discussed.

Robinson-Young, P. 1992. **"Recreation's Role in Gang Intervention."** *Parks and Recreation* 27 (3): 54–56.

This article examines the importance of recreation programs that target youths at risk for gang involvement. It suggests goals, functions, and services to help professionals develop recreation programs in their communities. The author suggests that assessment of the need for this type of program should involve surveys, interviews, observations, and discussions with known gang members. Other suggestions: In deprived areas without recreation agencies, mobile recreational units and recreational storefront programs can be successful; a variety of strategies can reward young people for positive behavior and encourage them to participate in positive recreational activities; and recreational activities for high-risk youth should be fast-paced and exciting to keep their interest.

Sampson, Robert J. 1986. **"Effects of Socioeconomic Context on Official Reaction to Juvenile Delinquency."** *American Sociological Review* 51: 876–885.

Many studies that examine juvenile delinquency look at factors such as race and socioeconomic status of youths and their families as important variables in the way that the legal system deals with delinquents. In this study, Sampson looks at 'the individual and neighborhood socioeconomic context of official reaction of juvenile delinquency" (page 877), by using data from the Seattle Youth Study, which includes self-reports of delinquency. Prevalence and frequency of delinquency were measured. Results from this study indicate that police were more likely to report delinquent behavior when the young person involved was from a lower-class neighborhood than when he or she came from a middle- or upper-class neighborhood. These findings are consistent even when other factors, such as prevalence and frequency of delinquency, race, family structure, and gang membership, are controlled. Sampson concludes socioeconomic status and the circumstances of the particular situation influence police reactions to these youth.

Spergel, Irving A. 1991. *Community Mobilization: Technical Assistance Manual.* Chicago: University of Chicago, School of Social Service Administration.

This manual describes the critical steps necessary to mobilize local communities to combat the juvenile gang problem. Spergel emphasizes the role and responsibility of community leaders or coordinators of community networks. Four important strategies are described, including the provision of opportunities, social-intervention activities, suppression tactics, and organizational change and development strategies. The gang problem must be identified and someone or some organization must take the lead in mobilizing the community. Primary community agencies, political leaders, and grassroots leaders must work together. Specific goals must be developed, activities should be designed and implemented to involve all necessary community agencies, local leadership should be encouraged, funding sources should be identified, and programs should be monitored and evaluated, Spergel says. References, a glossary, charts, and relevant technical assistance manuals are included.

————. 1992. *Grass-roots Organization: Technical Assistance Manual.* Chicago: University of Chicago, School of Social Service Administration.

Spergel developed this manual to describe the principles and steps involved in organizing a local neighborhood to combat the youth-gang problem. The roles of the neighborhood organizer, organizer trainer, and local community leaders are described, including ways they can mobilize the energy and resources of parents, local citizens, neighborhood groups, and local agencies. The scope and seriousness of the problem should be determined and then plans should be developed to eliminate the problem. Goals, objectives, and strategies that are appropriate within the neighborhood context should be developed. Funding sources should be located. Evaluation of the program and activities should also be conducted.

————. 1992. **"Youth Gangs: An Essay Review."** *Social Service Review* 66 (1): 121–140.

According to Spergel, the social-work and human-service communities have focused little attention on the problem of youth gangs in the past 30 years. He believes that a broad national policy to help solve the problems of youth gangs must include the involvement of social-service agencies. Spergel reviews the literature (ten studies and books) on gangs to help social-service personnel understand the depth and breadth of the problem. The type of research method selected for a study is critical, he says, because the characteristics of the selected method may determine the reliability, validity, and applicability of the findings. The definition of a gang and ways in which a gang is different from other youth groups is important in designing a study. Most of the studies reviewed emphasize certain factors that lead to gang participation: membership in the underclass, lack of opportunity, poverty, and social disorganization. Underclass theories are proposed by most researchers who believe that poverty and a lack of opportunity for families in the lower classes contribute to participation in gangs by children from these families. Social disorganization theory suggests that social change and the resulting disorganization weaken social controls that normally prevent youth from becoming delinquent and joining gangs. Spergel believes that these theories still do not explain why only certain youths join gangs and not every youth growing up in poverty, in ghettos, or as a member of a racial minority will join a gang. Differing analytical frameworks determine differing behavior patterns in gangs examined by the researchers whose works Spergel reviews. More research must be conducted to determine those personality/psychological characteristics that can distinguish gang members from non–gang members. The research reviewed does not concentrate on characteristics of female gang members. Few studies look at policy and program issues, although some discuss the failure of policy and programs in some areas. More studies need to be done that can lead to the development of detailed policy and program procedures, Spergel says.

————. 1993. *Gang Suppression and Intervention: An Assessment.* Chicago: University of Chicago, School of Social Service Administration.

Spergel and his associates at the School of Social Service Administration conducted this survey of the literature in the field of gang prevention and intervention as part of an attempt to develop and test approaches that appear promising in solving the youth-gang problem. This document is divided into two parts. The first part covers the nature of the problem and includes definition issues and data sources, the scope of the gang problem, the group character of the gang, gang demographics, and social contexts of gang development. Part two focuses on organizational responses to the gang problem, and includes examples of existing and evolving strategies to solve the youth gang problem, policies and programs of local organizations, government initiatives (federal, state, and local), historical strategies, social intervention strategies, a discussion of police suppression strategies, legal-system responses, probation- and correction-systems strategies, the importance of social and economic opportunities, community organizational issues, and recommendations for future policy.

Swart, William J. 1991. **"Female Gang Delinquency: A Search for 'Acceptably Deviant Behavior.'"** *Mid-American Review of Sociology* 15 (1): 43–52.

Most research conducted on gangs and gang behavior focuses on males. When the roles of females are studied, usually they are examined in the context of their support role to the males in the gang, that is, providing sex, carrying weapons, or spying on other gangs, among other activities. This article examines the complex reasons why females join gangs and their roles within these gangs. Studying the function that the gang plays as a peer group and the role that this group has in promoting or encouraging females to exhibit delinquent behavior, Swart reviews other similar research conducted by Anne Campbell, Peggy Giordano, Ruth Horowitz, and Lesley Smith and develops an alternative explanation for female gang-member behavior. Delinquent behavior, such as sexual promiscuity, drug use, and aggressive and violent behavior, as well as the role motherhood plays in slowing or restricting delinquent behavior, are discussed. Finally, Swart concludes that society's ambivalent attitudes toward women in general also influence attitudes toward women participating in gangs; these attitudes play a major role in defining what is acceptably deviant behavior for female gang members.

Thornberry, Terrence P., Marvin D. Krohn, Alan J. Lizotte, and Deborah Chard-Wierschem. 1993. **"Role of Juvenile Gangs in Facilitating Delinquent Behavior."** *Journal of Research in Crime and Delinquency* 30 (1): 55–87.

The research discussed in this article attempts to explain why gang members are more likely than non–gang members to commit serious and violent offenses. Using data from the Rochester Youth Development Study, the authors compare three models suggested for why gang members commit more crimes. These models include a selection model, a social-facilitation model, and an enhancement model incorporating aspects of both the selection and social-facilitation models. The selection model suggests that youths who join a gang are already delinquent or have a high propensity for delinquent behavior. The social-facilitation model suggests that gang members are basically the same as other youth, but that the group processes that occur within the gang create an environment in which delinquent behavior is encouraged and supported. The social-enhancement model combines elements of both of the other models, suggesting that gang members are recruited from youth who are already capable of delinquent behavior or who are already delinquent, and then the atmosphere within the gang encourages and enhances this behavior.

Toy, Calvin. 1992. **"Coming Out To Play: Reasons To Join and Participate in Asian Gangs."** *Gang Journal* 1 (1): 13–30.

The reasons that youth join gangs are explored in this study of Asian gangs in the San Francisco area. Research included interviews, questionnaires, and field observation of gang members. The author concludes that social factors and cultural conflicts have the greatest influence on gang behavior. Broken families lead to delinquent behavior and the seeking out of peers for emotional support. Many gang members were encouraged to join because they had been victims of ethnic discrimination or violence. Many members remained in the gang because they were afraid of additional victimization and felt the need for protection. Members may leave the gang as they mature and find that the gang provides little reward for them.

Vrgora, F. 1992. *Gangs: The Death of Our Society.* Washington, DC: National Institute of Justice.

This document describes the characteristics of major gangs in the United States, including distinctive features and behavior patterns, ways to tell whether or not a child is involved in gang activity, and ways to prevent children from becoming involved with a gang. Some conditions that contribute to children joining gangs include lack of parental supervision and the unavailability of jobs for young people. Major gangs discussed include the Crips, Bloods, Disciples, Vice Lords, white supremacy gangs, Latino gangs, and the Mafia. Signs of gang activity include wearing gang-related clothing, having gang tattoos or unexplained bruises, and staying out all night. The report includes a glossary, a list of suggested community gang-prevention activities, a list of community resources and organizations, and references.

Winfree, L. Thomas, Kathy Fuller, Teresa Vigil, and G. Larry Mays. 1992. **"The Definition and Measurement of 'Gang Status': Policy Implications for Juvenile Justice."** *Juvenile and Family Court Journal* 43 (1): 29–37.

The authors randomly selected 373 9th and 11th grade students in two senior high schools and two junior high schools in Dona

Ana county, New Mexico, and asked them to complete a questionnaire. The study examined three variables: involvement in gangs, self-reported delinquency, and personal-biographical characteristics. The authors used two measures of determining membership in a gang: self-definition and exhibition of gang characteristics, such as participation in initiation rites or use of external symbols of gang membership: tattoos, wearing gang colors, or using hand signs. Using the self-definition, the authors identified 68 "wannabes," 45 former gang members, and 56 current gang members. Using the more restrictive definition (initiation rites and symbols), the authors identified 116 wannabes, 18 former gang members, and 31 active gang members. Males were more likely to report activity in a gang than were females. There is a significant relationship between the number of hours that a student spends studying and gang membership; the more hours a student spends studying the less likely he or she is to be an active gang member. A significant relationship did not exist between living in a single-parent family and being an active or former gang member. The authors suggest that future research concerning the prevalence of the gang problem must pay attention to the conceptual definition of gang membership; otherwise the findings may not be helpful in learning more about youth-gang membership and activities.

Zevitz, Richard G., and Susan R. Takata. 1992. **"Metropolitan Gang Influence and the Emergence of Group Delinquency in a Regional Community."** *Journal of Criminal Justice* 20: 93–106.

Most people are aware of the existence of serious gang problems in major metropolitan areas in the United States. What is less known is the extent of the gang problem in smaller communities throughout the country and whether or not gangs in large metropolitan areas influence the existence or structure of gangs in smaller communities. This study addresses this issue by examining Kenosha, Wisconsin, located between Milwaukee and Chicago, both cities with documented gang problems. Data were collected from four sources, including tape-recorded interviews with 23 self-reported gang members and with key community members who work with troubled youth; police, welfare, and school case files; and newspaper reports of local gang activity. Self-reported gang members ranged in age from 13 to 17, all but two were male, and all were either African American or Hispanic. Many police officers, as well as workers in the Kenosha juvenile-justice system, believed that the majority of gang members in Kenosha had moved there from Chicago or other communities in northern Illinois. However, none of the 23 gang members interviewed agreed that they were transplants from the Chicago area; they said that any connection with Chicago gangs was in name only. Eight gang members were from Chicago, but viewed their current gangs as Kenosha gangs; the influence of Chicago gangs appeared only in symbolic areas. Analysis of police data did confirm a Chicago gang connection, although analysis of data from the Department of Social Service and school records does not support this connection. The authors conclude that as gangs appeared in Kenosha, authorities and news sources found it easier to explain their appearance as outside their control and influence—that it is easier to blame others than take responsibility.

State and Local Government Reports

Albuquerque Mayor's Council on Gangs. 1995. *Priority Recommendations and Projected Costs.* Albuquerque: Mayor's Council on Gangs.

The Mayor's Council on Gangs has developed a series of action steps for the community to implement in order to reduce the incidence and prevalence of youth-gang crime. Community agencies involved include professionals in the police department, prosecutor's office, judicial system, probation office, corrections, parole offices, and schools, along with community-based agencies and grassroots organizations. The authors of the report believe that only a coordinated effort among all agencies involved can help reduce the number of gang members, gangs, and gang-related crimes in their community. Some of the key steps proposed include the Serious Habitual Offender Comprehensive Action Program (SHOCAP) and bootcamp programs that hold youth responsible for their criminal acts; social workers working with school teams to help students who are facing suspension, are truant, or consistently disruptive; developing ways to help youth train for and find employment; training teachers and other youth-service providers in the best ways to work with gangs; encouraging middle-school activities to reduce gang influence and activity; mentorship programs to help students develop positive values and prevent them from joining gangs or engaging in violent behavior; and increasing the number of police officers patrolling the community.

Arkansas Attorney General's Youth Gang Task Force. 1995. *Summary Report: Attorney General's Youth Gang Task Force.* Little Rock: Attorney General's Office.

Arkansas, like many other states, has been faced with a growing problem of gang activity and violence. Little Rock, the state capital, has gained national attention because of its high rate of crime. In 1994, the attorney general of Arkansas convened a state task force to study and propose solutions to the increasing problems. Public hearings were held throughout the state to gather input from citizens about what should be done. Recommendations were made based on the testimony of many people at these hearings. Schools should widen the scope of services they provide and become community centers for youth. The entire community should be involved in the educational process. Community task forces on gang and youth violence should be formed. Law-enforcement agencies should provide additional training in gang and youth violence for all staff members, develop a statewide tracking system, increase community involvement, and strengthen the relationship between law-enforcement agencies and the school system. The state legislature should increase the penalty for murders committed in drive-by shootings, enhance penalties for drug violations near public housing projects, and increase the penalties for car-jacking. A statewide speakers' bureau should be developed, along with a statewide media campaign to provide public-education programs and public-service announcements. These and other recommendations from the task force are discussed in this document.

Blancarte, S., and B. J. Azeka. 1992. **"Pluralistic Approach to Gang Prevention: The Long Beach Model."** *Journal of Physical Education, Recreation, and Dance* 63: 31–33.

This article describes a multicultural approach used to prevent gangs in Long Beach, California, which has grown from a predominantly white, homogeneous community to a multicultural one. This growing diversity has created strains in the community. The mayor and city council appointed a task force on gangs in 1986 to study the problem and recommend ways to prevent or intervene in gang activities. The program developed as a result of this task force includes classroom anti-gang instruction, recreational programs, employment training, collaboration with the schools and the parks and recreation department in a peer counseling program, service-provider training to deal with at-risk youth, case-management services for high-risk youth, a resource directory, independent program evaluation, and parent education.

Boys' and Girls' Clubs of America. 1993. *Gang Prevention through Targeted Outreach.* New York: Boys' and Girls' Clubs of America.

This manual has been developed to help Boys' and Girls' Clubs understand the problems of youth gangs, determine the extent of gang activity in their local areas, develop ways to recruit at-risk youth before they become actively involved in gang activity, and develop ways to focus efforts and resources on providing services to at-risk youth. The introduction discusses how club directors should focus on understanding the program's approach to preventing gang activity, communicate the importance of this type of program to the community, appoint a coordinator, train staff members, lead networking efforts, assess and act on policy implications, and examine budget limitations. Subsequent sections cover gang types, characteristics, activities, and reasons for joining; the elements of a prevention effort; planning the prevention and intervention program, including setting objectives and developing an action plan; and a listing of resources available to those planning a prevention program. Interview guides, youth-gang prevention case management forms, recommended sources for funding information, organizations involved in youth activities, printed resources, worksheets for program planning and assessing program needs, and a list of resources available from the Boys' and Girls' Clubs of America are provided.

Brown, J. 1994. **"One City's Response to Youth Gangs."** *Prevention Researcher* 1 (2): 4–6.

This article describes a comprehensive program developed in Portland, Oregon, to reduce youth violence and gang activity after the city experienced increased numbers of juveniles involved in violent crime and gangs. Focusing on three types of organizations that are involved with juveniles, including the justice system, human-services organizations, and the city's political leadership, a community mobilization approach was developed to conduct suppression activities and social intervention, provide non-violent opportunities and activities, and encourage organizational change and development. The city created gang-enforcement units using multidisciplinary team approaches to address the gang problem. The Multnomah County Juvenile Justice

Division developed a Gang Resource Intervention Team (GRIT) to provide services to youth involved in gang activities and to their families. Community programs have been developed to offer youth advocacy, resource generation, outreach activities, and prevention services. A public outreach effort has been developed to help educate parents, the public, and youth.

California Attorney General's Office. 1994. *Gangs: A Community Response.* Sacramento, CA: California Attorney General's Office.

As a result of the spread of youth-gang activity in California from the cities to the suburbs and rural areas, the California Attorney General's Office developed this book to offer guidance to communities on ways to recognize the signs of gang involvement and prevent gang activity. A variety of approaches have been developed by youth workers and gang members to prevent gang activities and intervene when gangs are present in communities; these approaches often stress developing a partnership among concerned individuals, community organizations, and government agencies, and include police representatives, educators, churches, local government agencies, recreation agencies, and local businesses who work with parents and children in a variety of capacities. This article covers ways to identify gang activities within the family, the school, and the community; reasons why youth join gangs; the types of gang activities in which youth may participate; ways to prevent gang activities; anti-gang laws in California; and gang-prevention program resources.

California Department of Justice. 1993. *Gangs 2000: A Call to Action. The Attorney General's Report on the Impact of Criminal Street Gangs on Crime and Violence in California by the Year 2000.* Sacramento, CA: California Department of Justice.

This document, produced by California Department of Justice gang specialists, examines the current status of gang activity in the state and forecasts trends in this activity up to the year 2000. They show that gangs control some communities, many members have total disregard for human life, and gangs were responsible for killing or wounding hundreds of people in California in 1991. Law-enforcement agencies have added programs and stepped up enforcement strategies, and they have recognized that efforts to reduce gang activity must also include greater community involvement in prevention and intervention and the creation of activities to prevent young children from joining gangs. An executive summary provides an overview of the report and its findings. Profiles of gang activity within the Hispanic, African American, Asian, and white communities are presented, including background information through the 1980s and trends and patterns for the 1990s. Report topics include criminal incidence and statistics, career criminals, and organized crime; an examination of the impact of gang-related crime on the criminal-justice system (law enforcement, prosecutors and the courts, incarceration, and probation and parole); economic issues related to the increase in gang-related arrests and incarceration; trends in gang-related crime and growth of gang activities; and prevention efforts. The latter topic includes the goals of gang prevention, prevention strategies, promising approaches, and challenges to the police, schools and communities. A list of resources is provided, including those state and local agencies providing information to the analysts, gang experts throughout the state, a list of 94 agencies that responded to a research survey, and a bibliography.

Chesney-Lind, Meda, Mary Beth Leisen, Joe Allen, Marilyn Brown, Anna Rockhill, Nancy Marker, Rhonda Liu, and Karen Joe. 1995. *Responding to Gangs in Hawaii. Evaluation of Hawaii's Youth Gang Response System.* Honolulu: Center for Youth Research, University of Hawaii at Manoa.

Part 1 of this report examines trends in juvenile crime and arrests, offers statistics from the Gang Reporting Evaluation and Tracking program, discusses self-reported gang participation, reviews the results of a content analysis of newspaper stories covering gang activities between 1984 and 1994, discusses troubled schools and neighborhoods, provides statistics on school-based gang activities, and provides police department and social-service agency perceptions of the gang problem in the state. Part 2 evaluates the Youth Gang Response System, including the structure, function and operation of the system as well as an evaluation of the law-enforcement task force. Part 3 describes the activities and evaluation of five youth programs developed to combat delinquency. These programs include recreational programs offered by the Boys' and Girls' Clubs of Honolulu, an after-school tutoring program, YMCA outreach services, the School Attendance Program, and the Positive Alternative Gang Education program, which offers a joint police-school effort to prevent children from joining gangs.

Children's Cabinet Institute. 1991. *White Paper: Nevada's Youth Gangs.* Reno: Children's Cabinet, Inc.

The Children's Cabinet Institute, a think-tank for programs to benefit children and families in Nevada, developed this paper to provide a status report on the growing youth-gang problem in Nevada. The committee involved in developing this document agreed on a basic philosophical approach to dealing with the extent of such activity: early intervention, prevention, and diversion of at-risk youth are the most effective ways to control youth criminal activity; government and community-based agencies should support and strengthen families, but not substitute for them; local, neighborhood-based solutions are the most effective ways of dealing with youth crime and gang activity; and an effective response must be comprehensive, integrated, and balanced between prevention and enforcement activities. A summary of data and trends in youth crime and gang activity is presented, and recommendations are discussed. These recommendations are specific for community-based organizations, schools, business, local government staff, executives, legislators, probation and parole officers, law-enforcement personnel, judicial personnel, corrections staff, and the media.

Colorado Springs Public Safety Association. 1994. *Gangs: The Epidemic Sweeping America.* Northville, MI: Midwest Publishing, Inc.

The Colorado Springs Public Safety Commission has developed this gang-awareness handbook to provide a basic understanding of gangs and gang violence. The handbook includes an introduction from the Colorado Springs Police Department's Chief of Police, and it defines and describes gangs, relationships between gangs, guns and drugs, myths about gangs, types of gangs, and the ways that parents can prevent their children from joining gangs. Information is provided on what police departments and other community agencies are doing to combat gang violence in their communities. The handbook also covers such topics as use of graffiti and programs to rid communities of it, gangs and rap music, gangs and schools, a description of the Gang Violence Reduction Project in Los Angeles, things other communities are doing to reduce gangs and gang violence, and a list of common slang terms used by gang members. An interview with a former gang member is also provided.

Feyerherm, William, Carl Pope, and Rick Lovell. 1992. *Youth Gang Prevention and Early Intervention Programs: Final Research Report.* Portland, OR: Regional Research Institute for Human Services.

Produced for the Boys' and Girls' Clubs of America, this report summarizes the findings of an evaluation of gang-prevention and -intervention programs operated by 33 Boys' and Girls' Clubs throughout the country. Funded by the Office of Juvenile Justice and Delinquency Prevention of the U.S. Department of Justice, this research documented strategies used at 30 prevention program sites and three intervention program sites. Successful Boys' and Girls' Club programs provided expanded hours of operation; had additional funding resources to help support a prevention or intervention program; mainstreamed youth into their regular services and activities; had the support of an effective community network for outreach, recruitment, and referrals; had appropriate record-keeping and data-collection systems in place; encouraged family participation in the program; and offered teen programs to keep youth involved in positive activities. One section of the report provides a variety of program data, separated by program type, and includes statistics on intake and retention, source of referral, age distribution, gender distribution, race and ethnicity distribution, factors determining what youth are at risk for gang involvement, attendance records of youth in programs, and discipline and rewards provided to youth. The task force believes that additional efforts should be made to make the public aware of the prevention and intervention programs offered by the Boys' and Girls' Clubs of America.

Johnson, Ulric, and William J. Kreidler. 1995. *Gang Violence Prevention: A Curriculum and Discussion Guide.* Pleasantville, NY: Sunburst Communications.

Produced for students in grades 7 through 12, this curriculum has been developed to make children aware of the harsh realities of gang membership. It relates why youth are attracted to gangs, corrects myths and misinformation about gangs, and emphasizes the similarities between the dependency on violence that gang membership encourages and a drug or alcohol dependency. This guide also helps students explore healthy alternatives to membership in a gang. It is contained in a three-ring binder and contains a 62-page curriculum and seven student handouts.

Lakewood Police Department. 1994. *Street Gangs*. Lakewood, CO: Lakewood Police Department.

This informative pamphlet on street gangs provides a great summary of current information relating to gangs. Starting with the Lakewood Police Department's policy on gangs, the reader is provided with a wealth of information on the community impact of gangs, gang membership, organization, recruitment, roles and initiations, and behavior. The pamphlet describes athletic clothing, dress styles, nicknames, tattoos, and hand signs that are common to gang members; characteristics of various gangs, including skinheads, Crips and Bloods, Hispanic gangs, Asian gangs, and other Denver-area gangs; and gang-related topics such as drive-bys, drugs, prison gangs, graffiti, rap music, and street language. The pamphlet also summarizes statutes and criminal acts. This document is an excellent community resource.

Levine, C. 1992. *Blueprint on Gangs: A Coordinated Approach to a Growing Problem*. Salem: Oregon Crime Prevention Research Center.

Developed by the Oregon Crime Prevention Research Center, this manual describes the factors that promote or encourage gang development, signs of gang activity, and the history of gangs in the Portland area. It presents strategies for local community agencies to use in combating gangs and describes gangs in the Portland area. Most of the gangs are loosely organized, and members are recruited through intimidation, financial inducements, family involvement, and peer pressure. A list of community organizations that may be involved in the development and operation of anti-gang activities includes schools, churches, social service organizations, recreation agencies, law-enforcement agencies, the juvenile-justice system, other government agencies, health-care providers, the media, local businesses, and other community groups. A list of community resources is included.

McConnell, E. H. 1994. **"Youth Gang Intervention and Prevention in Texas: Evaluating Community Mobilization Training."** *Journal of Gang Research* 2 (1): 63–71.

This article describes a curriculum, based on a community-coalition model (also used by the U.S. Department of Justice), that was developed for the state of Texas to provide training to teams and individuals from communities that noticed an increase in gang activity. Training conferences were held in Corpus Christi, El Paso, and Fort Worth. In order to measure the effects of the training program, a three-part evaluation design was developed; it consisted of a pre-test and post-test administered to conference participants, participants' evaluations of the training, and a participant survey administered to determine changes that occurred as a result of the training. Results of the evaluation suggested that the training was successful in its organization, issues covered, relevance, usefulness, opportunities, length, classroom rapport, instructor's knowledge, recommendations of the instructor, and meeting its stated objectives. However, recommendations were made to improve the curriculum and its presentation.

New Mexico State Department of Public Safety. 1994. *New Mexico Street Gangs: 1994 Update.* Albuquerque: New Mexico Department of Public Safety.

The Criminal Information and Analysis Bureau of the New Mexico State Department of Public Safety developed this document concerning the problem of gangs throughout the state as an update to its 1993 report on gangs. Since that time, gangs have made inroads onto several Indian reservations, and teenage girls have been joining gangs in increasing numbers. Girl cliques in some high schools terrorize other students and are extremely aggressive, violent, and protective of each other. They are the cause of at least three or four conflicts each week in which police are involved. Farmington, Las Cruces, Santa Fe, and Roswell also report several girl gangs in their cities. Many cities throughout New Mexico are also seeing increased amounts of gang graffiti; Albuquerque has passed legislation to promote anti-graffiti strategies. In an interview, the head of the Albuquerque Police Department Gang Unit discusses the scope of the gang problem, drug use, turf gangs, taggers, graffiti, skinhead groups, Asian gangs, female gangs, and ways that communities can deal with the problems associated with gangs. As the number of gang members grows, the arrest rate of these juveniles also grows, and the state correctional system is seeing more gang members in correctional facilities. These young people are becoming hard-core criminals at an earlier age than ever before, some as young as 9 years old. The closing section provides information on community resources and descriptions of several programs throughout the state.

San Antonio Youth Initiatives. 1994. *City of San Antonio Youth Initiatives: A Status Report Prepared for the Mayor and City Council.* San Antonio, TX: San Antonio Youth Initiatives.

San Antonio's Youth Initiatives Program was initiated in 1992 to stem the tide of violence, gang affiliation, and juvenile crime in the city. Its purpose was to mobilize city and community resources to develop positive activities and a variety of opportunities for youth as alternatives to juvenile crime and gang participation. During the first two years of operation, the total crime rate decreased by more than 10 percent each year. More than 240,000 youth were served by the program and juvenile victimization during curfew hours decreased by 42 percent in 1993 and 32 percent in 1994. Focusing on youth, the city placed increased funding and expanded services high on its list of priorities. This document reports on departmental programs and offers an executive summary of youth-related ordinances, a report on the nighttime youth curfew ordinance, a status report on the daylight youth curfew and graffiti and weapons ordinances, and a summary of initiatives proposed for 1995.

Smyth, J. P. 1991. *Youth Gangs.* New York: New York City Board of Education.

This document provides lesson plans for New York City safety officers to help prevent and eliminate youth-gang activities in and around the schools. It reports on the impact of youth-gang activity and provides suggestions for students about how to recognize gang activity and what to do when it occurs. Teaching methods recommended include videos, group discussions, and lectures. Each course segment comes with detailed teaching instructions, and procedures for reporting gang activity are provided.

Takata, S. R., and C. Tyler. 1995. **"Community-University Based Approach to Gang Intervention and Delinquency Prevention: Racine's Innovative Model for Small Cities."** *Journal of Gang Research* 2 (2): 25–38.

The city of Racine, Wisconsin, like many small cities, has experienced problems with juvenile delinquency and gangs. Seventy people signed a petition complaining about juvenile crime and gang activities in a particular neighborhood, and a professor at the local university was selected by a city task force to collect statistics and other data on juvenile crime and gang participation in the city. Recommendations were made and two projects were initiated to study community collaboration and to conduct a youth-needs assessment. This article reports on Racine's activities and, from this city's experience, develops guidelines for other small cities that are interested in developing a community-university-based model for gang intervention and delinquency prevention. After a community's attention has been focused on juvenile crime, community leaders should be brought together to network on gang-related issues. The local college or university (if one is located in the city) should be involved in providing guidance by gathering statistics on gang activities and developing a report on any gang activities that are found to exist. Projects should be proposed that help deal with the issues examined in the study and funding sources should be identified.

Tarrant County Citizens Crime Commission. 1991. *Gangs in Tarrant County: Strategies for a Grass Roots, Holistic Approach to Gang-Related Crime.* Fort Worth, TX: Tarrant County Citizens Crime Commission.

The Gang Task Force in Tarrant County developed recommendations for combating local gang activities. A grass roots action plan was developed that addresses prevention, intervention, and enforcement activities. This report suggests that prevention is the most effective and efficient way to control gangs; if children can be prevented from joining gangs in the beginning, gang activity will slowly disappear. At-risk children are targeted for prevention activities. Strategies are recommended for school activities, youth agencies, neighborhoods, businesses, community-based organizations, police departments, government agencies, religious institutions, and the media. A bibliography is included.

Tognetti, B. 1991. *Strategy for Addressing Illegal Youth Gang Activities by a Mid-Size Police Department.* Sacramento: California Commission of Peace Officer Standards and Training.

This report documents a study of the activities that mid-size police departments throughout the United States can employ in addressing the problems of illegal youth-gang activities. The study included an extensive literature search and site visits to mid-size police departments that have anti-gang programs or gang units. The report identifies emerging trends of gangs and their activities and recommends a comprehensive, cooperative strategy that involves law enforcement, other components of the criminal-justice system, local government officials and departments, schools, and several community resources. Activities and policies described include zero-tolerance law enforcement, city council commitment to gang-intervention and -prevention policies, graffiti abatement, a police-school liaison, youth outreach programs, news media involvement, an area-wide law-enforcement task force, and multidisciplinary criminal-justice coordination. A transition management plan is also presented.

Trump, K. S. 1993. **"Tell Teen Gangs: School's Out."** *American School Board Journal* 180 (7): 39–42.

This article describes the results of a program implemented in the Cleveland, Ohio, public schools to eliminate juvenile gangs from the school system. The program gathered information on youth gangs and presented this information, along with recommendations for dealing with specific gang problems, to parents, the community, and the news media. It suggested the development of student handbooks, staff training in gang prevention, community-wide strategies, and methods for dealing with the news media. The pros and cons of implementing a dress code are discussed. The student handbook should include responsibilities and rules for students as well as describing the consequences of failing to follow the rules. Staff should be trained in ways to identify gangs, what motivates youth to join gangs, prevention strategies, and ways to teach conflict resolution skills to students.

Willis-Kistler, Pat. 1988. **"Fighting Gangs with Recreation."** *Parks and Recreation* (November): 45–49.

This article describes the efforts of programs developed by four cities in California to reduce violent gang activity. The Anaheim City Council appointed a task force to review information on gangs and the State Task Force study and to recommend ways to reduce youth crime and gang activity. Project SAY (Save-A-Youth), created by the city, suggested that a cooperative effort be developed among such community-service organizations as the YMCA, the Parks, Recreation and Community Service Department, Boys' and Girls' Clubs, the Salvation Army, and the Police Department. Among other programs, Project SAY has implemented boxing and weightlifting programs and summer camp programs. The city of Paramount offers programs for educating youth on the dangers of gang activities and provides a variety of recreational activities, including a summer mountain camp. In Westminster, city officials found that most gang activity centered around one city park. The city responded by making several physical changes to the park that created a safer area for recreational activities and by offering a variety of services to youths and their families. The city of Whittier wanted to increase services to youth in a variety of areas, including community involvement in recreational activities. It developed the Whittier Youth Network (WYN), a recreation program staffed by two full-time recreation coordinators. After-school programs have grown, with programs offered in schools and parks.

Selected Nonprint Resources

7

Videos

Bad Girls
Type: VHS
Length: 48 min.
Date: 1989
Cost: $250; rental: $75
Source: Coronet/MTI Film and Video
108 Wilmot Road
Deerfield, IL 60015
(800) 777-8100
Fax: (708) 940-3640

Statistics from metropolitan areas throughout the country demonstrate that girls are being arrested for a variety of crimes, including participation in gang violence and drug wars, burglary, theft, violent assault, and murder; the arrest rate grew ten times faster for girls than for boys between the years 1983 and 1987. In this startling documentary report, host Deborah Norville interviews several of these "bad girls" and the professionals who are working to help them turn their lives around. Throughout the video, police officers, members of the clergy, mental-health workers, and other professionals provide insightful comments. The program visits what are considered to be successful rehabilitation programs, such as Nebraska's Boys Town (which despite its name now serves girls as well). The video provides an eye-opening, candid examination of this disturbing social problem and provides estimates of its extent and causes. It can be useful in stimulating constructive classroom discussion of remedies. For junior and senior high school students.

Cancelled Lives: Letters from the Inside . . .
Crime/Violence Prevention
Type: VHS
Length: 41 min.
Date: 1991
Cost: $149.95
Source: The Bureau for At-Risk Youth
645 New York Ave.
Huntington, NY 11743
(800) 999-6884
Fax: (516) 673-4544

For students in grades 7 through 12, this emotional video offers teenagers an intimate, compelling look at what it is like to be behind bars. It features interviews with young boys and girls who have experienced the criminal-justice system first-hand and are serving time in juvenile facilities, as well as interviews with men and women serving time in prison. This video is excellent for use in conjunction with other prevention activities for at-risk children and teenagers, including predelinquent youth and juvenile offenders. It includes a discussion guide.

Choose Not To Lose: The Reality of Gangs and Drugs
Type: VHS
Length: 18 min.
Date: 1992
Cost: (write for current cost)
Source: Cook County State's Attorney Office
500 Richard J. Daley Center
Chicago, IL 60602
(312) 890-2700

This video, narrated by former Chicago Bears football player Dave Duerson, is intended for young people who are at risk for joining gangs and using drugs. It portrays and discusses the consequences of gang and drug involvement and encourages viewers to choose positive alternatives. Shots of youths lying bleeding in the streets, being loaded into ambulances, and being treated for gunshot wounds in emergency rooms offer vivid evidence of what can happen to those who become involved in gang activities. Bodies that are being wheeled into the morgue demonstrate the finality of gang violence. Former gang members and prison inmates emphasize the cost of joining a gang or using drugs. Actor Edward James Olmos describes his childhood in a gang-infested neighborhood. He emphasizes to the viewers that he had a choice, and they have a choice: to stay out of gangs and not use drugs. If they choose gangs or drugs, they are choosing a dead-end life. Several young children talk about the pressure they feel to join gangs because then they can belong to something and feel needed and protected. Finally, former gang members, prison inmates, and juvenile-justice professionals warn students that gangs and drugs will destroy them.

Gangs: Be Aware!
Type: VHS
Length: 24 min.
Date: 1993
Cost: $198.00
Source: Intermedia
1300 Dexter Avenue North
Seattle, WA 98108
(800) 553-8336; (206) 284-2995
Fax: (800) 553-1655; (206) 283-0778

This video presents the stories of four young men involved in gang activity. The first, Kevin "Pudge" Jackson, was a member of an Evanston, Indiana, gang and was killed by rival gang members. His story is told by his foster mother, Evanston police officers familiar with his activities, and video of Kevin talking about what he wanted to do with his life. The stories of the next two young men are briefly profiled; one landed in jail soon after the video was made, and the other is now out of jail and jobless after being incarcerated 18 times by age 21. The final young man is Michael Langford, who was also killed by rival gang members. Michael had lived with his grandmother since he was seven years old. She did not have any trouble with him at home, but he was always in trouble in school. He never told his grandmother that he was in a gang, and when she asked him about his activities, he lied to her. She wanted desperately to believe that he was not involved in gang activity, so she never questioned him closely. This video helps young people understand the hopelessness of being in a gang—as Michael's grandmother says, "It's only jail or death."

The Gang's Not Here
Type: VHS
Length: 30 min.
Date: 1995
Cost: $79.95
Source: The Bureau for At-Risk Youth
645 New York Ave.
Huntington, NY 11743
(800) 999-6884
Fax: (516) 673-4544

This video tells the story of Adams Junior High School. In 1993 this school had a reputation as a war zone. Gangs had become prevalent throughout the school, and fighting was an everyday occurrence. However, things have changed at Adams. A new principal, Celestine Sanders, instituted a zero-tolerance policy toward violence, gangs, and gang members. Disputes now are usually resolved by the students themselves before these disputes have a chance to become violent. Programs were developed to teach the students conflict resolution skills, and counseling and peer mediation programs were started. This video is for children, parents, and caregivers. It demonstrates how student-managed prevention programs along with developed policies against violence can really work, even in a school with students who have a history of conflicts and suspensions.

Gangs
Type: VHS
Length: 30 min.
Date: 1988
Cost: $350; rental: $85
Source: Coronet/MTI Film and Video
108 Wilmot Road
Deerfield, IL 60015
(800) 777-8100
Fax: (708) 940-3640

This video tells the fictional story of two brothers in East Los Angeles who disagree with each other about participating in gangs. It is a poignant drama that offers a forceful statement on the dead-end nature of gang life. The story shows how the enticements of quick wealth, recognition, and a sense of camaraderie and protection can lead teenagers away from school and family and toward a life that focuses on drugs, theft, and other criminal activities. It also demonstrates the futility of wars with rival gangs, who are seen as enemies only because they live in a different neighborhood. The video was directed by Jesus S. Trevino, an East Los Angeles native who has filmed several documentaries on prison gangs. It is appropriate for junior and senior high school students, college students, and adults.

Gangs and Violence: Schoolwide Strategies for Prevention and Intervention
Type: VHS
Length: 15 to 18 min. each
Date: 1996
Cost: $299.95
Source: American Guidance Service (AGS)
4201 Woodland Rd.
P.O. Box 99
Circle Pines, MN 55014-1796
(800) 328-2560
Fax: (612) 786-9077

This series for students in middle school consists of three videos for teacher training and a presenter's guide for teachers plus three student videos with teacher's guides. The series encourages students to develop a sense of pride in themselves, helps them understand the need to belong to a group, and provides them with an understanding of the importance of refraining from gang activity. To that end, the three in-service videos provide teachers and other staff members with effective means for intervening in violent activities and show them how to work with parents and the community to prevent school violence; the three student videos demonstrate several methods for avoiding violence, gang activity, and gang membership. The teacher/staff/ parent videos include *Gang and Group Violence, Preventing Gang and Group Violence,* and *Intervention Strategies and Teamwork.* The latter demonstrates when and how to intervene in violent activities. The student videos include *You Have the Power,* which shows students how to overcome intimidation and confrontation; *The Language of Personal Power,* which demonstrates the benefits of using language to solve conflicts rather than fighting or fleeing; and *Getting Help,* which shows students how to avoid or get out of gangs, report gang activity, remain safe from gangs and retaliation, and contact police.

Gangs, Cops and Drugs, Part I
Type: VHS
Length: 49 min.
Date: 1989
Cost: $250; rental: $75
Source: Coronet/MTI Film and Video
108 Wilmot Road
Deerfield, IL 60015
(800) 777-8100
Fax: (708) 940-3640

With 70,000 gang members belonging to more than 700 gangs, Los Angeles has become a hotbed for drug-related violence. This segment investigates the deadly combination of gangs and drugs and shows how the Los Angeles Police Department, the Federal Drug Enforcement Agency, and other groups are combating the destruction created by gangs and drugs. This video is quick-paced and provides junior and senior high school students in sociology, psychology, and government classes with valuable material to consider when they are studying gangs and violence as a social problem. It was produced by NBC News and provides an effective and poignant view of America's own war zone.

Gangs, Cops and Drugs, Part II
Type: VHS
Length: 49 min.
Date: 1989
Cost: $250; rental: $75
Source: Coronet/MTI Film and Video
108 Wilmot Road
Deerfield, IL 60015
(800) 777-8100
Fax: (708) 940-3640

This video examines the destructive effect of gang warfare in Los Angeles and also provides a broader view of the effects of gang-related crime on the rest of the nation. It includes footage of a live television forum that connected William Bennett, former U.S. education secretary and director of the Office of National Drug Control Policy, and a panel of law-enforcement and academic professionals with a New York studio audience. The audience primarily includes people who have survived some form of drug warfare: former gang members, victims of gangs and gang violence, and mothers who are trying to keep their children from joining gangs or being affected by destructive gang activities. This video was produced by NBC News and is appropriate for junior and senior high school students.

Gangs, Guns, Graffiti
Type: VHS
Length: 30 min.
Date: 1989
Cost: $295; rental: $65
Source: Pyramid Film & Video
Box 1048
Santa Monica, CA 90406-1048
(213)828-7577
(800) 421-2304

Gangs, Guns, Graffiti provides a graphic view of the consequences of participating in gang violence. Interviews with actual gang members, victims of gang violence, and prosecutors offer a realistic picture of life in the streets and the devastating role that gang violence can take. Viewers gain an understanding of ways that gang members work, how they think, how they use graffiti to get their message across to other gang members, and the roles of violence, loyalty, guns, and drugs in gang life. The video is primarily for at-risk juveniles in junior and senior high schools as well as adults who combat gang activity in their communities. It is also recommended for anti-gang programs, parent- and community-education programs, law-enforcement agencies, staff training for new professionals working with young people, and teacher in-service training programs.

Gangs: The Fatal Attraction
Type: VHS
Length: 21 min.
Date: 1993
Cost: $150; rental: $75
Source: Coronet/MTI Film and Video
108 Wilmot Road
Deerfield, IL 60015
(800) 777-8100
Fax: (708) 940-3640

This video provides a basic introduction to gangs and explains the many reasons why certain young people are attracted to gangs. It should enhance the ability of parents and other adults involved with these children to recognize many of the early signs that children may display when they are beginning to become involved in gang activity. Gang members tell their stories and discuss such topics as gang initiation rites, the roles that female members play in the gang, the use of nicknames, how and why gang members retaliate against other gangs, and what it takes for a member to quit a gang. This video was produced by the Los Angeles County Sheriff's Department for adults interested in this topic.

Gangs: Not My Kid
Type: VHS
Length: 29 min.
Date: 1990
Cost: $250; rental: $75
Source: Coronet/MTI Film and Video
108 Wilmot Road
Deerfield, IL 60015
(800) 777-8100
Fax: (708) 940-3640

This eye-opening video, hosted by actress Tyne Daly, begins by documenting the life of a gang member from his birth in a gang-infested area to the time when he becomes involved in gang activities. The viewer sees how peers pressure young people to join gangs, use drugs, and commit violent acts to show allegiance to a gang and its activities. The video then shifts to several mothers who take a personal stand after becoming concerned with their children's behavior and participation in gangs. By telling their personal stories, this documentary shows the effect that gang violence has on urban family life. It specifically explores the ways that members of MAGIC (Mothers Against Gangs in Communities) in Los Angeles are dealing with their day-to-day concerns for their children. In this case, the expression "not my kid" has become a rallying cry to encouraging people to participate in community activities and make a personal commitment to keep children from joining a gang and help combat the influence and presence of gangs. This video is for junior and senior high school students, college students, and concerned adults.

Gangs: Rambo
Type: VHS
Length: 26 min.

Date: 1993
Cost: $150; rental: $75
Source: Coronet/MTI Film and Video
108 Wilmot Road
Deerfield, IL 60015
(800) 777-8100
Fax: (708) 940-3640

This video features Silvia Nunn, a member of the Bloods gang whose street name is Rambo. She tells her own story, providing personal insights into the reasons why many young people end up joining gangs. She describes gang activity, the emotions that she feels, and the personal rewards she receives from being a member of a gang. This video was produced by the Los Angeles County Sheriff's Department and is appropriate for adults who want to understand the allure of a gang.

Gangs: Reasoning, Reaction, Rhetoric
Type: VHS
Length: 20 min.
Date: 1993
Cost: $150; rental: $75
Source: Coronet/MTI Film and Video
108 Wilmot Road
Deerfield, IL 60015
(800) 777-8100
Fax: (708) 940-3640

This video describes the role of the law-enforcement professional in suppressing gang activity in local neighborhoods. Police officers and gang members participate in a discussion of what they believe are fair measures that these officers can take in response to gang activity. Gang members also provide their opinions on what they consider the most effective means of preventing and stopping gang activity. This video was produced by the Los Angeles County Sheriff's Department for adults who are concerned about gang activity or who work with prevention and intervention programs.

Gangs: Signs and Symptoms
Type: VHS
Length: 16 min.
Date: 1995
Cost: $69.95

Source: The Bureau for At-Risk Youth
645 New York Ave.
Huntington, NY 11743
(800) 999-6884
Fax: (516) 673-4544

Recognizing early signs that children are beginning to participate in gang activity helps parents, teachers, and members of the community identify those children most at risk for becoming involved in a gang. This video demonstrates and explains a variety of gang-related behaviors and helps viewers recognize the early signs and symptoms that can distinguish gang activity from other, more benign, activity. Some of these signs are in the physical appearance of youths, the body language that they use, the signs that they flash, their tattoos and graffiti, and the use of weapons. Signs and symptoms of drug abuse are also described.

Gangs: Tags, Tacs, Terminology
Type: VHS
Length: 20 min.
Date: 1993
Cost: $150; rental: $75
Source: Coronet/MTI Film and Video
108 Wilmot Road
Deerfield, IL 60015
(800) 777-8100
Fax: (708) 940-3640

In this provocative video, gang members talk about participating in a gang and what it means to them. They discuss their nicknames, how they got them, and what a nickname means to a gang member; reasons and ways they use tattoos; the respect they receive for having scars from wounds inflicted during gang violence; how and why they use hand signals; the importance of wearing certain colors and certain clothes; and a variety of gang slang. This video was produced by the Los Angeles County Sheriff's Department for adults who are concerned about gang activity and those who work with young gang members.

Got II Come Up
Type: VHS
Length: 23 min.
Date: 1994

Cost: $219
Source: Intermedia
1300 Dexter Avenue North
Seattle, WA 98108
(800) 553-8336; (206) 284-2995
Fax: (800) 553-1655; (206) 283-0778

Subtitled "A Day in the Life of a Young Man," this fictional video takes the viewer through a day with Cameron, a young black teenager who must decide whether or not he will participate that evening in a gang initiation ceremony that involves hijacking a car. We see Cameron getting up in the morning and going off with his friends, and it is clear that he is not going to school; he and his friends are hanging out. Cameron and others participate in a discussion with adult youth workers about what it means to be a man, what it means to be a gang member, and what type of respect is really important to each young man. Interspersed with Cameron's activities are scenes of him struggling with the decision he must make that evening. Once he tells his friends that he will not participate in "jackin'" a car, scenes of him at home with a girl friend and others alternate with flashes of his friends, now in jail. Developed for young people in grades 6 through 12, this video emphasizes the importance of pride, respect, responsibility, and personal choices.

Graffiti: The Language of Gangs
Type: VHS
Length: 21 min.
Date: 1995
Cost: $69.95
Source: The Bureau for At-Risk Youth
645 New York Ave.
Huntington, NY 11743
(800) 999-6884
Fax: (516) 673-4544

Graffiti is an important part of gang life. Gang members use graffiti to get their messages out to other gangs and often to bait and incite them. It frequently leads to violent behavior, acts of revenge, wars between gangs, and injuries or death for some gang members. This video explains specific symbolism involved in graffiti and takes the viewer through the process of understanding it. Professionals and parents working to eliminate and prevent gang activity and violence will find this video helpful.

Homeboys
Type: VHS
Length: 27 min.
Date: 1990
Cost: $250
Source: Coronet/MTI Film and Video
108 Wilmot Road
Deerfield, IL 60015
(800) 777-8100
Fax: (708) 940-3640

Homeboys provides a chilling look at the violence in the lives of gang members and their lack of a sense of a future life. Throughout the United States, life is bleak for many inner-city residents who lack hope for a better future. Through interviews the video reveals the motivations, rituals, rewards, and perils of life for the urban underclass. Young men who are currently in jail or prison for crimes they committed as gang members tell their stories, effectively communicating their feelings to the viewer. They talk about guns in schools, the advantages they see in selling and distributing drugs, and the murders that are committed by gang members in the course of their violent activities. They discuss these and other issues matter-of-factly, as if these occurrences are so common that they can't understand why other people get so upset about them. Viewers are provided with an excellent opportunity to see gang activity as gang members see it. Their stories offer a shocking and provocative portrait of life on the streets. The video was produced for junior and senior high school students, college students, and adults who work with or are interested in gangs and gang activities.

In Us We Trust
Type: VHS
Length: 30 min.
Date: 1995
Cost: $79.95
Source: The Bureau for At-Risk Youth
645 New York Ave.
Huntington, NY 11743
(800) 999-6884
Fax: (516) 673-4544

Many programs encourage young students to solve their problems and conflicts peacefully. This video takes the viewer to elementary schools in several urban and suburban areas and describes the efforts these schools are making to prevent violence within their walls. Children and adults are encouraged to take positive action against violence by organizing a variety of school and community programs. One of the programs described is "Peace Pie," which provides children with many choices, such as talking with an adult or simply walking away, for effectively handling disputes without resorting to violent actions. Through their experience with these programs, students are encouraged to participate in other violence-prevention activities.

It's Your Choice
Type: VHS
Length: 19 min.
Date: 1995
Cost: $69
Source: The Bureau for At-Risk Youth
645 New York Ave.
Huntington, NY 11743
(800) 999-6884
Fax: (516) 673-4544

For use in grades 6 through 8, this video provides an effective portrait of life inside a maximum-security prison. In the video, a group of students make their way into this prison to interview two inmates about their lives and their problems. Topics discussed range from drinking and drugs to shoplifting and gangs. The inmates describe the mistakes they made while growing up and the effects that these mistakes have had on their lives. They advise the students on how to avoid making poor choices in their lives so that they won't end up in prison.

**Mario's Gang: A Parent's Guide
to Separating Teens from Gangs**
Type: VHS
Length: 25 min.
Date: 1995
Cost: $95
Source: The Bureau for At-Risk Youth
645 New York Ave.
Huntington, NY 11743
(800) 999-6884
Fax: (516) 673-4544

Part of the Bureau for At-Risk Youth's *Parenting Difficult Adolescents* series, this video draws on real-life situations and uses skits to illustrate ways that parents and teenagers can resolve problems and settle their differences. Narrated by Emmy Award-winning journalist Ellen Kingsley, it focuses on many difficult parenting issues, especially efforts to keep children from joining gangs. Seven troubled teens and their parents are shown attempting to resolve many common contemporary life issues. The renowned Family Life Theater dramatizes situations, and child therapists offer comments concerning these scenarios in an interactive audience setting. Parents are taught how to recognize problems, resolve disagreements, and set limits with their children, as well as how to determine when they need to seek professional help. This video is an excellent resource for school counselors, social workers, parenting groups, and family workers. The series was produced for the U.S. Department of Health and Human Services and the Bureau for At-Risk Youth.

McGruff's Gang Alert

Type: VHS
Length: 16 min.
Date: 1994
Cost: $165
Source: AIMS Media
      9710 DeSoto Ave.
      Chatsworth, CA 91311-4409
      (800) 367-2467
      Fax: (818) 341-6700

In this video for students in primary and intermediate grades, McGruff, a canine character in a popular television cartoon, explains the major reasons why children should not join street gangs. These gangs can harm the community and disrupt the lives of their members, he says. McGruff offers dramatizations from his "files" to demonstrate how gangs take away a young person's ability to make his own decisions. Reasons that many young people give for joining a gang, including feelings of loneliness, wanting to be part of a group, and peer pressure to commit crimes, are discussed. McGruff explains that no matter what a kid's reasons may be for joining a gang, being in a gang is always a dead end. He also explains to viewers the reasons why they should not let others make decisions for them and tells them what they should do if gang members approach them. This video is also available in Spanish.

Real Men Don't Bleed
Type: VHS
Length: 20 min.
Date: 1991
Cost: $350; rental: $75
Source: Coronet/MTI Film and Video
           108 Wilmot Road
           Deerfield, IL 60015
           (800) 777-8100
           Fax: (708) 940-3640

Teenagers today face a variety of challenges and pressures to do what the rest of their friends are doing. Living in an inner-city neighborhood adds many more pressures to a child's life. This video explores the types of situations that are faced by many inner-city youths on a daily basis, including gangs and gang violence. It offers young men alternatives to the macho image that many of these teenagers feel they must maintain. This video is an excellent resource for teenagers from any background because most teenagers will face many similar pressures in the process of growing up. Teenagers are provided with alternatives to the fight-or-flight choice that is the most common reaction to confrontational situations. This video is appropriate for junior and senior high school students, college students, and concerned adults. A video-disc version is also available for $165.

Refusal Skills for Teens
Type: VHS
Length: 18 min.
Date: 1990
Cost: $89
Source: The Bureau for At-Risk Youth
           645 New York Ave.
           Huntington, NY 11743
           (800) 999-6884
           Fax: (516) 673-4544

This video, part of the *Teens in Crisis* violence-prevention video series, teaches teenagers how to resist the many temptations they face, both in school and with their friends, including the pressure to join gangs, try drugs, and use alcohol. Realistic scenarios show teenagers using strong refusal skills in situations that viewers may face. Viewers are shown how to handle each situation as it arises. For students in grades 7 through 12.

Resisting Pressure to Join Gangs
Type: VHS
Length: 18 min.
Date: 1990
Cost: $89
Source: The Bureau for At-Risk Youth
645 New York Ave.
Huntington, NY 11743
(800) 999-6884
Fax: (516) 673-4544

This video is part of the *Teens in Crisis* series. It provides teenagers with effective guidelines on ways to resist pressure to join a gang, emphasizes that pressure to join gangs is negative peer pressure, shows realistic alternatives to life in a gang, and suggests things teens can do to achieve a sense of belonging without being forced into a gang. For students in grades 7 through 12.

Street Peace: Violence Prevention Video and Curriculum
Type: VHS
Length: 60 min.
Date: 1995
Cost: $189.95
Source: The Bureau for At-Risk Youth
645 New York Ave.
Huntington, NY 11743
(800) 999-6884
Fax: (516) 673-4544

Students from urban areas with high crime and violence rates provided guidance for this video. A 45-page manual with eight lessons comes with the video, which contains 22 short segments that encourage students to participate in discussion and skill-building activities. Real teens tell their own stories or recreate real-life situations and then offer solutions to violence-related issues. Three groups of lessons are provided. The first concerns violence, cultural and gender sensitivities, and values and goals. The second provides information about peer pressure and decision making, communication and negotiation, and triggers and options. The third group concerns peer mediation activities and setting new norms. The video is intended primarily for inner-city and urban teenagers.

**Sweetwater and June: Gang Membership
and Its Consequences**
Type: VHS
Length: 30 min.
Date: 1992
Cost: (write for current cost)
Source: Karol Video
P.O. Box 7600
Wilkes-Barre, PA 18773

This drama uses the experiences of two juvenile gang members to show the grim consequences of gang membership. Sweetwater persuades June to go along with his impulsive criminal behavior. One night he is bored, so he steals a car at gun-point and then participates in a drive-by shooting in another gang's neighborhood. A witness describes the stolen car to police officers who locate the car and arrest the two juveniles. The police book June and then release him into the care of his mother pending the disposition of his case. On their way home, June and his mother are killed by the gang members who were shot at earlier by Sweetwater. Meanwhile, the police continue to hold Sweetwater at a detention center, where he must participate in a group counseling session. Sweetwater gets into a fight with another juvenile detainee and the officers return both boys to their cells. Through the cell wall, the two talk about the futility of their lives and debate whether or not it is too late for them to change. Feeling depressed about his life and his future, Sweetwater hangs himself in his cell. The video leaves conclusions up to the viewer. It comes with a pamphlet that provides a list of learning objectives, discussion questions, and suggested activities.

That Old Gang of Mine
Type: VHS
Length: 50 min.
Date: 1994
Cost: $125
Source: The Bureau for At-Risk Youth
645 New York Ave.
Huntington, NY 11743
(800) 999-6884
Fax: (516) 673-4544

In this powerful video, former gang members talk about their lives and experiences. The interviewees include males and females, whites, Hispanics, African Americans, and others who explain why they joined a gang, who they hurt, what they did while in the gang, and the price they have paid for their behavior. All of them are in jail or prison in California as a result of their actions. The video includes a leader's guide and is aimed at students in grades 6 through 12, as well as teachers and parents.

Urban Turf . . . Grades 7 and Up
Type: VHS
Length: 26 min.
Date: Not available
Cost: $95
Source: The Bureau for At-Risk Youth
645 New York Ave.
Huntington, NY 11743
(800) 999-6884
Fax: (516) 673-4544

Many young people join gangs because the gang provides the identity and sense of family that they can't find elsewhere, especially among their own families. These young people often do not realize the negative aspects of joining a gang. This video teaches children that gangs are often involved in illegal activities such as dealing drugs, stealing cars, and organized crime and that some teenagers who join gangs engage in violent initiation rituals. It discusses problems created by street gangs, alternatives to gangs, and possible solutions to the problems created by gangs. The video comes with a leader's guide.

Violence Prevention: Inside Out
Type: VHS
Length: 45 min.
Date: Not available
Cost: $135
Source: The Bureau for At-Risk Youth
645 New York Ave.
Huntington, NY 11743
(800) 999-6884
Fax: (516) 673-4544

This video offers a comprehensive view of violence in a variety of forms, including domestic violence, sexual assault, gang-related violence, and institutional violence. It also explores various facets of violence, including how it starts and how it affects the people involved, and offers ways to prevent it at home, in school, and in the community. Interviews with youths in juvenile-detention centers, treatment programs, schools, and on the street illustrate the cycle of violence. For students in grades 7 through 12. A leader's guide is included.

What About Gangs?
Type: VHS
Length: two videos, Part I is 18 min. and Part II, 40 min.
Date: 1993
Cost: $179.95
Source: The Bureau for At-Risk Youth
          645 New York Ave.
          Huntington, NY 11743
          (800) 999-6884
          Fax: (516) 673-4544

Part I of this two-part series is aimed at students in grades 6 through 9. It focuses the decision whether or not to join a gang, offers other options for viewers, and suggests ways to counter the growth of gangs in local communities and schools. It also discusses issues important to students and their families, including low self-esteem, dysfunctional families, and fears of gang violence. Part II was developed for parents, teachers, and administrators and features a panel discussion about gangs. Panel members include Jerry Simandi, a member of the Chicago Police Department's Gang Task Force, sociologist Joan Moore, a teacher and counselor, gang expert Xavier Cartada from Miami, a community activist, and a school principal. Each panel member offers valuable information and suggestions for educators to help reduce gang violence.

Online Searches

Center for the Study and Prevention of Violence
Institute of Behavioral Science
University of Colorado
910 28th Street
Campus Box 442
Boulder, CO 80309-0442
(303) 492-1032
Fax: (303) 443-3297

The center provides information and assistance to groups and individuals studying the causes of violence and ways of preventing violence, especially youth violence and gang activity. The center's Information House gathers information on research, programs, curricula, videos, books and journal articles, and other sources of information about causes of violence and prevention strategies; this information is included in an online database. Custom searches can be performed.

Internet Resources

**Alliance Working for Asian Rights
and Empowerment (AWARE)**
P.O. Box 28977
Santa Ana, CA 92799-8977
(714) 597-9766
Internet: http://sun3.lib.uci.edu/%7Edtsang/awarefs.htm

AWARE was founded in 1993 as a grassroots effort focusing on Asians and Pacific Islanders in Orange County and providing community support and advocacy. Because of growing gang activity in Orange County and other counties and cities in California, AWARE believes that police are stopping young Asians and other people of color and taking photographs of them based on an ill-conceived notion that many of these young people are gang members, solely based on their clothing and skin color. This site documents incidents of suspected and confirmed police harassment of innocent Asians and other people of color, a "Know Your Rights Card," and contacts for more information.

DARE (Drug Abuse Resistance Education) Program
Lake Township Police
27975 Cummings Road
Millbury, OH 43447
Internet: http://www.dareing.com/dare/dare.html

This site offers information about the DARE program, lesson objectives, upcoming events, a bulletin board, links to other DARE-related pages, mailing lists, a parent's page, a pen pal page, and a DARE quiz to test the reader's skills.

Front Rangers Cycling Club
Internet: http://pages.prodigy.com/Front Rangers

This organization was founded in Denver in 1993 by master racers, cycling enthusiasts, and Denver police officers; their purpose was to attract young people who are at risk for unhealthy lifestyles. Their goals include providing an alternative activity to drugs and gangs, introducing young people to cycling, providing positive role models, enhancing the image of law enforcement personnel, promoting bicycle safety, and promoting a healthy lifestyle.

Juvenile Justice Clearinghouse
Office of Juvenile Justice and Delinquency Prevention
National Institute of Justice
U.S. Department of Justice
P.O. Box 6000
Rockville, MD 20849-6000
(800) 638-8736
Internet: http://www.ncjrs.com

The clearinghouse is a comprehensive resource for information on a variety of juvenile justice topics, including gangs. Juvenile justice professionals and anyone else seeking information on juvenile justice topics can speak with an information specialist concerning specific requests for information. Access is provided to the NCJRS library, which is one of the world's most comprehensive sources of criminal justice and juvenile justice literature. An electronic bulletin board can be found on the Internet, which provides timely information on a variety of topics of interest to juvenile justice professionals.

Mothers Against Gangs
Internet: http://www.winternet.com%7Ejannmart/nkcmag. html

Mothers Against Gangs developed this site to address the issue of crimes committed by today's youth. They realize that not all young people who are in a group are members of a gang; most children want to belong to some type of group. This site provides information on education and motivation, lobbying and legislation, and advocacy activities and includes a mission statement, educational resources, comments, an art gallery, writing showcase, and an entrepreneur's network.

National Graffiti Information Network
P.O. Box 400
Hurricane, UT 84737
(801) 635-0604

Fax: (801) 635-7324
Internet: http://www.infowest.com/NGIN/index.html

This site provides information about gangs, graffiti, and other vandalism for private individuals and organizations, corporate agencies, and municipal organizations. A wide variety of information is offered, including photos and research, field surveys, educational options, on-location field research, instructional materials for organizing a community to fight gangs and graffiti, contact sheets for the development of a regional task force, and a speakers' bureau. Foundation and corporate grant sources are also provided.

National Youth Gang Center (NYGC)
Institute for Intergovernmental Research
P.O. Box 12729
Tallahassee, FL 322317
(800) 446-0912
(904) 385-0600
Internet: http://www.iir.com/nygc/nygc.htm

The NYGC is operated and funded by the Office of Juvenile Justice and Delinquency Prevention (OJJDP) in the U.S. Department of Justice and provides statistical data collection and analysis focusing on gangs, an analysis of gang legislation, gang literature review, identification of promising gang program strategies, and consortium coordination activities, including the annual National Youth Gang Symposium. This site offers detailed information about the NYGC and its activities.

Texas Youth Commission
Office of Delinquency Prevention
4900 N. Lamar Blvd.
P.O. Box 4260
Austin, TX 78765
(512) 483-5269 or (512) 483-5336
Internet: http://www.state.tx.us/TYC/catalog.html

This site offers a listing of programs and research papers focusing on a variety of topics, including delinquency prevention, gangs, child abuse, families, intervention, mediation, mentoring programs, parenting programs, recreation programs, rehabilitation research, and restitution programs. Copies of these documents are available from the Texas Youth Commission at the above address.

University of the Pacific
Enhancement Course Program
440 West First Street, Suite 102
Tustin, CA 92680
(800) 762-0121
Internet: http://www.xmission.com/gastow/up-oll/gang-guide.html

The Enhancement Course Program developed this site to provide a directory of common gang signs and graffiti. The developers realize that no site can be comprehensive because so many gangs exist and signs may mean different things to different people. This site provides a sampling of gang signs and graffiti and relates primarily to Hispanic and black gangs in California.

Youth and Child Resource Net
267 Lester Ave., Suite 104
Oakland, CA 94606
(500) 675-KIDS or (500) 446-KIDS
Internet: http://www.slip.net/%7Escmetro/childco.htm

This site provides information on many programs serving children and youth, including national hotlines, gang prevention and intervention programs, a child and family interactive network, antidrug programs, and sites on youth violence. It was developed and is maintained by the National Children's Coalition.

Index

Karen L. Kinnear holds an M.A. in sociology and is a professional researcher, editor, and writer with over 20 years' experience in sociological, economic, statistical, and financial analysis. Among her previous publications are *Violent Children: A Handbook* and *Childhood Sexual Abuse: A Handbook*.